All My
Best Friends

Also available in Large Print
by George Burns:

How to Live to Be 100—Or More
Dr. Burns' Prescription for Happiness
Dear George
Gracie: A Love Story

GEORGE BURNS

All My
Best Friends

Written with
David Fisher

G.K. HALL & CO.
Boston, Massachusetts
1991

Published in Large Print by arrangement with
G. P. Putnam's Sons.

British Commonwealth rights courtesy of G.P. Putnam's Sons.

G. K. Hall Large Print Book Series.

Set in 16 pt. Plantin.

Library of Congress Cataloging-in-Publication Data

Burns, George, 1986-
   All my best friends / George Burns, written with David Fisher.
     p. cm.—(G.K. Hall large print book series)
   ISBN 0-8161-5016-8.—ISBN 0-8161-5017-6 (pbk.)
   1. Burns, George, 1896-   . 2. Comedians—United States—
Biography. 3. Entertainers—United States—Biography. 4. Large
type books. I. Fisher, David, 1946-   II Title.
[PN2287 .B87A3 1991]
792.7'028—dc20
[B]   90-46438

"MOST OF WHAT I SAY IS TRUE.
THE REST IS SHOW BUSINESS."

*G. K. Hall and Company, Publishers,
is very proud to present between our covers today,
the inimitable . . .*

GEORGE BURNS:

1

(APPLAUSE)

Thank you, thank you very much. You know, a funny thing happened to me on the way to this page. My life in show business. So far. And, so far, so good. I've been working in show business for eighty-six years, if this keeps up maybe I should consider making it my career. Listen, when I started the only types of entertainment we had were vaudeville, the burlesque, minstrel shows, the theater, silent movies and the hole in the wall between our bathroom and the Wisnewskys' bedroom. The hole in the wall was the most popular. The only forms of mass communication we had were the Western Union and women. And Western Union wasn't very good for comedians, unless the punch line to their jokes happened to be dot-dot.

During my life in show business I've seen the end of vaudeville, burlesque, the stock companies and minstrel shows and the birth of talking movies, radio, television, and the recording industry. I've known and worked with and loved a lot of the people who created modern show business, and that's what I want to tell you about.

1

Welcome to my new book, and thank you for coming. I hope you didn't have too much trouble getting here today. Now, this book is a little different than anything I've ever done before. And believe me, at my age it's hard to find anything I haven't done before. And even harder to do it. I've been a very fortunate man. I've had one of the longest show business careers in publishing history. Seven books. And I shared it with the pretty little girl who was my partner onstage and offstage for forty years, Gracie Allen. I could write a whole book just about Gracie. In fact, I already have. It's called *Gracie: A Love Story*. Maybe you've heard of it?

(APPLAUSE)

Thank you. I'm sure Gracie would thank you too. So that's seven books I've written. Not bad for somebody who's only read three. Well, this book isn't about me and it isn't about Gracie. It's about my friends, the people I grew up with in show business; the people show business grew up with. Look, I've been a singer, a dancer, an actor, a straight man, a comedian, once I even threw fish to a trained seal. I've done so many things that even the audience got confused—they must have, because when I was a singer they laughed and when I was a comedian they didn't. But when I tossed fish to the seal they knew what I was. Desperate.

But during my career I've also been lucky

enough to sing with Al Jolson, dance with Fred Astaire and stand onstage next to Jack Benny while he stared at the audience and said absolutely nothing better than any comedian who ever lived. And I've worked with Groucho and Harpo, and Jimmy Durante and Bob Hope and Georgie Jessel and Eddie Cantor and Ed Wynn and Milton Berle and Fanny Brice and so many others. We all started together in vaudeville and spent our lives together in show business. Now, a few of you might not be too familiar with some of the people I'm going to be telling you about. But these were the performers who were there at the beginning of radio and television and talking movies and the victrolas. Whatever type of entertainment you like, these were the people who did it first, and maybe best. I've admitted I lie a lot. Believe me, that's true. I was making a career out of lying even before the politicians made it fashionable. All right, maybe that's not true, even I'm not that old. But when I tell you my friends were the giants of show business, I'm telling you the truth.

Al Jolson, for instance. He called himself "The World's Greatest Entertainer," and he was right. Here was this Jewish kid from St. Petersburg, Russia, whose father was a cantor in the synagogue, and he used to walk onstage in blackface and get down on one knee and sing "I got a Mammy in Alabammy," and people believed him. I just don't think you can have any more talent than that. Sometimes, when Jolie was starring in a Broadway show at the Winter Garden, he'd stop the show, walk to the footlights and tell the audience, "You know how dis ends. The horse, he wins the race, and the boy get de girl. Now, you wanna see that or you wanna hear Jolson sing?" Then he'd have candy served to the audience, invite the rest of the cast to sit onstage, and for the next two or three hours sing the songs he'd made into hits, songs like "Mammy," and "Swanee," "April Showers," "Red, Red Robin," "Toot, toot, Tootsie," "California, Here I Come," "Sonny Boy," "Rainbow 'Round My Shoulder," and "Brother, Can You Spare a Dime." And then, if he still felt like singing, he'd invite the entire audience to a nearby restaurant and continue the show. Nobody ever dominated a theater like Jolson. And nobody was ever as quick to admit it as he was, either.

Maybe the only thing as big as Jolson's talent was his ego. He couldn't believe that there would be an empty seat in the theater when he was performing. Once, when he was starring in the show *Bombo* at the Winter Garden, there were four empty seats in the front row. He just could not stand to see those empty seats. So finally he stopped the show and said to the audience, "Ladies and gentlemen, I'd like you to take a minute and bow your heads in a moment of silence for these four people who aren't with us tonight. I don't know what happened to them, but they must be dead, or they never would have missed Jolson."

And Jack Benny, my closest friend, who created the best-known character in show business history. Everybody in America knew all of Jack Benny's weaknesses; he insisted he was a great violinist but he was really terrible, he claimed to be only thirty-nine years old for about forty years, and he was the cheapest man in the country; he was so cheap that instead of bringing his date flowers, he brought her seeds. Jack's character was so firmly established in the minds of the audience that he could get laughs without saying a word. Once, I remember, he was asked to throw out the first ball at a World Series game. But he broke up the whole ball park when he looked at the ball and, instead of throwing it, he put it in his pocket and sat down.

Jack had a show on radio and television for more consecutive years than anyone else in history. When he no longer wanted to do a weekly show, he did specials, but he never called them that. "To me," he said, "a special is when they knock down the price of lettuce from ninety-nine cents to seventy-nine cents."

I worked with Georgie Jessel and Eddie Cantor, next to Jolson the two greatest stars of vaudeville. When vaudeville died Jessel became "America's Toastmaster General," and made a career out of speaking at dinners and funerals. There's no connection between the two, by the way, unless my sister Goldie was doing the cooking. Jessel gave the eulogy at so many funerals that people used to claim the most feared question in show business was Jessel asking, with an anxious look in his eye, "So, how you feeling?"

Jessel loved speaking at funerals, sometimes he'd do two in one day, and he was just great at it. I remember when the great actor Sam Bernard died. Georgie and Sam had been good friends, and Georgie gave a beautiful, very touching eulogy at Sam's funeral. Everybody was crying. About three days later Georgie came walking into the Friars Club and he had on his striped pants again. Anytime you saw Jessel in those striped pants it meant he was appearing at a funeral. "Who died?" I asked him.

"Louie Mann," he said, referring to the theater-chain owner. "I'm just on my way over to the funeral."

I didn't understand that at all. "I don't get it, Georgie. Just a few days ago you told me you didn't like Louie Mann."

"I didn't," he explained, "but I've got some great stuff left over from Sam Bernard."

Offstage, Georgie was probably the funniest man I ever knew, as well as the most married. I don't know if there's a connection between those two. But he was always going out with pretty, young girls. When he was forty-two years old he married a sixteen-year-old actress who admitted, "I love Georgie more than any man I've loved in my whole life."

Eddie Cantor had more energy than any performer who ever appeared on the stage. Maybe Eddie didn't sing so well, and he wasn't a great dancer, and most of his jokes really weren't that funny, but he did so much so fast that the audience didn't have time to notice. Slow-motion instant replay could have killed Cantor's career. Onstage he'd open his "Banjo eyes" so wide they looked like they were going to pop out of his head, prance across the stage, clapping his hands, he'd sing a verse, roll his eyes, tell a joke, do a few quick steps, leap into the air, prance back across the stage. . . . Whatever it was that he did, he did it so well, and audiences loved him so much, that Flo Ziegfeld made him the star of the Ziegfeld Follies at a higher salary than any comedian had ever been paid. And for a fellow who didn't sing so well, he made some of the most popular recordings of all time, like "Makin' Whoopee," and his theme song, "If You Knew Susie." Eddie must have had a lot of energy offstage too. He and his wife, Ida, who he claimed was "Sweeter than apple cider," had five children—five girls. A large part of Eddie's act in radio consisted of complai . . . commenting about the problems of living with six women.

That was funny. Jessel and Cantor were best friends, and Cantor's biggest problem was Jessel's biggest fantasy.

Unlike so many performers who created instantly recognizable characters—Jack Benny was cheap, Milton Berle stole jokes, I didn't do anything—Eddie was just a great entertainer with five daughters and a lot of energy. That meant he had to start fresh with every audience; they wouldn't believe him if he suddenly claimed he was so cheap he had his garbage cleaned so he could use it again. He was once trying to explain this to the great Broadway actress Katharine Cornell. "See, Miss Cornell," he said, "when you're onstage you're creating a character. You've got to get into it everytime. What do I have to get into? The trombone player's lap!"

Then there was Ed Wynn, who was billed as "The Perfect Fool." He wasn't, of course, nobody's perfect, but he was a great fool. Wearing a ridiculous costume, big round-rimmed black glasses, some sort of silly hat several sizes too small for his head and shoes with three-inch-thick soles, Wynn would come onstage carrying an incredible collection of props and gadgets, which he would demonstrate while telling bad jokes and worse puns. It was Ed Wynn, for example, who invented the eleven-foot pole that you used to touch people you wouldn't touch with a ten-foot pole, and the overcoat with sharp spikes to be worn on the subway, and the bicycle with a piano where the handlebars were supposed to be so you could have music when you went bike riding, and the glasses with windshield wipers to be worn when eating grapefruit. Wynn was so popular that when the great Palace Theatre opened in 1913 he served as host, introducing the acts on the bill and taking part in several of them—making Ed Wynn the first master of ceremonies in show business history.

After vaudeville he became a major radio star as "The Fire Chief," still telling his bad jokes and terrible puns. "I was carrying a jar of jelly wrapped in a newspaper," he'd tell his famous announcer, Graham McNamee, in a high-pitched, lisping voice, "and I fell on the floor and it broke. So you should see the jam Dick Tracy's in today."

Wynn's career faded in the 1940s and 50s, but he made a great comeback as a serious actor in *Requiem for a Heavyweight,* which led to featured roles in movies like *The Diary of Anne Frank,* and *Mary Poppins.*

And what can I say about Milton Berle that he already hasn't said himself? Milton is one of the most talented performers in show business. When he was twenty-three years old he was the youngest MC ever to work the Palace Theatre, and three decades later became "Mr. Television," the most popular television star in history. Onstage, Milton's act was every bit as good as Jessel's or Cantor's. In fact, it wasn't only just as good, it was the same. "The Thief of Badgags," as he was nicknamed, has made a career out of being accused of stealing other comedians' best material. Once he was introduced as "The man who always steals the show—one joke at a time," and even he used to say, "I went to see Frank Fay at the Palace. He was so funny I almost dropped my pad and pencil."

Look, I love Milton. He's a very talented man and I've always admired his act. In fact, I admired it when Eddie Cantor did it, when Bob Hope did it, when Ed Wynn did it. . . . But seriously, folks, in all the years I've known Milton, and that's a

9

long, long time, he's never stolen a single line from me. So at least you know he has pretty good taste.

When I talk about the giants of show business, I can't overlook Jimmy Durante's nose. Calling Durante's nose large is like calling Jack Benny "thrifty," it just doesn't make the point. "The Schnozzola," as Jimmy was affectionately known, actually had his nose insured by Lloyds of London against an accident that might make it normal, and while other stars made imprints of their hands and feet in the cement outside Grauman's Chinese Theatre in Hollywood, Jimmy left the impression of his nose. The only problem with that today is that a lot of people think it's a pothole.

During his career The Schnozz was the most imitated performer in show business. Even more than Jolson. Maybe that's because audiences loved him so much, and because he was so easy to do. He spoke, and sang, in an unmistakable voice that sounded like gravel being mixed in a food processor, and he fought a lifelong battle with the English language. He did things to the English language that even Jessel wouldn't have done with Mae West. It was Durante who claimed to get "a little neuralgic" for the old days, and admitted that most of the books he read were "non-friction," and was proud to be so successful he didn't have to worry about "the kiss of debt." When an English teacher accused him of splitting an infinitive, he said, after somebody explained what that meant, "I don't just split 'em. When I goes to woik on 'em, I breaks 'em up in little

10

pieces." Maybe no one ever dominated a stage like Jolson, but no one ever destroyed one like Durante. When a member of his band would hit a wrong note or miss a cue, as they always did, Jimmy would scream, "Stop da music! Stop da music!" then complain to the audience, "Surrounded by assassins," or "I'm a victim of da small print in my contract," or, "Evvvvery-body wants a get inna de act." Jimmy could do things to a song that no other performer would have dared. Good things, I mean. And his versions of songs like "You Gotta Start Off Each Day With a Song," "Ink-a-Dink-a-Doo," and "September Song" were big hits. But Durante's most famous trademark, besides his nose, besides his wrecking the language, was his finish. In a business where your finish is the most important part of your act, Jimmy had one of the most memorable finishes in history. In a low voice he would thank the audience and say goodnight, then add, "And good night, Mrs. Calabash, wherever you are."

Nobody ever knew who Mrs. Calabash really was, and Durante never explained—except Jessel, who claimed he used to go out with her.

So this book is about these people. And it's also about some other friends of mine that you've probably heard of, people like Bob Hope, the Marx Brothers, Carol Channing, Walter Matthau, Al Jolson . . .

Okay, I know I mentioned Jolson twice, but that's because he always claimed to be twice as big a star as anyone else.

It's really about them all. It's about the people who were brave enough to get up onstage, or stand in front of a microphone, or look into a camera, and try to entertain an audience, because as far as I'm concerned, they were all my best friends.

I started out in show business about the same time a lot of these great stars were starting out. None of us knew we were going to be creating modern show business. I don't think anybody really expected to become a star, maybe Berle; but we had a hunger for something more important than fame.

Food.

Almost all of us grew up in very poor families. Poor? As Matthau says, "Compared to us, poor was already rich." We were the children of immigrants. We had nothing in common. That's what we all had, nothing. Cantor was brought up by his grandmother in a basement on Henry Street. Berle's family was evicted from a tenement in Harlem. Durante grew up in an apartment in Little Italy that was so bad they tore it down to put up a tenement. I grew up on Rivington Street on New York City's Lower East Side with four brothers and seven sisters. We were so poor that I couldn't even afford to have my own dreams. When they invented the automobile Izzy dreamed that someday he would be a car salesman; when I got old enough I dreamed that I would be a used car salesman. There was only one rich family on our block. They lived in the building on the corner and we knew they were rich because they had lace curtains on their windows. Sometimes I'd get up very early in the morning and take whatever little garbage we had out of our garbage can and put it in theirs, and put their garbage in ours, because I wanted the neighbors to think we were doing well.

The kids in my neighborhood would do anything to make money. Sing, dance, steal, anything. Believe me, if school had paid better, there would have been a lot more smart kids coming out of the Lower East Side. One kid, I remember, had a great money-raising bit. He'd lost half his index finger, right down to the middle knuckle, when a sewer grate fell on it. All he had was this flat stub. So he'd stand on the corner holding that stub against his forehead, and it really looked like the rest of his finger was sticking in his head. People were amazed, and they'd usually give him a few pennies. And if they didn't, he'd get even with them by holding his stub under one nostril.

None of us ever let school get in the way of our education. We knew that there were only two ways to make enough money to be able to move uptown and wear spats; become a gangster or an entertainer. And both of them were considered equally respectable. I'll tell you how people felt about show business—When Ed Wynn decided he was going into show business his father disowned him. When Jack Pearl, who became famous on the radio as "Baron Munchausen," was a kid he was so wild his parents said, "We knew he would either be crazy or an actor." Walter Matthau's father had deserted his family when Walter was very young, and his mother had struggled to raise the family. Years later, after Walter had become one of the great comic actors in the world, making millions of dollars a picture, he asked his mother how she felt about his success. "If you had had a decent father," she told him, "you could have been a doctor, or a lawyer."

I went into show business when I was seven years old. I put together a little harmony group and we called ourselves The Pee Wee Quartet. I was the lead singer and business manager, Mortsy Weinberger was the tenor, his brother Heshy was the baritone and a kid named Toda sang bass. We'd sing on street corners, outside saloons and on streetcars and ferry boats for throw money. At the time I thought people were throwing money to us to sing; later I realized they were throwing it at us to stop. Sometimes, when we weren't doing so well in show business, we'd go up to the roof of a tenement and use a long wire with a loop on the end to steal seltzer bottles that people had left out on their fire escapes. We'd break the lead tops off the bottles and melt them down. Lead was selling for about six cents a pound and on some days, with our singing ability, if we could lift ten bottles we'd make about sixty cents.

But even with a potentially profitable career in lead melting ahead of me, the only thing I really wanted to do was go into show business. Who knows why. From that first time when I opened my mouth and started singing, and heard the wonderful sound of laughter, I was hooked. Believe me, there is nothing that feels as good as standing onstage and hearing the laughter and applause of an audience. Nothing.

I was a better dancer than a singer. Soon as I was old enough I started going to the local dance halls every Friday and Saturday night. Admission was twenty-five cents for girls and thirty-five cents for men. I loved to dance, and I knew all the moves. I loved to dance even more than I loved sex. First of all, it was a lot easier to find a partner. And I was much better at it.

So I began my career as a singer and a dancer. A lot of great comedians started out as musicians. Immigrant parents believed that knowing how to sing or play an instrument was a sign of respectability, and a lot of them made big sacrifices to pay for an instrument and lessons. For instance, the Marx Brothers' mother, Minnie Marx, insisted that all of her sons play an instrument. Groucho played the guitar. Chico was an excellent pianist. Harpo played the harmonica, clarinet, the harp, two songs on the piano and the bicycle horn. Ed Wynn played the piano, but only in the key of B-flat. If B-flat had been more popular, Ed Wynn might have become a famous musician. Jimmy Durante's father, who had a little barbershop on Catherine Street, wanted Jimmy to be a concert pianist. The closest Jimmy ever came to classical music was making a record with opera diva Helen Traubel. When the record came out Helen said, "It's a pleasure to record with a great *artiste* whose voice sounds exactly the same whether the record player needle is good or bad." Jack Benny's father, a saloonkeeper, wanted Jack to become a classical violinist. Jack got so good that some of his neighbors in Waukegan, Illinois, took up a collection to send him to Europe to study there. At least, that's why they said they wanted to send him out of town. Jack also learned to play the trumpet while he was serving in the Navy, but I know how much he loved playing the fiddle his whole life. I guess that proves the old saying, "You always hurt the one you love."

A funny thing though, the greatest musician I've ever seen, Al Jolson, started as a comedian.

In those days it wasn't hard to break into show business; you showed up at the theater on time, you were in show business. There was no radio, no television, no talking movies. Show business consisted of live shows. Every town in America had vaudeville houses and theaters and clubs and saloons, and they all had live entertainment. You really needed only one thing to break into the business—desire. You had to want to do it very badly. And that's how I did it.

It's so different today. Today a young comedian can do stand-up for a few weeks at a comedy club and get invited to be on Johnny Carson's television show. If, after he's done his routine, Johnny invites him to sit next to him on the couch, the kid immediately gets a three-picture deal and a TV series pilot. Me? When Johnny invites me to sit on his couch, I'm just thrilled to be able to sit down.

Getting booked in small-time vaudeville wasn't difficult because there were so many theaters with bills to fill that booking agents were always looking for new acts. As long as you had glossy pictures for the lobby somebody would give you a chance. I had pictures and a lot of new acts. None of the acts I did lasted long enough to get old. Whatever type of act the booking agent was looking for happened to be the type of act I did. I sang, I danced, I worked with Captain Bett's seal, I worked with a dog, I did a song-and-dance act with a dog; I worked alone, I worked with a partner, I took absolutely any job I could get. I've already told you I lie a lot, but believe me, I was awful. If I was going to make something up, I would tell you I was good. But even I'm not that big a liar.

I'll tell you how bad I was. I did a dancing act when I was Brown of "Brown and Williams." No, that's not the original "Brown and Williams," but after Brown left to become Edwards of "Edwards and O'Brien," and Williams, who had previously been LeFleur of "Lefleur, Prideaux and DePass," the "Three Swingin' Frenchmen," left to join Cobb in "Garrison and Garrison," I became Brown of "Brown and Williams." Originally, "Brown and Williams" had been a song-and-dance act, but we danced on roller skates. But other than that, this was the original "Brown and Williams."

All right, maybe that's not exactly true. The

truth is that Cobb never was in "Garrison and Garrison."

I didn't care who I was. As long as I could put on my makeup and go out onstage I was happy. I was so proud to be in vaudeville that most of the time I wouldn't even take off my makeup after the show so people would know I was in show business. Sometimes, when I wasn't working, I'd put a red ring around my collar so that people would think I'd been wearing makeup and know that I was in show business.

I think we all felt that way. Benny, Berle, Groucho, Jessel, Fred Allen, Jack Haley, Jesse Block and Eva Sully, all my best friends. We were in love with show business, with the excitement of getting onstage. Nothing else mattered to us. The only politics any of us cared about was why the Orpheum Circuit had booked "Flora D'Aliza's Educated Roosters" instead of "Camilla's Pigeons." The only thing any of us knew about sports was what boxing champion or olympic medal winner or six-day bike race winner or baseball star was playing Hammerstein's. The only thing that really mattered to any of us was getting the next booking.

There were so many different ways to break into show business. Acts came from the honky-tonks, the legitimate theater, the Broadway theater, traveling shows, nickelodeons, anyplace there was an audience. The beautiful singer Blossom Seeley, who eventually became a headliner with Benny Fields, started as a teenager singing in waterfront saloons on San Francisco's Barbary Coast. "Baby Blossom," as she was billed, used to wear a big tiger's head between her legs when she performed. The tiger's mouth opened and closed and she worked it with a string in her hand. Men would throw silver dollars to her and she'd catch them in the tiger's mouth. I said to her once, "That must have been pretty tough to do. When you were doing it, did you ever drop any coins?"

"Are you kidding?" she told me. "I could make change."

Durante broke into show business banging out Scott Joplin, Harvey Brooks and Mike Bernard ragtime numbers on the "pianna" at Little Italy socials and between bouts at a local boxing club. "Ragtime Jimmy," as he was known, didn't sing or tell jokes or talk, he just played that pianna. When he was seventeen years old he broke into show business as the house piano player at Diamond Tony's, a Coney Island clip joint, playing, as he used to say, "From nine a clock in da evenin' till I got subconscious." One of the singing waiters at Diamond Tony's was a kid named Eddie Cantor and the two of them got to be close friends. The waiters worked mostly for throw money. Ragtime Jimmy would play a hot tune, the waiters would sing and the customers would throw nickels to them. The waiters were too busy to stop and pick up the money, and none of them could afford a tiger's head, so they'd kick it over to the piano and Jimmy would scoop it up without missing a

19

note. Cantor was known as the best nickel-kicker at Coney Island.

Sometimes customers would request songs that neither Durante nor Cantor knew, but these guys were not about to let a nickel get away. So if a customer asked to hear a song like "I'll Be Waiting for You Bill When You Come Back From San Juan Hill," Durante would fake the melody and Cantor would sing, "Oh, I'll be waiting for you Bill . . ." and then he would start ad-libbing, "These loyal girls, their hearts pure as pearls . . . waiting for their Bills, to come on home to them from that ole San Juan Hill. . . ." If the customer was drunk enough he might not even notice that they were making up the song. But if he did complain that that was not THE "I'll Be Waiting for You Bill When You Come Back From San Juan Hill," Cantor would look shocked, open up those old Banjo-eyes wide as possible, and say innocently, "You mean there are two of them?"

Durante and Cantor always claimed that their greatest contribution to American culture was convincing a delivery boy for Feltman's Franks, Nathan Handwerker, to open up his own hot dog stand. That was the beginning of Nathan Famous. I don't know if that story is true or not, I'm not the only one who lies, you know. I will tell you that Feltman sold his frankfurters for ten cents and Nathan sold his for a nickel, and Cantor was the best nickel-kicker in Coney Island.

Eventually Durante put together a band, "Jimmy Durante's Original Jazz Novelty Band," that featured Jimmy playing in what he called "the classic razzmatazz style—heavy chording in the bass, and light finagling in the treble." The band opened at Harlem's Club Alamo then played speakeasies all over the city. Durante wasn't making too much money, but he had his pianna, his friends, and he was in show business. Jimmy didn't say a word in the act, but Cantor knew how funny he was and kept trying to convince him to start talking. "Just say a few words while you're playing," he suggested.

Jimmy was actually a shy man, maybe because of all the teasing he'd taken from kids about the size of his nose when he was growing up. "Oh, I couldn't do that," he told Cantor, "I'd be afraid the people'd laugh at me."

When Jimmy finally did start talking he found out that he was right—the people laughed at him. He formed an act with a ballad singer, Eddie Jackson, and the two of them opened a speakeasy, The Club Durant, on West 58th Street just off Broadway. Business was slow until a vaudeville actor and soft-shoe dancer, Lou Clayton, joined them and the trio of Clayton, Jackson and Durante became the hottest nightclub act in New York. Let me put it this way: their act made the Marx Brothers look sophisticated. Basically it consisted of throwing insults, lamps, telephones, dishes, whatever they could pick up, at each other, the people who worked for them and the customers. Jimmy's big finish was ripping apart his pianna piece by piece and throwing it at the band. The more things they threw at the customers, the more popular they got. That was about the only act I didn't try in vaudeville—throwing things at the audience. Once, supposedly, Durante's father came to the club, and after the show Jimmy asked him, "Well, Pop, how'd you like my woik?"

"Lissen, son," his father said, "les not get inna argument."

When prohibition agents closed the Club Durant the trio worked all over the country. There wasn't a piano that was safe from them anywhere. But Jimmy was the star of the act, and eventually he went into vaudeville as a single. Still ripping apart pianos. But Clayton and Jackson, "My Vice-Presidents," as Jimmy always called them, stayed on his payroll forever.

Cantor was great at recognizing real talent. After he worked with me and Gracie at the Palace Theatre he immediately asked Gracie to be on his radio show by herself. That was our first big break in radio.

Eddie had started in show business just like I did, working on the streets of New York for throw money. He did impersonations of famous performers. Since there was no radio or television or talking movies at that time, nobody knew what these famous performers really sounded like. I'll tell you what they sounded like, they sounded like Eddie Cantor. Or they sounded like Eddie Cantor speaking in a low voice, or they sounded like Eddie Cantor speaking in a falsetto. The great thing about doing impersonations was that you didn't have to have great material. If your jokes were bad or your songs were off-key, you could blame it on whomever you were impersonating.

In those days weekly amateur contests were very popular and Cantor's career really started when he entered the amateur show at Miner's Theatre on the Bowery. He ran around the stage, he clapped his hands together, he sang, he danced, he told a few jokes, he ran around the stage some more and by the time he was finished the audience was exhausted. He won the five-dollar first prize. From there he hooked on to a touring burlesque show as a blackface comedian, and was eventually hired by Gus Edwards to do a Jolson impersonation for one of Edwards' touring companies. I think Eddie was twelve years old.

A lot of very talented people started their careers with Gus Edwards: Cantor, Jessel, Phil Silvers, Berle, Groucho, Ray Bolger, Walter Winchell, Jesse Block, Hildegarde, The Duncan Sisters, The Human Top . . . Edwards produced kid acts, usually under the "Gus Edwards Presents" name, and sent them out on the different vaudeville circuits. Edwards was also a fine songwriter, writing songs like "School Days" and "Sunbonnet Sue."

Gus Edwards was a very well respected producer and his acts did very well. The kids who started with him were always very proud of that. In fact, I remember one night when Jessel got into an argument with someone at the Friars Club, and that person screamed at him, ". . . your people killed Christ!"

"Well, I had nothing to do with it," Jessel told him. "I was with Gus Edwards."

Georgie Jessel broke into show business with Jack Weiner, who became a very successful talent agent, and Walter Winchell, the famous gossip columnist. Jessel's mother was a ticket seller at The Imperial Theatre, a nickelodeon on 116th Street in Harlem, and she talked the owner into hiring the three boys to plug songs. Colored slides would be projected on a screen and "The Imperial Trio" stood next to the screen and sang the right lyrics.

Jessel used to claim that the trio sang "in all eight flats." After a few weeks Weiner and Winchell were fired and the theater manager advertised, "It's worth 5¢ alone to hear little Georgie Jessel sing." More than thirty years later Winchell told that story in his newspaper column, then added, "And that's still true."

Jessel joined Gus Edwards when he was ten years old and headlined several acts on the Orpheum Circuit, including "Kid Kabaret," with Cantor. When Jessel's voice changed he left Gus Edwards and tried to make it as a single. Sime Silverman, the famed publisher of *Variety*, reviewed his act, pointing out, "George Jessel is growing. In the passing of his cuteness, he'd better get some talent."

Jessel made his first appearance in the legitimate theater when he was hired at the last minute to replace a sick actor in a revue called "The Gaieties of 1919." He didn't even have time to learn all his lines. When he made his entrance the leading man looked at him and said, "And here comes Jack the Rounder now."

"Oh," Jessel shrugged, "I wouldn't know anything about that. I was just hired this morning."

Edgar Bergen, probably the greatest ventriloquist in history, really started at the bottom of show business, stoking the furnace in the basement of a local picture house in Decatur, Michigan. One day he bought a thirty-five-cent book that promised to reveal the secrets of magic, hypnosis and ventriloquism. Most people don't know this, but the first ventriloquists were the high priests in the ancient days. These priests would make voices come out of their idols, usually saying things like, "Give all your money to the priest." Supposedly, in Europe, people who could throw their voices were considered to be witches and a lot of them were burned at the stake. Fortunately for Bergen, it wasn't that tough in Decatur, unless your act was really awful.

Bergen was very unusual for a vaudevillian, he graduated from high school. I got to the fifth grade. Durante made it to the seventh grade, Benny made it all the way to his sophomore year in high school. Jessel spent eight months in school. And Harpo was thrown out of school in second grade. I mean, he was literally thrown out of school. The other kids threw him out of the window. That must have been some rough second grade. But Bergen actually graduated, proving that his partner, Charlie McCarthy, really was the dummy in the act.

Charlie McCarthy started his career in show business as a tree.

Fred Allen, the great humorist, also did some ventriloquism. His dummy, Jake, did impersonations of well-known performers—while those performers' records were played offstage. But Fred Allen broke into show business as a juggler in amateur shows in Boston. He was a terrible juggler; you know, he would juggle one ball at a time. When he tried to juggle too many tennis balls, or plates, or cigar boxes, he'd end up dropping them. So he did the really smart thing—he called himself a comedy juggler. People thought he was trying to be bad. Now *that's* what I should have done. As Freddy James, "The World's Worst Juggler," or "Freddy James and his Misses," he'd tell bad jokes as different objects smashed on the stage. "Did you hear about the guy who was run over by a brewery wagon?" he'd ask as he tossed three tin plates in the air. "It was the first time the drinks were on him." Clink, clink, clink.

I met Cary Grant when he was still calling himself Archie Leach and was sharing an apartment with costume designer Orry-Kelly in New York. We were all starting out together, Archie and Orry-Kelly and Jack and me and Gracie. Gracie and Orry-Kelly stayed close friends for their whole lives. Archie started in show business as a five-dollar-a-week stilt-walker in Coney Island, he sang light opera in St. Louis and finally broke into vaudeville as a bit player in a sketch called "The Woman Pays," starring an actress named Jean Dalrymple.

Even though we only grew up a few blocks apart, I didn't really get to know Walter Matthau until we worked together in the movie version of *The Sunshine Boys*. I was a little older than he was. In fact, I still am. Walter broke into show business as an ice cream and soda vendor and occasional "super," or stage extra, in the Yiddish theater. On the Lower East Side and East Greenwich Village the Yiddish theater was the only theater that mattered. Every famous play was done in Yiddish. It was really something to see Shakespeare in Yiddish. The translation would be something like, "Oi, the ghost of the King is due here any minute and the castle is such a mess." There's a very famous story they tell about the time John Barrymore came to New York to play Hamlet on Broadway.

Stop me if you've read this one before; but believe me, it's not the story, it's the way I write it.

Anyway, when Barrymore got off the train at Grand Central Station he got picked up by a little Jewish cabbie from the Lower East Side. This cabbie looked in the mirror and recognized the actor from photographs he'd seen in the newspaper. Naturally he was very impressed. "Excuse me," he said, "you should beg my pardon for asking, but what are you doing in New York?"

"I am playing Hamlet on Broadway for eight weeks," Barrymore told him.

"No kidding?" the cabbie said. "On Broadway, huh? That's something. So tell me, you think they'll unnerstand it in English?"

When Milton Berle was five years old he cut a piece of fur from his mother's handwarmer, pasted it under his nose, picked up a cane then walked like a drunken sailor—and won a quarter and a loving cup for his imitation of Charlie Chaplin. This was a very famous moment in show business history: the first time Milton Berle did somebody else's act.

Milton was born to be in show business. That was his mother's plan. Milton's mother, Sarah Berlinger, was probably the most famous stage mother of all time. Almost before Milton could walk she had him modeling as the boy in the Buster Brown shoe ads. When he was six she took him to Fort Lee, New Jersey, to work at the Biograph Studios in the silent films. Milton was the little boy on top of the moving train with Pearl White in *The Perils of Pauline*. He worked with great stars like Marie Dressler, Mabel Normand, Ruth Roland and Douglas Fairbanks. Senior. Fairbanks "saved" Milton's life in several serials, something a lot of people never forgave him for. Then Milton went to Hollywood and worked with Chaplin in *Tillie's Punctured Romance* and Mary Pickford in *Little Lord Fauntleroy* and *Rebecca of Sunnybrook Farm*. He made about fifty films.

Milton's mother dedicated her life to his career.

Once, when he was working in the Catskills, she broke up a baseball game to tell the other kids, "Milton has to be captain because it's his bat and ball, and besides, he's going to be a big Broadway star someday."

Milton worked as hard as anyone in show business, doing whatever he had to do to keep working. He broke into small-time doing kid acts, or "flash acts," as they were known. Milton was known as "The Shimmy Kid," "The Child Wonder" and "The Wayward Youth"; he taught himself to sing, dance, dance on his toes, do acrobatics, work on the trampoline, juggle, ride a unicycle; he did card tricks; he even did a kind of unique ventriloquism—he made other people's material come out of his mouth. By the time he was fourteen years old he was playing next-to-closing at the Palace.

When he got too tall to do kid acts he had to start all over again in small-time. He changed his name several times; I think he was Williams of "Brown and Williams" when it was a target-shooting act. Maybe not. He worked with a quick-change artist. He worked with Blossom Seeley and Benny Fields. He even worked with Phil Silvers, who was a tenor singing from the box. Song pluggers, like Silvers, were paid by sheet music publishers to stand up in the audience, when called on by the performer onstage, and sing a song to try to convince people to buy the sheet music. Sarah Berlinger thought Silvers was a very nice boy, so she let her Milton go out with him one night.

Phil took him directly to a whorehouse.

Milton never missed a performance, and neither did his mother. She'd sit in the audience for every show leading the laughter and applause. Once, Milton says, as he was doing his opening monologue, the man sitting next to her tried to put his hand under her skirt. She didn't say a word until the show was over. When Milton asked her why she didn't yell, she told him, "I didn't want to miss a cue."

Sarah Berle would hire people to sit in the audience and laugh at Milton's jokes. When Berle was working in Brooklyn one day, she paid a young comedian named Henny Youngman fifty cents to laugh at Berle. Youngman said that Berle was so good he would have done it for forty cents. Berle came onstage and said, "Good evening, ladies and gentlemen . . ."

"Oh no," Youngman said to the person sitting next to him, "he stole my opening."

Milton was always working, even when he wasn't onstage. Sometimes when he was waiting for a train he'd go up to a stranger, take out a deck of cards and demand, "Go ahead, take a card." One night at a party somebody did that same thing to Groucho. So Groucho took a card, said "Thanks," then put it in his pocket and walked away.

Harpo and Groucho were good friends of mine, but I knew all five Marx Brothers. They were also born into show business. Their grandfather had been a German magician and ventriloquist who had toured Europe in a covered wagon for fifty years. Their uncle, Al Shean, who started as a pants presser on my block, Rivington Street, was one of vaudeville's great comedians, Shean of "Gallagher and Shean." It was Minnie Marx, the boys' mother, who was determined that they would be in show business.

Chico was the oldest and he was a talented piano player. Harpo was born next and he could play two songs on the piano, "Love Me and the World Is Mine," and "Waltz Me Around Again, Willie." Chico and Harpo looked very much alike and whenever a piano-playing job came up Chico would go audition for it. If he got it, Harpo would show up for the job and play his two songs over and over, fast, slow, medium, fast and slow, while Chico was busy auditioning for the next job. By the time Harpo got fired, Chico already had another job lined up for him. Groucho started his career as a soprano in the Episcopal Church—he was the only Jewish kid in the whole choir—but was suspended for puncturing the organ bellows with the alto's hatpin. That shouldn't have surprised anyone, Groucho spent his whole life letting the hot air out of windbags. Groucho made his professional debut in North Beach, New Jersey, standing on a beer barrel to sing "Don't Break the News to Mother."

Minnie Marx put together a singing act called "Fun in Hi-Skule" starring Groucho, Harpo and

Gummo Marx, and featuring a pretty girl she hired. Chico, meanwhile, was playing piano in honky-tonks and wrestling all challengers at one dollar a match. When he was fired for throwing a paying customer through the front window, he went to Waukegan, Illinois, to catch up with the rest of the family. While the Marx Brothers were singing in Waukegan, Minnie Marx offered the job of musical director of the act to a member of the local house orchestra. And if that young man's father had let him take the job, the world might never have heard of . . . Benny Kubelsky.

Okay, maybe the world never heard of Benny Kubelsky. But everyone had heard of . . . you'd better imagine a little drumroll here, this is a very dramatic part . . . Jack Benny! Jack's real name was Benny Kubelsky. He was also Ben K. Benny for a little while. I think he might have also been Brown of "Brown and Williams" just after Thomas J. Wooley, the great peglegged dancer, had been Brown.

But can you imagine that, Minnie Marx wanting to hire Jack Benny as musical director of the Marx Brothers act? That would be like hiring Durante to be grammar coach.

The Marx Brothers really did start as a musical act. No kidding. Minnie wouldn't allow it. The best thing that could be said about their singing ability was that they always showed up on time. In Springfield, Ohio, for example, the tenor in an illustrated song bit didn't show up and Harpo volunteered to fill in for him. The theater manager accepted, and after hearing Harpo sing he fined him ten dollars.

Even the boys couldn't take their singing seriously, and sometimes when Minnie wasn't around they'd burlesque their own act. When she showed up unexpectedly in Cedar Rapids, Iowa, and caught them, she started screaming. She reminded them that the mortgage to their house was held by a tough landlord named Greenbaum, and if the act was canceled she wouldn't be able to pay Greenbaum and they'd lose their house. "Don't forget Greenbaum," she warned. And they never did. So from that time on, whenever their act started to get out of control, one of them would shout, "Don't forget Greenbaum!" And then things would really get out of control.

The real inspiration for their act, which I guess you can describe as indescribable, came from a wild mule in Nacogdoches, Texas. The Marx Brothers were onstage singing when somebody ran into the theater and announced that an angry mule was kicking a store apart. Given a choice between the Marx Brothers and a wild mule, the entire audience walked out. Groucho was furious, and when the audience came back inside he started insulting them. "Nacogdoches," he told them, "is full of roaches." The audience thought Groucho's insults were almost as good as watching that mule kick the store apart. Groucho was a pretty smart fellow; he knew that he either had to make the mule a permanent part of the act or keep the insults in. The mule, as it turned out, was already booked—I think he was Williams of "Brown and Williams" just before the famous aerialist Bobby Boswell, when it was still a high wire-animal act. But after that night in Nacogdoches the Marx Brothers became a vaudeville comedy act. Seriously.

I never did find out what happened to the mule. Or Greenbaum.

Al Jolson's father also wanted him to go into the family business; he wanted him to be a cantor. Religion was very important to many of the immigrants, in a lot of cases they'd left Europe and Russia to escape religious persecution. Jack Benny's father, for example, was an Orthodox Jew. One Yom Kippur Jack embarrassed him by showing up in the middle of the service. Meyer Kubelsky picked up a prayer book, a siddur, and smacked Jack in the face with it. That night, Mr. Kubelsky, trying to apologize, walked into his son's room and told him, "You know, in our religion it's considered a great blessing to be hit by a siddur on Yom Kippur."

Jolson sang in his father's choir, but he used to sneak away to work in Baltimore burlesque houses like the Bijou and Kernan's, singing songs with lyrics like "I'll leave my happy home for you, for you're the nicest girl I ever knew. . . ."

Jolie ended up running away from home to serve as a mascot for a regiment in the Spanish-American War. He must have done a pretty good job, we won the war. He never personally claimed credit for that though, and knowing Jolson, that was surprising. Jolson was a lot of things, none of them were "shy." He ran away from home three times and ended up living in the St. Mary's Home for Boys, the same place that Babe Ruth lived.

Like the rest of us, Jolson had some tough times when he was starting out. He did whatever he had to do to eat. For example, whistling was very popular at that time and Jolie was a wonderful whistler, so after moving to New York he earned throw money by imitating the whistle of the Italian organ-grinders. For a while he worked in a circus sideshow as a ballyhoo man, bringing in the rubes by promising to show them wonders like The Incredible Lizard Man, The Amazing Tatooed Lady, The Unbelievable Headless Horse, Milton Berle doing his own material. . . . Okay, I lied about the headless horse.

Jolson hung around outside the theaters like we all did, just waiting for a chance. He finally made his stage debut as a member of the mob in Zangwill's *Children of the Ghetto* at the Herald Square Theatre. I wasn't there, but I'll bet Jolson was the best mobster in theater history.

He broke into the small-time with his brother Harry doing a two-act called "The Hebrew and the Cadet," playing the cadet. After that act folded, Jolie and his brother put together a sketch with singing, dancing, comedy and whistling and played the Sullivan-Considine Time as "Jolson, Palmer and Jolson." Jolie played a bellboy in the act, and he worked in whiteface until J. Francis

Dooley of "Dooley and Sales," a very good mixed comedy team, told him to try it in blackface.

Working in "black," covering your skin with burnt cork and painting on wide white lips, was an important part of vaudeville. The blackface comedian had started in the minstrel shows of the 1800s and been carried over to variety shows and then to vaudeville. It had no racial meaning at all, even great black stars like Bert Williams put on blackface. Performers wearing black didn't imitate blacks, most of them spoke in their ordinary voices. The only thing that blackface meant was that the person wearing it was working in show business. At different times just about everybody blacked up; Jolson, Jessel, Cantor, Jack Benny, I wore it a lot of times. When Cantor blacked up and became a star in the Ziegfeld Frolics, his manager, Max Hayes, decided the whole world should put on blackface. All the acts he handled put it on, his wife, his secretary, even his dog.

About 1930 Gracie and I were on the bill at the Fifth Avenue Theatre with Jack Benny, and at the finish Jack and I did a minstrel number with Kramer of "Kramer and Morton," a blackface comedy duo. Benny was "Mr. Interlocutor," the man in the middle who asked the questions, the straight man, and Kramer and I were the end men, who answered them. Only the end men, Kramer and I, were in blackface. But to make Jack laugh, each show I made my white mouth a little bigger. By the sixth show my mouth included both ears. Benny thought it was great, even if the audience didn't get it. I didn't care about the audience, they didn't get most of my jokes. I was trying to break up Jack. The theater manager cared. "Maybe you make Jack Benny laugh," he told me, "but you don't make the audience laugh. From now on I want you to try something different—be funny for the audience."

I don't think anyone ever summed up my career in vaudeville any better.

Supposedly, the great blackface comedian Frank Tinney once tried to deduct $750 in expenses from his income tax, claiming he'd spent that much money on burnt cork. When the IRS agent asked him how he could possibly spend $750 on corks in one year, he told him, "Why, my dear man, I only use champagne corks."

Jolson was the most famous blackface performer of all time. Two years after putting on black for the first time Jolie was working next-to-closing in Lew Dockstader's Minstrel Show. Not long afterward he was "discovered" by J. J. Shubert and booked into the brand-new Winter Garden Theatre. The rest, as they say, is history. And if it isn't really history, it's show business.

Jack Benny was my closest friend in the world. And of all the great qualities he had, and there were so many, there was one thing that set him apart from everybody else. He really thought I was funny.

Jack was a deprived kid. Unlike me and Jolson and Jessel and Cantor and Berle, he had a very middle-class childhood. He actually grew up in a happy home, not the best place for a comedian. Fortunately, he was able to overcome it.

Jack Benny's ability on the violin was legendary. Everybody knew he had none. Once, supposedly, he was rushing to the White House to meet his friend President Harry Truman, carrying his fiddle case under his arm. He was stopped at the front gate by a security guard, who asked, "What's in the case, Mr. Benny?"

Jack was always a great ad-libber. "It's a machine gun," he said.

"Thank goodness," the guard told him. "For a minute I was afraid it was your violin."

Evvvvery-body wants a get inna de act!

Jack really did break into show business as a serious musician. If that sounds funny, you should have heard him play. But when he was only twelve years old he was working in the pit band of the local vaudeville house in Waukegan. In school, the only thing he cared about was playing in the orchestra, but he was kicked out for wisecracking; while they were rehearsing Schubert's Unfinished Symphony, he said that the Waukegan High School Orchestra was going to finish it off once and for all.

When the vaudeville theater closed, Jack teamed up with an older woman pianist and went on the road with a musical act, "Salisbury and Benny—From Grand Opera to Ragtime." Believe me, when Jack played it, the opera wasn't so grand. The ragtime was pretty ragged though. Jack didn't say a word in the act, he was always funniest when he said nothing, but he got laughs by playing the ragtime numbers with the little finger of his bow hand extended straight out, then staring at it as if he had no control over it.

Some things never changed in the fifty years Jack and I were friends; he always could get more laughs with his little finger than I got with my whole act.

When Salisbury went back to Waukegan, Jack teamed with pianist Lyman Woods in a whole new act, "Benny and Woods—From Grand Opera to Ragtime." They opened with a classical number, Brahms' "Hungarian Dance," but finished with popular songs of the time like "Oh! You Beautiful Doll," and "Everybody's Doin' It."

It was a pretty good act. They worked their way up from the Gus Sun Circuit to the Western Vaudeville Circuit, the Pantages-Time and, finally, the Sullivan-Considine Time and the Orpheum Circuit. Jack played the Palace for the first time in 1916. "Benny and Woods" was in the number-two spot, following an acrobatic act, but it was The Palace. "A pleasing turn for an early spot," *Variety* reviewed.

It took a world war for Jack to really get laughs. During World War I he enlisted in the Navy and was assigned to the Great Lakes Naval Station. A revue was being put together to tour the Midwest raising funds for Navy Relief and Jack was asked to play in the band and double in a comedy sketch. As "Corporal Izzy There," in "The Admiral's Disorderly," Jack first introduced a bit he used later in his vaudeville act. As he came onstage he'd stop and ask the audience, "How's the show going so far?"

Fine, they would respond.

"Well," he'd tell them, "I'll fix that." "The Great Lakes Revue" was a big hit.

When the war ended, Jack went back into vaudeville, this time as a monologist, a stand-up comedian. His act was called "Ben K. Benny, Fiddleology and Fun." Jack was Ben K. Benny. He became Jack Benny when Ben Bennie, a great vaudeville comedian, complained to the Vaudeville Managers Protective Association that he had his name first, forcing Jack to change his name to Jack Benny.

In his act Jack played a couple of tunes on his fiddle, told a few jokes he'd taken out of humor magazines—including one or two of the then-popular cheap jokes about Scotsmen, and finally did two vocals, "After the Country Goes Dry, Goodbye Wild Women Goodbye" and "I Used to Call Her Baby, But Now She's a Mother to Me." It didn't take Jack long to realize that the less he played the violin the more the audience enjoyed his act. Eventually he started using the fiddle as a prop. He'd carry it onstage, put it under his chin, lift his bow hand—and stop to tell a story. "I took my date to a very expensive restaurant last night," he'd say, "and I told her a great joke. She was laughing so hard she almost dropped her tray." The basis of the whole thing was threatening to play his violin. And when he stopped playing it for good he became a big hit. And he stopped playing it for the good of everyone.

Once he established his character he realized that if he didn't speak, if he just stared out at the audience with those mournful eyes of his, the audience loved him even more. This was some great act this guy had; Jack Benny carried a violin that he didn't play, a cigar he didn't smoke, and he was funniest when he said nothing. He did absolutely nothing and the people absolutely adored him.

Maybe *that* was my problem, I did something.

2

Once, Blossom Seeley and Benny Fields were finishing a run at The Boston Music Hall and had reservations on the midnight train back to New York. But their last show ran late and they had to make a later train. The midnight express derailed outside Providence, Rhode Island, and a lot of people were killed or seriously injured. Word got out that Blossom and Benny had been on that train. But the next night they walked into Lindy's for dinner, looking just like they were alive. The maître d' turned pale white. When they asked him what was the matter, he held up a copy of the *New York Sun*, which had a big headline reading, BLOSSOM SEELEY DIES IN PROVIDENCE

Blossom was stunned. "That's ridiculous," she said. "I *never* died in Providence. They always loved me there."

Anybody who ever worked in vaudeville would know exactly what she meant. To a vaudevillian, everything in life had something to do with your act. For example, the success of your act was measured by the amount of time you were allotted by the theater manager. If two vaudevillains met and one of them asked, "How you doing?" the other one would tell him, "About fourteen minutes."

There was never anything like vaudeville. Except for the big stars, being in vaudeville meant doing three shows a day and five shows on Saturday and Sunday, often to half-filled houses. It meant carrying your whole life around in a steamer trunk, spending most of your time on trains or in hotel rooms so small that your shadow had to wait for you outside, cooking over illegal hot plates that had to be snuck into the hotel or eating in one-arm joints or all-night hash houses; it meant never being able to save any money and always being worried about being canceled or getting the next booking, and it meant never, ever being home for any holidays and rarely seeing your family unless they were part of the act . . . but only if you were very lucky. I think that to most of us, probably the only thing that was worse than working in vaudeville was not working in vaudeville.

I think I loved being in vaudeville more than any other part of my career. Vaudeville meant show business, and I wanted to be in show business. Vaudeville was that place where people who said they would do anything to be in show business, did.

When I started out there were more than 5,000 vaudeville theaters in the country. Every city had several theaters and most small towns had at least one. And if they didn't have a real theater, they had a lodge hall, a storefront, a high school auditorium or an "airdome," an outdoor stage. There were so many theaters on the vaudeville circuits that if a performer had fourteen good minutes he could work six years without changing a word or playing the same theater twice. Before I met Gracie I worked in places so small that before the show I had to help the theater manager set up folding chairs for the audience. And the audiences in those small towns were tough, too—they even booed the way I set up chairs.

In retrospect, small-time vaudeville was fun—but as Groucho might say, everyplace else it was very tough. Think about it. We'd do anything to save a few bucks. Until the Marx Brothers were in their twenties Minnie Marx would claim they were children and buy half-fare train tickets for them. Once, when they were discovered smoking cigars and playing three-card stud by a conductor, she explained sweetly, "Children seem to grow up so fast these days."

Fanny Brice always traveled with a hot plate, pans and food so she could cook in her hotel room. One night she was in Cincinnati with Cantor and W. C. Fields and she insisted on making a spaghetti dinner for them. Fields took two bites and started foaming at the mouth. "Oh dear," Fannie said, "you can tell me, there's something wrong with the spaghetti, isn't there?"

Fields blew a bubble. "Actually, I'm not that hungry," Cantor said. Turned out it wasn't the spaghetti, it was the cheese. When she'd packed, she accidentally put soap powder in her grated-cheese jar.

Fortunately, Bill Fields always carried a little something with him for just such emergencies and used it to wash down the soap. Actually, Bill always carried a lot of something with him. And from the day Fanny told me that story, I always wondered if that's where the phrase "soap bar" came from.

May I have your attention please—heckling is not permitted in this chapter.

Admission to a lot of these small-time theaters was next to nothing, and in most cases the audience got their money's worth. The same kind of acts that played big-time played small-time, but the performers just weren't as good. The ventriloquists moved their lips, the jugglers dropped their balls, the acrobats dropped their partners; let me put it this way, it was in small-time that Jack Benny made a living as a violinist.

Because big-time acts never played the small towns, a lot of performers survived by imitating famous big-time acts those audiences would never see. They really didn't have to be very good, without television there was no basis for comparison. So any performer who sang "Yankee Doodle Dandy" through his nose was George M. Cohan. If an actor put on big white glasses, clapped his hands, waved his arms and sang, "If You Knew Susie," he was Eddie Cantor. A woman could become Fanny Brice by wearing a short skirt, leaning against a prop lamppost, and smoking a cigarette while singing "My Man." Anyone who put on a straw hat, stuck out his lower lip and sang "Mimi" in a bad American accent was Maurice Chevalier. If you could twirl a lariat and chew gum at the same time, all you had to do was say, "Well, seems to me that the Washington Monument's the only thing they got in that town that has any point to it," and you got to be Will Rogers. Any performer who couldn't sing could pretend he was talking on the telephone to his mother, then sing an off-key version of "My Mother's Eyes," and everybody in the audience knew he was Georgie Jessel. And if you couldn't even sing well enough to be Jessel, you could put on a hat, paste on a false nose and become Durante. There was only one Jolson, and a lot of people were him: They just blacked-up, got down on one knee and sang "Mammy." The performers who were being imitated didn't mind, and even if they did there was nothing they could do about it back then. Once, the great actor David Warfield suffered through a few minutes of a bad imitation of his act. Finally he turned to his companion, sighed, and said, "One of us is lousy."

I did impersonations when I was working with Billy Lorraine. "Burns and Lorraine," we billed ourselves, "Two Broadway Thieves." At least we were honest. Billy did Jolson, Cantor and minstrel show star Eddie Leonard. I did the great hoofers George White and Pat Rooney and George M. Cohan. Believe me, imitations were very easy to do.

Now big-time was just the opposite. Big-time was first class. We only did two shows a day, the dressing rooms had running water—some small-time theaters had running water too, but in big-

46

time the water came out of faucets—the theaters were beautiful and we were paid thousands of dollars a week. Everything about the big-time was better; the ticket takers, the backstage crew, the huge orchestra, the acts, even the audience. Most of the big-time theaters had a reserved-seat policy and people would buy subscriptions to the theater, guaranteeing them the same seat for the same performance every week. And going to vaudeville was special, people would dress up for the show. At the San Francisco Orpheum, for example, people would wear evening clothes.

The greatest big-time theater was the Palace on West 47th Street and Broadway in New York City. Once you played the Palace your career was made. No matter where you appeared after that you got top billing, "Direct from the Palace . . ." Every top star played the Palace—except Jolson. Jolson played the Winter Garden. He appeared at the Palace only once. Because of New York's blue laws, vaudeville was not permitted on Sundays. Instead, the Palace would host "concerts." Now, maybe these concerts looked like vaudeville, and maybe they sounded like vaudeville, but the big sign out front said CONCERT, so that's what it was. That's all right, I was once billed as a singer.

The biggest stars playing in New York would show up at the Palace on Sunday nights because their theaters were dark, and it became a tradition to introduce them to the audience and ask them to stand up and do a small bit. Many years later Ed Sullivan did the same thing on his Sunday night television show. So one Sunday night Palace MC Dave Apollon called on Jolson. Naturally, Jolson was very reluctant to perform for the audience. Sure, he was. Like my sister Goldie was reluctant to go out with a man still breathing. So Jolson stood in the aisle and sang for the audience, and that was the only time he ever performed at the Palace.

Incidentally, if anyone knows a single man for my sister Goldie, he doesn't have to be breathing *that* deeply.

Gracie and I were on the last great bill that played the Palace before they added movies to the show, and it was during that run that Eddie Cantor got the biggest laugh I ever heard in vaudeville. Cantor and Jessel were onstage ad-libbing and Jessel topped Cantor. Cantor then took off his shoe and hit Jessel over the head with it. I mean, he really hit him. The audience loved it. Jessel rubbed his head and walked to the footlights. When the audience stopped laughing, he said, "Ladies and gentlemen, something very painful has just happened to me. No, I don't mean getting hit on the head, I mean I've just discovered, after all these years, that I'm working with an idiot. You see, I said something very funny and you were kind enough to show your appreciation with your laughter. Mr. Cantor couldn't think of anything intelligent enough to top it, so he resorted to the most base form of humor, he hit me on the head with his shoe. And that pains me. Because a great comedian, and until this very minute I'd always considered Mr. Cantor a great comedian, must be witty enough to rise to the occasion . . ." and he went on and on about how hitting somebody over the head with a shoe was no way to try to top a joke. Cantor stood right behind him the whole time, just listening, not saying a single word. Finally, Jessel finished, and he turned and looked at Cantor and said, "So now what do you have to say for yourself?"

Cantor hit him over the head with his shoe again.

A typical big-time vaudeville bill included eight acts, while a small-time show might have four or five acts and a movie. When B. F. Keith created modern vaudeville he had intended it to be a show that ran continuously all day. "Come when you please," he advertised, "and stay as long as you like." At first a lot of people thought that policy wouldn't work because nobody would leave the theater. P. T. Barnum, the great showman, had solved the same problem when he ran his circus by hanging a big sign over the exit reading, THIS WAY TO THE EGRESS! But the continuous-run policy never caused any problems in small-time, maybe because of the quality of the acts. Let me put it this way: how many people really wanted to sit through "Brown and Williams" twice?

In the small-time the silent movies were known as "chasers," because if the acts didn't empty the theater, the movies would chase the audience. Most big-time theaters had a reserved-seat policy that prevented any problems.

The position on the bill was very important to a performer. The better spot you played, the more you would be paid, and the better chance you'd have for higher-paying bookings. Once, Gracie and I were supposed to be fourth, but when I showed up and checked the blackboard I saw we were in the second spot. I didn't want to play in the spot because it would have been a demotion. I called Gracie and told her she was sick. But just as I was telling the theater manager that Gracie was sick and we couldn't go on, he glanced at the blackboard. "Oh no," he said, "that's not right. 'Burns and Allen' are supposed to be fourth, the singer is number two."

"I think I hear the doctor calling," I said. I called Gracie and told her that a miracle cure had been discovered—a better spot on the bill.

Every show began with the house orchestra playing an overture, usually a medley of the current popular hits. The opening act was always a dumb act. A dumb act was an act that had no talking. For example, a 120-pound woman named Martha Farra did a strong-man act in which she laid down on a bed of nails and lifted a car with twelve men sitting in it. Now that was really a dumb act. Gracie and I, on the other hand, did an act in which she played dumb, but it was not a dumb act because we talked.

Dumb acts were jugglers, acrobats, animal acts, bicycle acts, aerial acts, roller and ice skating acts, club-swinging, hoop-rolling, boomerang-throwing, roping and whip-snapping acts, tram-

50

poline acts, swimming and diving "tank" acts, sharpshooters, strongmen, even contortionists. Their spot on the bill had nothing to do with how good they were; they could be the greatest hoop-rolling act in vaudeville, but they were still a "dumb" act and they were going to open the show. And a lot of these acts were absolutely amazing. I'd watch an acrobat bounce down a flight of stairs on his head and I'd wonder, how can he do that? And then I'd wonder, why would he do that? I always wanted to know who thought up bits like juggling people with your feet or sitting in a tank of water with a bucket over your head, playing the trombone. They used to tell a story about Kartella, who a lot of people believed was the greatest high-wire walker in show business. He would finish his act by balancing upside down on his head, on the high wire, while playing the clarinet. Supposedly, someone once brought a friend to see the act, and after that great finale asked, "What'd you think of that?"

The friend thought for a minute and said, "Well, he's no Benny Goodman."

Gracie and I once worked with the great juggler Serge Flash, who would finish his act by putting a fork in his mouth and catching food thrown to him from the audience on its prongs. Serge only had one rule—no puddings.

Fred Allen broke into vaudeville doing a comic variation of Serge's act—he'd put a fork in his mouth and attempt to catch a turnip thrown from the audience. He was so bad he couldn't have

51

caught a compliment. He'd always miss. That was his big finish, getting hit on the head by a thrown turnip.

The second spot was usually a singing or dancing act. When "Brown and Williams" was a song and dance act we worked in this spot. The dancing acts did every type of dance—clog dancing with wooden shoes, the old soft-shoe, tap-dancing, the buck and wing, roughhouse dancing that involved a lot of tossing partners, rope-skipping, the shimmy, the turkey trot, Charleston, black bottom, jitterbug, varsity drag, Lambeth Walk, even ballroom dancing. There were several specialty dance acts— "monopede" or one-legged dancers like Peg Leg Bates, and "monopede teams" in which each partner had one leg. There was a team that dressed like prisoners and performed with their legs chained together with a weighted ball and chain. There was a stilt dancer and a snowshoe dancer. Supposedly Bob Hope started as part of a dance act with Siamese Twins.

I did several different dance acts. One thing that I always wanted to do, and never had the opportunity, was tap-dancing. I had a great tap number choreographed, but I never found the right spot for it in my act. Maybe this is the moment I've been waiting for. So, with your permission, Mr. Conductor:

Tap. Tap tap. Taptaptaptaptaptaptaptaptaptaptap . . . watch me now . . . taptaptaptaptap. Tap tap, taptaptaptap, tap tap.

Tap.

Thank you, you're very kind. I'll tell you, that's not as easy as it used to be. Believe me, I'll bet that's the best tap-dance anybody's written in years.

The third act on the bill was a sketch, a one-act play. A sketch could be anything from heavy drama to slapstick comedy. Sketches allowed some of the great actors from the legitimate theater, people like the Barrymores, Sarah Bernhardt and Lily Langtry to tour without having to bring an entire company of actors and big sets with them. The Marx Brothers, who eventually became the highest-paid act in vaudeville at $10,000 a week, found their characters in sketches. For example, Groucho started as a German-dialect comedian— of course the day the German Navy sank the *Lusitania* he became a Hebrew-dialect comedian. Even after the Marx Brothers went into the movies they'd test scenes they were going to use in their movies in vaudeville, constantly adding new material and throwing out things that didn't work.

And as Gracie would say, that's why her brother George was not one of the Marx Brothers.

Gracie and I broke into the big-time as a disappointment act—when a scheduled act couldn't make it a disappointment act filled in—at the Bushwick Theatre in Brooklyn, following Ethel Barrymore in her classic dramatic sketch called "The Twelve Pound Look." We had absolutely no chance; old people came to see Ethel Barrymore before they died, young people came to see her before she died, the result was that everybody lived and "Burns and Allen" died.

The headliners usually appeared in the fourth and fifth spots. A big-time bill might include as many as three headliners. Headliners didn't even have to be good, they just had to be able to attract paying customers to the theater. A major headliner was someone like Sophie Tucker, "The Last of the Red Hot Mamas." Nobody could belt out a song like Sophie; they used to say her voice was so strong she could audition for a part in Hartford without ever leaving New York. Cantor and Jessel were headliners, they played the Palace more often than any other performers. Frank Fay was a headliner, he held the record for most consecutive weeks as MC at the Palace. Ed Wynn was a big headliner. Blossom Seeley and Benny Fields were headliners—Blossom was actually the first performer to get down on one knee while singing, even before Jolson—but she made a big mistake, she got up; Benny was the first star to sing through a megaphone. Lou Holtz was a big, big draw. Edgar Bergen and Charlie McCarthy, Fanny Brice, Durante, The Marx Brothers, they were all headliners. The Cherry Sisters were headliners too. Now, there were at least 25,000 acts working in vaudeville, so it would be impossible to single out one act as the very worst.

The Cherry Sisters were the worst act in vaudeville. If anybody asks, tell them that George Burns can do the impossible.

There were originally five Cherry Sisters, but

two of them went off on their own and became known as "The Vegetable Twins." The Cherry Sisters did a singing act that was so awful that they had to stand behind a net while performing so they wouldn't be hurt by the fruit and eggs thrown at them by the audience. They sang songs like "She Was My Sister and Oh, How I Missed Her," and the classic, "Corn Juice." They were so bad that they could have gotten down on *both* knees and it wouldn't have helped. They were so bad that Serge Flash could have put four complete table settings in his mouth and he couldn't have protected them. Once, they sued the *Des Moines Leader* for slander after that paper's theater critic had written, "Their mouths . . . opened like caverns and sounds like the wailings of damned souls issued therefrom. . . ." The judge in the case saw their act and found for the newspaper.

Not only didn't you have to be good or bad to be a headliner, you didn't even have to be a performer. The vaudeville stage was the only place people could see, "live and in person," the same celebrities they were reading about in the newspapers. Famous criminals, particularly women who were involved in "crimes of passion," appeared in vaudeville after being acquitted or after being released from prison. Women who swam the English Channel and anyone who flew across the Atlantic Ocean were big draws. After Charles Lindbergh became the first person to fly solo across the Atlantic he turned down a $100,000 offer to play a West Coast theater for one week.

The famous evangelist Aimee Semple McPherson got $5,000 a week, and flopped—although *Variety* decided, "She wears a white satin creation, sexy but Episcopalian." Most of the boxing champions toured in vaudeville, "Gentlemen Jim" Corbett even became a popular monologist after retiring from the ring. A lot of baseball players, including Babe Ruth and Ty Cobb, appeared in vaudeville during the winter. Giants pitcher Rube Marquard married Blossom Seeley and they worked together long before she met Benny. In their act he put on a dress and pretended to be pitching for her female baseball team. Maybe that wasn't a dumb act, but you had to admit it was pretty silly. Giants manager John McGraw recited a monologue and both Lefty Gomez and Dizzy Dean did comedy routines. Marathon winners, jockeys, pool and billiard champions, six-day-bicycle-race winners, tennis players and even football star Red Grange headlined shows. The famous blind and deaf writer Helen Keller appeared in vaudeville, touching the lips of members of the audience to "hear" their questions.

There was an intermission after the fifth act. The sixth act "opening intermission" featured the largest act on the bill. It might be anything from a "flash" act, a musical act featuring as many as fifteen beautiful girls, lavish costumes and elaborate sets—an act that made a big flash—to a big animal act. The smaller animal acts usually played first on the bill. There were lion acts and tiger acts and panthers and leopards, cats and dogs, elephants, monkeys, baboons, gorillas, horses, donkeys; there were bears and chickens, pigeons, cockatoos, boxing kangaroos, alligators, pigs, lambs, mice, snakes and seals. These animals did everything from posing to answering questions by tapping their feet. A lot of people believed that the big cats weren't really dangerous because they were old or had had their teeth removed. But as every vaudevillian believed, "A lion can still gum you to death."

A lot of performers didn't like to follow animal or kid acts, but the wonderful comedian Benny Rubin built an entire routine around following a dog act. Benny would be announced as a dancer; he would come onstage dressed in a formal outfit and start dancing. He was a talented dancer, but after doing several complicated steps he'd suddenly slip, and fall. He'd get up slowly, apologizing to the audience, and staring at a spot on the stage—his meaning was clear, the dog act had left a little souvenir behind. Benny would brush off his jacket, the music would start again and Benny would continue dancing. And then he'd . . . slip. And start to get up and . . . slip again. His whole bit consisted of slipping all over the stage on those souvenirs. Then, toward the end of the routine, he'd do two minutes of serious dancing, finally finishing with a showy move very popular with dance acts at that time—he'd kick up his heels and, with the palms of both hands, simultaneously slap the soles of his shoes. And then he . . .

. . . would remember. He'd stop completely,

and slowly, verrrry slowly, and with a look of great disgust on his face, look at his palms.

Personally, I always thought he was very lucky he didn't follow Powers Elephants.

The seventh spot, "next-to-closing," was the top spot on the bill. This was the star's spot. It was every vaudevillian's dream to play next-to-closing on the Orpheum Circuit. It was also the toughest spot, because the audience expected the most. If a comedian working next-to-closing came out and said, "A funny thing happened to me on the way to the theater tonight . . ." there would always be a heckler in the audience warning him, "At these prices it better have."

The greatest acts in vaudeville history played next-to-closing. That was when Smith and Dale would come onstage and do one of their classic "Dr. Kronkhite" bits, the most famous comedy routines in vaudeville. Smith played the aggressive patient who barged into Dale's Dr. Kronkhite's office. "How do you do, sir," Smith would begin. "Is this the office of Dr. Kronkhite?"

"Yes," Dale would reply. Both of them spoke with a heavy Jewish accent.

"Are you a doctor?"

"I'm a doctor."

"I'm dubious."

"I'm glad to know you, Mr. Dubious. Mr. Dubious, would you mind waiting, I got a patient in the other room. I'll be right back."

Dale would exit and suddenly a scream would

be heard offstage. "That's all I want to know," Smith would say, and start to leave the office.

Dale would reenter and catch him. "Here, here, where are you going?"

"I'm going home, I forgot something."

"What? What could you forget?"

"I forgot to stay there."

I guess Georgie Jessel and Eddie Cantor played next-to-closing at the Palace more than any other acts. Jessel was a great monologist. His most famous routines were imaginary telephone calls to his mother. Georgie didn't originate that idea, "Cohen on the Telephone" did it first, but Jessel made it popular.

"Hello, Momma," Georgie would begin, "it's me, Georgie. That's right, Georgie from the money. Where do you think I'm calling from? Hollywood, it's long distance. Of course it's expensive, but don't worry about it. I'm visiting. I'm at Eddie Cantor's house. How are you feeling? Oh, you see spots in front of your eyes? Well, why don't you wear your glasses? Because they're up on your forehead? That isn't the Brooklyn Bridge, you know, you can just pull them down. Good, you got your glasses on now. How is it? You can see the spots better with your glasses?

"So how did you like that beautiful present I sent you? That beautiful bird. You cooked it? Mother, that was a South American parrot, he speaks five languages. You're right, he should have said something. Momma, put my sister Anna on the phone.

59

"Anna? Look, honey, I know this isn't the time or place to lecture you, but after all, I'm your older brother and I love you dearly. And if I'm not thinking of your future, who is? Now what's gonna be with that fella of yours? You're getting married in December? How do you know? Oh, he said it would be a cold day when he married you. Put your mother back on."

Lou Holtz was another comedian who appeared next-to-closing on some of the greatest bills in vaudeville. I know that as soon as I mention the name Lou Holtz one word jumps into most of your minds: Who? Lou Holtz isn't very well remembered today, maybe because he never successfully made the transition to radio, and that's a shame because he was a great comedian. Just as important, he was a regular in my Thursday-night card game at the Forrest Hotel on 49th Street with Jack Benny and Jesse Block, Benny Fields, Ted Lewis and whoever else was in town. Lou Holtz was the kind of man valued in any card game— a rotten player with money. Believe me, if you ever played cards with Lou Holtz, you wouldn't have forgotten him so fast.

I'll tell you how big Lou Holtz was at that time—he was the first comedian to book the Palace for ten consecutive weeks, and he did it at $6,000 a week. He was one of the best dialect comedians in the business; he'd tell long stories about a character named Sam Lapidus in a classy Jewish accent. Dialect comedy was very popular in vaudeville—any accent you could hear on the streets of New York you could hear on the vaudeville stage. And nobody got offended. Today . . . today it's very tough to tell any kind of ethnic stories. People are so sensitive. If you want to tell ethnic stories you have to be so careful, they have to be things like: these two Polish guys are walking down the street and one of them said nothing to the other one. Or, Pat and Mike walked into a bar and ordered mineral water. Or, this Jewish mother answered the telephone and it was her son, the doctor, calling.

But Lou Holtz's Sam Lapidus wasn't like that. I think a lot of immigrants identified with Lapidus because he was constantly trying to make sense of things in this country he didn't understand. I'll give you an example. In one famous story Lou told, Lapidus and his friend had just finished their meal in a fancy restaurant and the waiter had placed finger bowls in front of them. Sam had no idea what it was:

"For what good is it?" Lapidus asked. "It can't be soup, soup we already had it. It can't be water—water is already in the glasses, and with lemon on the side this has got me biffled completely. I think I will ask the vaiter."

"Oi," his friend said, "please, don't humiliate me."

"Waiter," Lapidus said, "so excuse me the intrusion, but for what are these two articles?"

The waiter explained that they were called finger bowls, and they were to be used to wash fingers.

61

"Ah-ha!" Lapidus's friend said triumphantly, "see, I warned you. You ask a foolish question, you entitled to a foolish answer."

The closing act on the bill was always another dumb act. People used to say that the closing act played to the haircuts, because the audience would usually start leaving after the headliner took his curtain calls, and all the closing act saw was the back of people's heads.

The whole bill was held together by the master of ceremonies. The MC would introduce the acts, fill the time between acts by ad-libbing, gag with the acts before they performed and do his own bit. A good MC could make average acts seem like stars, telling the audience, "The only reason he's here with us tonight instead of being next-to-closing at the Palace Theatre in New York was because the Wabash River washed out," or, "I know you're going to appreciate them because they send their whole salary to their poor, crippled children . . ." or, "If 'Brown and Williams' are successful here tonight, they're going to be booked on the Orpheum Circuit and maybe, just maybe, be able to pay the bank and save their farm."

Ed Wynn was the first MC at the Palace, working the show when the theater opened in 1913, but most people would agree that Frank Fay was the greatest MC in vaudeville history. That was an amazing thing too, because Frank had a tremendous handicap to overcome—his character. He didn't have one. I'll tell you what kind of guy Frank Fay was; he once hired a lawyer to defend him against another lawyer; who was suing him because he hadn't paid his attorney's fees in a divorce case—and after Frank won that case he didn't pay the second lawyer either. All right, so maybe he wasn't all bad. But he was an egomaniac, he was constantly starting fights and he was an alcoholic. Outside of that, he was a sweetheart.

Fay had a lot of nicknames. "The Great Fay," "The King," "Broadway's Favorite Son," and anything else he could think of to call himself. It was Fayzie who once had a long conversation with a friend about the act he was doing, then said, "Look, that's enough about me, let's talk about you. What do *you* think about my act?" It seemed like he was always in a fight with somebody. Once, he got into a brawl with comic Ted Healy and Healy knocked him out with one punch. Well, actually, Healy didn't knock out Fay, he knocked out Fay's teeth, and Fay immediately stopped the fight to search for his teeth. Fay did, however, score a one-punch kayo over his wife, Barbara Stanwyck.

But it was something to see Fay work onstage. You just had to admire his talent. One year he spent twenty-six weeks hosting shows at the Palace. One of the things he did onstage was analyze the lyrics of popular songs. When "As Time Goes By" was a big hit, for example, he quoted the line "The world will always welcome lovers . . ." then wondered, "If that's true, why do they have house detectives?"

I think Fay's real strength as an MC was his

63

ability to ad-lib. He was very smart onstage. Once, for example, he was working at the Shubert when a small fire broke out in the balcony. There was a lot of smoke and people started to panic. Fay calmed everybody down, telling them, "Now just wait a minute, where do you think you're going? Nobody runs out on me. So just sit down and relax." And people trusted him, at least people who weren't lawyers trusted him, and they calmed down.

All the great comedians used to love to go to see him and give him a bad time. He could handle it. Once Berle was heckling him, and challenged him to a duel of wits. "I can't," Fay explained, "I never fight an unarmed man." During another show Groucho was giving him a tough time; this was just after Zeppo had quit the act. Every time Fay opened his mouth Groucho tried to put some words into it. Finally, Fay asked Groucho to come up onstage. Groucho refused. Fay insisted, "Come up here so the audience can hear both of us." When Groucho refused again, Fay looked right at him and said quietly, "See you really do need Zeppo."

Gracie was the first woman to serve as mistress of ceremonies at the Palace. When she was offered the job I turned it down—sure, let Bergen speak for his dummy *on* stage—but Jessel accepted it for her. Gracie would walk onstage with strings tied around her fingers, "To remind me not to forget what I'm trying to remember."

"Gracie," I would say to her, "your memory is

so bad that if your head wasn't fastened to your shoulders you'd forget it."

"I know, George," she'd agree, "it runs in the family. My uncle had to go back to Arizona for his lungs."

Gracie had her own way of introducing an act. "The next act is a charming boy with a wonderful voice. I know you'll be crazy about him on account of I am, so let's give him a big hand . . . Gene Harvey." Now, Gene Harvey, or whoever, would come out and Gracie would say, "Gene, I just thought of a wonderful story. It seems that once there was this traveling salesman who was kind of cool towards his wife. In fact, he didn't like his wife at all. As a matter of fact, Gene, he hated his wife. What I mean is, he really despised her. So for twenty years every time he traveled he took his wife with him. Finally one of his friends asked him, 'Joe, if you hate your wife like that, why do you always take her along?' And Joe said, 'I hate her so, that I'd rather take her along than have to kiss her goodbye.' Ladies and gentlemen, Gene Harvey. . . ."

Of course, she couldn't use that introduction for anybody but Gene Harvey.

Finally the vaudeville would end and the audience would leave the theater—unless Sophie Tucker was on the bill. After every show Sophie would set up a folding table in the lobby and sit behind it selling copies of her book or her records. Sophie only accepted cash. No checks. She told me that all the money she made went to charity.

Now, Sophie was a wonderful woman; smart, talented, sassy, and I'm not saying that she kept any of that money, but Sophie also used to tell me, "Remember, Natty, charity begins at home."

I think one of the most exciting things about vaudeville was that anybody could be in it. It wasn't restricted to people who could sing or dance or fly through the air—anybody who could do anything that somebody else would pay to see could be in vaudeville. In addition to the normal acts on every bill, there were often novelty acts or "freak" acts—one-of-a-kind, step-right-up-and-buy-your-ticket types of acts. Even the sophisticated Palace Theatre once booked "The Twelve Speed Maniacs," a team of a dozen men who would assemble an entire Ford Model T in exactly two minutes. Their big finale was driving it offstage.

Female and male impersonators were popular in vaudeville. At the end of their performance they would always take off their wig to prove to the audience that they were really the opposite of what they were pretending to be. Sometimes, though, after taking their bows, the female impersonators would take off a male wig and confuse the audience by looking as if they were really the woman they'd pretended to be when they first came onstage. I suppose you could call that bit a "Jessel"—Georgie always wanted to be the man between two women.

Remember, hecklers will be ejected from this book.

If you could do anything better, faster, longer, more often, higher, worse or differently than anyone else, you could work in vaudeville. For example, "The World's Fastest Typist" had a great act. She'd type 200 words a minute, then pass the perfectly typed pages out to the audience to be inspected. For her finish she'd put a piece of tin in her typewriter and imitate a drum roll or the clackety-clack of a train picking up speed.

Anything could be the basis of an act. Mind reading, mental telepathy and hypnotism were popular. Posing acts pretended to be statues— maybe they did nothing, but they did it beautifully. One performer ate paper, wood, flowers, light bulbs and matches, while another man bit railroad spikes in half. There was a couple who danced wearing snowshoes, a woman who jumped over lighted candlesticks, and several people wrote forwards, backwards and upside down; there was an Australian speed-woodchopping act, a man who got taller as his act progressed and there was "Dates," who could name the exact date any major event in history took place. There was even . . . "The Wrestling Cheese," a slab of cheese that could not be lifted off the stage, and a Chinese act that put chopsticks through their noses.

Uh, Milton? I think I have an idea for you.

A lot of different types of artists toured in vaudeville. There were quick-sketch artists who could turn out several drawings a minute, "shadographists" who cut silhouette profiles out of black paper; there were artists who painted with colored sand and artists who blew colored soap bubbles and artists who sculpted in clay and ice. And, naturally, there were escape artists.

There were also a lot of musical novelty acts. Two men played "The Anvil Chorus" by clanging horseshoes on anvils, complementing their "music" by creating an impressive display of colored sparks. One musician played two clarinets at the same time, another one played the piano and the violin simultaneously. There was a wheelbarrow player, a performer who played a skeleton as if it was a xylophone and another one who played his face—making "music" by hitting his teeth, cheeks and the side of his head. A barbershop quartet played the comb and all the other things you'd find in a barbershop, another act played the tools found in a sawmill. A sharpshooter played the chimes by shooting at them from the theater balcony, someone else made music by throwing snowballs at tambourines—although he was forced to take summers off—and another musician played the piano with a banana and a lemon. One performer sang "I Am Smoking" while smoking a cigar and blowing smoke rings, and a real Jewish cantor was a big hit singing "Mother Machree."

What the Palace was to the great performers, Hammerstein's Theatre in New York was to these novelty acts. Today, when an athlete wins a big game, the Disney people pay him a lot of money to claim, "Now I'm going to Disneyland." Personally, it looks to me like he's going to the locker room. But in the old days, whenever an athlete won a big event, his coach or manager would tell him, "Hurry up, take a shower and put on your clothes. You're booked at Hammerstein's." That's true, and this time I really mean it.

Willie Hammerstein was the greatest showman in vaudeville, booking anyone who would draw customers. When two women shot and wounded a male socialite, Willie bailed them out and booked them for a week as "The Shooting Stars." The world's tallest man, a 9'2" giant, played Hammerstein's; the first hootchy-kootchy dancers in America made their debut at Hammerstein's; and Evelyn Nesbit, the woman who became world famous when millionaire Harry K. Thaw shot architect Stanford White for stealing her affections, set attendance records at Hammerstein's. A few years later Jessel took a shot at the guy who'd stolen Norma Talmadge from him, but all he got out of it was probation and a big fine.

Willie Hammerstein was a very smart fellow. I'll tell you what he did. He enclosed the roof of his theater in glass and presented the *really* unusual acts up there. Unfortunately, there was no air conditioning so in the summer Hammerstein's Roof got very hot. So Willie put a heater in the elevator that took people up to the roof and had it going full blast, that way no matter how hot it got on the roof, when people stepped out of the elevator they felt it was much cooler.

I miss vaudeville. I miss the acts, the theaters, the audiences, the fun we had and, maybe most of all, I miss the security. No matter how bad your act was, you could get booked. Believe me, if a wrestling cheese could work, I knew I'd never have to worry about getting a job.

Basically, the only things you needed to work in vaudeville were black and white lobby pictures, business cards and music in your key. The act didn't have to be very much, but you had to do something—unless you were doing a posing act, in which case you had to do nothing. And do it without moving for long periods of time. The hardest part of putting an act together was getting material.

Most comedians did the same thing I did when they were starting out, they found jokes in humor magazines and joke books and rewrote them to fit their acts. For example, Benny Ryan used to ask his partner, Harriet Lee, "Did you read about the big robbery in the paper the other day?"

"No," she'd say. Until Gracie changed things, women usually played straight man.

"It was terrible," Benny would tell her. "A man stole $100,000 and insects."

"A man stole $100,000 and insects?"

"That's what the story said, 'Man Steals $100,000 and Flees.'"

Now, if Jack Benny were stealing that joke, he'd say ". . . a man stole a dollar and insects . . ." Lou Holtz's Sam Lapidus might say, "Oi, you should only know from this meshugana robber . . ." And Jolson would tell audiences, "Maybe you read in the papers about the big robbery the other day? Well, it don't matter anyway, 'cause Jolie's gonna sing a few songs for you. . . ."

I'm going to admit something right now, a lot of performers stole their material from other acts. Keep it quiet. It's true, we would steal from anybody. Maybe with the exception of "The Wrestling Cheese." Berle was the smartest one of all. Not only did he steal jokes, he built his whole character around the fact that he stole material. So he got jokes out of stealing jokes.

The only way an act could protect its material was to register it with the Casey office. Pat Casey ran the Vaudeville Managers Protective Agency and everybody would write down their act, seal it in an envelope and send it to Casey for safekeeping. If there was a disagreement over who owned some material Casey would open the letter and notify the person who stole it to stop using it. The Casey office was part of a major booking agency, so everybody who wanted to work listened to him. Now, Gracie's brother didn't quite understand the concept. For a while he was a trombone player, so he blew his act into an envelope and mailed it to the Casey office. I tried to tell him that wouldn't do him any good but he didn't believe me. "What's the matter," he asked, "can't anybody in the Casey office read music?"

You think I spent forty years with Gracie and some of it didn't rub off?

Even Jolson stole material from other acts, but Jolson was so big he could get away with it. If he heard a joke he wanted to use, he'd send a wire

71

to the performer using it telling him to take it out of his act because it was his joke. Jolson was so important that even people who were using material they'd written figured they must have stolen it from Jolson's mind. Besides, it was an honor to be good enough to have Jolson steal your material. It was like owning a bank robbed by John Dillinger. And maybe it was only fair—everybody else was doing Jolson, why shouldn't Jolson do everybody else?

Of course, there were performers who took action when their material was stolen. When Bill Fields found out that a famous comic was using one of his bits he hired two tough guys to cut it out of that comic's act, literally, if necessary. And they used to talk about a comic named Harry Breen, who ran into a comedian who was using some of Breen's material. "You make your living talking, right?" Breen asked. The other comic agreed. "Good," Breen said as he punched him in the mouth, "try doing it with a lisp."

Performers would take material from anyplace they could find it. Harpo told me about a theater the Marx Brothers played in Fargo, North Dakota; the manager had hung up a big sign in the wings listing about 100 jokes and the warning, THESE JOKES HAVE ALREADY BEEN USED IN THIS THEATER—DO NOT USE THEM. And nobody used them there, but everybody wrote them down and put them in their act for their next booking.

Vaudeville not only gave us a chance to fail, five times a day, it allowed us to find our characters while we were failing. Remember, when we all started Harpo spoke and Durante didn't, I told jokes, Jack played the violin, Jolson stood up, Edgar Bergen put Charlie McCarthy in a closet and tried to make it as a Swedish-dialect comedian, Berle did his own material and Fred Allen got hit in the head with turnips, but those acts didn't work and we all had to try something different. I was probably the luckiest one of all, it wasn't hard for me to find my character. One day I looked to my left and Gracie was standing there. The audience helped us create our act; they laughed at our funny lines and didn't laugh at my lines. The audience created Gracie's character. Audiences were great, they let you know when they liked you and they told you when they didn't—and that was called heckling.

Every performer in vaudeville had to learn how to deal with hecklers. There were lots of standard responses: "The last time I saw a mouth like yours it had a hook in it," "You can go home now, your cage is clean," "Is that really your face, sir, or did your pants fall down?" "Sir, if I had your intelligence I wouldn't be wasting my time making a fool out of myself in a small town like this, you can go big time," and, "Listen, I don't come 'round to where you work and kick the shovel out of your hand." Milton was probably the best at dealing with hecklers, but then he probably had the most practice. He used to tell members of the audience who yelled at him, "Please, sir, I've only got ten minutes to make a fool of myself, you've got all night," and, "Didn't I see your face on a bottle of iodine?"

A performer always had to be careful dealing with a heckler, you really didn't know who you were dealing with. For example, the Jefferson Theatre on 14th Street in New York was one of the toughest houses in vaudeville. One night a local gangster who had only one arm, he was called "One Arm Tony," was sitting in the front row for Lou Holtz's show. He'd applaud by slapping his one arm against his thigh. When Lou went on, he didn't applaud, he yelled at him. Lou handled it very nicely, he looked right at the guy and said, "Who's that seal in the front row?"

Let me offer a little advice for any would-be performers, based on my eighty-six years in show business: Never call a one-armed gangster a seal.

Lou had to have a police escort to leave the theater that night and didn't play the Jefferson again for years.

Of course, sometimes there is no answer for a heckler. Sid Garry and I were once on a bill with a nice family act called "Jim Gibson and Company." At the end of their act, Jim Gibson would walk to the footlights and say, "Ladies and gentlemen, you've been a wonderful audience. Thank you so much on behalf of myself and the kids. Now, to show our appreciation, how would you like to hear my wife sing a song?" Usually everyone in the audience applauded, but one night a fellow in the front row said loudly, "I wouldn't."

Gibson was stunned. "What?" he said.

"Look, Mr. Gibson," the heckler explained, "I loved your act, it's great, I applauded my hands off. But you've played this theater before and I've heard your wife sing. So when you asked that question, I answered it."

As Durante would have said, "Evvvre-body wants a get inna de act."

3

I want to discuss something with you privately, page to person. Look around, is anybody reading over your shoulder? I want to tell you something I've never told anybody else in this book before. I . . .

I dare you to stop reading right now. Still reading? Sure you are, otherwise you wouldn't be reading this. See, I've just shown you the importance of a good opening to an act. Or a chapter. The thing I wanted to tell you was that I didn't have an opening for this chapter. But now I don't have to worry about it, it's already opened.

Jack Benny always said that the opening was the most important part of an act. We used to talk about it a lot. "It's how you start that's important," he insisted, "Once you get the attention of the audience it's not really important how you finish. You'll be a hit. You can always get offstage—there are two exits.

Maybe that's good advice when it comes to dating, open with flowers and you'll be a hit, but not when it concerns your act. Jack was wrong about that. The closing is just as important as the opening—in show business and in dating. Winning the audience is important, but the bookers remember how many curtain calls you took at the end. In vaudeville, if your act didn't have a big finish, your act was finished.

When Jack started as a single he had a very small opening. The curtain would rise and he'd be standing there with his back to the audience, playing the scales on his violin. That was smart, he knew that as soon as he stopped playing, his act would start getting better. Finally he'd turn around and look at the audience. "Oh," he'd say casually, "I guess I'm on."

Jack didn't become a star until he stopped playing the violin and began using it as a prop. I helped talk him into that, or out of it, and I don't really think I've ever received enough credit for that. We were working in Wilkes-Barre, Pennsylvania, and I knew he'd been thinking about going on-stage without his fiddle. "You don't need it," I told him, "just leave it here in the hotel."

He wasn't sure. "You really think I don't need it?"

"Jack," I said, putting my arm around his shoulder, "Jack, how long have you known me? Would I lie to you?"

He didn't say a word, he just looked at me with those big, sad, innocent eyes.

"All right," I admitted, "maybe I would. But not about this. You don't need the violin." I never said, trust me. He knew me too well for that.

So he believed me. Is that my fault? That night he went onstage for the first time in his life without his fiddle. He used his opening from "The

Great Lakes Revue," asking the orchestra conductor, "How's the show so far?" The conductor said it was fine. "Well," Jack promised, "I'll fix that." As he started talking he folded his arms, he intertwined his fingers, he touched his cheek, he put his hands under his chin, he hid them behind his back. He didn't know what to do with his hands. But without his fiddle to hold on to he couldn't concentrate. He finally had to borrow a violin from a musician in the orchestra to hold on to while he finished his act.

It was more than a year later before he tried working without his fiddle again. He had finally figured out what to do with his hands—he folded his arms, he intertwined his fingers, he touched his cheek, he put his hands under his chin, he hid them behind his back. His hands became an important part of his stage character. A lot of people could play the violin as badly as Jack Benny, but few people were ever as bad with their hands as he was.

Jack wasn't the only person who used a prop in his opening. When Fred Allen was starting his career as a monologist he'd come out dressed in a suit way too big for him. The pants dragged on the floor, the jacket hung down to his knees. He'd stand there for a little while, letting the audience see the suit, then explain, "I bought this suit up in New Rochelle, my hometown, and in New Rochelle I'm a much bigger man than I am down here."

Ed Wynn often used an elaborate opening.

In one show he did, when the curtain went up, an acrobatic act would be onstage twirling Indian clubs back and forth. As many as twenty Indian clubs would be spinning through the air. It was really impressive. Then Ed would stroll in from the wings carrying a stepladder. He'd set up the ladder between the acrobats, climb up five steps, and reach down and grab an Indian club out of the air. Then he'd climb down the ladder, fold it up, put it under his arm and walk offstage without ever looking at the audience. When he came back onstage he'd always get a big ovation.

But no matter what Wynn did, he'd do it wearing a silly costume. He always wore something that made the audience laugh. Years later Milton Berle often opened his television show the same way—except he'd be wearing a dress. I think he stole that particular opening from Loretta Young. Listen, I always thought it was fine to wear something funny—as long as the rest of your act was good enough to live up to your dress.

In vaudeville, Berle would come out and heckle the audience. Maybe he thought he'd beat them to the punch line. He'd open with a bad joke and when the audience didn't laugh, he'd ask, "What's the matter? You sore 'cause I'm working?" If that didn't get the response he wanted, he'd lean forward and cup his hand around his ear. "I know you're out there," he'd say, "I hear breathing."

Cantor had a cute opening bit. He'd come onstage with a deck of cards and ask for volunteers from the audience. He'd give cards to four or five people and tell them to stand up and hold them over their heads, but warn them not to let him see what they were. And then, while they were standing there holding these cards over their heads, he'd ignore them completely. He'd start singing, "Oh, How She Could Yacki Hicki Wicki Wacki Woo . . . She had the hula hula yacka bula in her walk." It wasn't exactly a love song. It took the audience a minute to realize that the card trick was that there was no card trick, just people standing up holding cards over their heads. . . .

Jessel had a casual opening. At times he would enter eating a frankfurter and ask the audience, "Does anyone have any mustard?" Frank Van Hoven, a comic magician, had one of my favorite opening bits. He'd come out twirling a cane. He'd flip it into the air and it would come down and stick in the stage, then a little American flag would pop out the top. "I know it's not much," he'd say, "but I thought somebody might like it."

"Harris and Holly," a standard comedy-with-music act, would be struggling to get a grand piano onstage when the curtain lifted. Holly was straining to pull it, but Harris was on the back end doing nothing. "Come on," Holly pleaded, "push this thing."

"You just keep on pulling your end," Harris told him, "my end'll follow."

Comic Bert Fitzgibbons did one of the great "nut" acts in vaudeville; it was called a nut act because he did nutty things. Nut acts included a lot of physical comedy. When Fitzgibbons was announced, he'd race down the center aisle from the back of the theater, leap onto the stage and smash a footlight with his cane, shouting, "Nobody sleeps when I'm on."

It was a nice opening and I'd even think about using it today, but by the time I reached the stage the audience would have gone home.

. . . Still holding the cards over their heads. . . .

Harry Rose, who was known as "The Broadway Jester," also did a nut act. He'd open by running out from the wings and leaping onto a platform the stagehands had constructed over a portion of the orchestra pit. But one day the stagehands forgot to put up the platform, and when Harry's entrance music began he came running out, leaped . . . and crashed onto the floor of the pit. The conductor just looked down at him lying there, then asked, "Want me to play your entrance music again?"

I'll tell you who had a clever opening, Bob Hope. Bob would come onstage and look around and then he'd . . . leave for Europe.

Jolson had the most famous opening line in show business. I think he used it for the first time when he appeared at a war bonds rally during World War I. Enrico Caruso was on just before him, and Caruso could sing. This was one of the very few times in his career he ever performed outside the opera. So he sang and he sang and the people just loved him. He finished by leading the whole audience in "Over There." Everybody in

81

the place was standing and singing and crying, they tore the place apart.

And then Jolson came on. Jolson always went on last because nobody could follow him. Now, Jolie hated to hear the audience applauding another performer and Caruso had just received one of the biggest ovations in show business history. So Jolson waited until the crowd had quieted down, and then he told them, "Ladies and gentlemen, you ain't heard nothin' yet!"

Musicians and singers and dancers could always get offstage with a rousing finish to one of their songs, magicians could just disappear, Powers Elephants did a Charleston, but comedians had a tough time finding a big finish for their act. When the Marx Brothers were doing their singing act, Minnie Marx taught them, "Always leave 'em with a song. If they go away whistling, you're a hit." And when they became a comedy act she insisted, "Always leave 'em with a laugh . . . as long as you send them home whistling."

People would do anything for a big finish. One famous sketch ended with a reenactment of Paul Revere's ride—the actors brought a live horse onstage and had him galloping on a treadmill. Both Fred Allen and Benny Fields had patriotic finishes—while the orchestra played patriotic music, they'd show a silent film clip that included American flags blowing in the wind, soldiers marching off to war, Presidents waving, kids saluting, it was impossible not to stand up and cheer.

And when the audience got up and cheered, Fred and Benny would take a bow and walk off.

Once though, Benny Fields was on a bill with Henny Youngman at the Flatbush Theatre in Brooklyn, and they weren't getting along. Youngman wanted Benny to cut a few minutes out of the show and Benny wouldn't do it. So, one matinee, while Benny was onstage for his big finale, the orchestra was playing, flags were waving, the soldiers were marching, Presidents saluting, kids waving, Henny walked onstage wearing a red, white and blue bathrobe and a large red, white and blue hat. He went right up to Benny Fields and screamed, "Go ahead and wave me, you no good son of a bitch."

The great British comedienne Bea Lillie had a wonderful finish. Bea could sing a little and at the end of her act she'd put on a sophisticated full-length gown and sing a sweet, sentimental love song. And then, as the last beautiful notes of the song were still floating gently in the air, she'd hike up her gown, revealing her roller skates, and skate offstage.

Lou Holtz was known for his finish, his "O Sole Mio," song. He'd sing endless comic verses to the tune of "O Sole Mio," and the whole audience would join him for the chorus, which was "O Sole Mio." It went something like this:

> *My wife ran away with the chauffeur*
>   *last year,*
> *Now I'm as nervous as can be,*

'Cause every time I hear an auto horn,
I think he's bringing her back to me.
O sole mio, O sole mio . . .

At first Jack Benny would end his act by playing a tune on his violin, so naturally he got a big cheer when he finished. But when he put down his fiddle, he needed another finish, so he started singing. Let me tell you about Jack's singing voice—it made his violin playing sound good. Jack's singing career started when he worked in vaudeville with a song plugger named Ned Miller. Back then music publishers would do anything to promote sales of their sheet music—when a song sold a million copies, that meant it had sold a million copies of the sheet music—including providing a singer to tour with vaudeville acts that would let them plug some songs.

To begin with, Jack would introduce Ned Miller as his "very nervous kid brother. He's backstage right now," Jack would explain, "but if you give him a warm welcome, he'll come out and sing a song for you. " A warm welcome? They could have thrown ice cubes and Ned would have come out to sing. Ice cubes? The Ice Age could have run through the theater and Ned would have come out to sing. Ned wrote and performed a wonderful song, "Why Should I Cry Over You," which did sell a million copies—with Jack's photograph on the cover of the sheet music. After a while Jack planted Ned in the audience, and Ned would heckle Jack throughout his act. Finally Jack would challenge him, "Okay, if you want to entertain these people, go ahead." Then Ned would stand up and surprise everybody by singing in a beautiful soprano voice. Whether Ned was onstage or in the audience, Jack would join him in singing the last few bars, and Jack was so off-key, but sincere, that the audience couldn't help laughing. And while they were laughing, Jack would walk offstage.

Jack probably had the shortest opening and finish to an act in vaudeville history. Believe me, this could be a true story. He was booked at The Academy of Music on 14th Street in New York, one of the toughest houses in the business. The master of ceremonies introduced him and before he could open his mouth the catcalls started: "Throw him a fish." "Nice fiddle, Nero." Jack knew he had no chance. So he waited until the audience quieted down a bit, then told them, "Nothing funny happened to me on the way to the theater tonight, so good night," and walked off and kept walking right out the stage door.

Durante's finishes were famous. He did one act, called "Wood," in which he read an "Ode to Wood" published by the lumber industry, while Clayton and Jackson piled things made of wood onto the stage. I mean, anything made of wood. They started with a pencil and ended up with tables, chairs, a canoe, anything. But when he worked as a single, he'd be sitting at a grand piano, singing one of his songs, and suddenly he'd start waving his arms and shouting at his backup orchestra, "Stop da music, stop da music!" The music would fade out and he'd throw the sheet music at them, screaming, "You're supposed to follow da music, not chase it all over da place!" Then they would start playing again, and again Jimmy would wave his arms, "Stop da music, stop da music! You know, I went inta the Automat today and I put a lead nickel inta the slot and whattya think comes out? The manager." Then he'd start playing again and again, stop da music, stop da music. "What's this?" he'd demand, grabbing the music rack and throwing it at his drummer, Jack Roth. "This board looks useless. It interferes with da vibrettos. Mr. Knabe musta put that there when Mr. Steinway wasn't looking." Again he starts playing and again he . . . stop da music, stop da music. "Some careless guy left this top up," he screamed, pulling out the prop and letting the lid crash down. "It's lettin' da music out too fast. I'll fix that." And again . . . stop da music, stop da music. He grabbed hold of the pedals and yanked them out, heaving them toward Jack Roth. "Away with da harps. I only play one instrument at a time." And . . . stop da music, stop da music. "Whatta coincidence," he said as he threw the keyboard cover over his shoulder, "this . . . is removeable." An . . . stop da music, stop da . . . The top went next, as he explained, "No wonder da notes sound smothered up. They can't breathe with this thing on." Stop da . . . the keyboard. "Maybe Iturbi needs a keyboard, but I play by ear!" Stop . . . one leg of the piano. "Run for da hills, folks, bedlum is runnin' amuck!"

Finally, all that was left was a heap of broken piano and Jimmy, standing in front of it, complaining, "The jernt wanted genius . . . but I warned 'em that this pianna wasn't made for da classical touch."

I'll tell you the worst finish I ever heard about in vaudeville. Hawthorn and Cook did a nut act called "Two Crazy Guys." One night their act did not go over at all and Cookie just couldn't take it. Maybe all the years of bad bookings, bad hotels and bad meals got to him, or maybe he just had too much to drink, because instead of doing the regular finish, he walked to the footlights and told the audience, "We want to thank you very much. You've been a very charming audience, and to show how we feel about you, on the way out my father's going to stand by the exit and beat the hell outta you."

Now that wasn't just the finish of their act, that was almost the finish of their career in vaudeville. Not only couldn't you say hell in vaudeville, you couldn't threaten to beat up the audience. And after that no one would book them. So supposedly Hawthorn hired six young children and took them to the office of Edward Albee. Albee built most of the great theaters in the big time. Hawthorn pleaded with him for a contract, asking him, "You don't want these wee ones to hate you for their whole lives, do you?"

And Hawthorn wasn't even Irish.

Jolson never had a real ending. I don't think he could bear the thought of an audience actually leaving. So he would just keep on singing. When the crew wanted to close the theater, he'd tell the audience, "I'm going over to Lindy's, and I'll probably sing a few more songs over there," and his concert would move to the restaurant. Jolson never finished, he just wore out the audience.

Because both Gracie and I had started out as hoofers, we ended our act by dancing offstage, pausing every few steps to tell a quick story about one of Gracie's relatives. Now, since I'm confessing in this chapter, I'm now going to tell you something I've never told anyone before. So don't tell anyone else, because you never know when I might need another good opening bit. The truth is that some of the stories we told about Gracie's relatives weren't true. We made them up; the relatives and the stories. There really was no Franklin Delano Allen. Or Thomas Alva Allen. Or King William IV Allen. But the stories I've told about my sister Goldie were all true. Well, at least most of them, I admit I lied about the affair with Gandhi.

It was several years later that we began using the closing that became so well known. After Gracie told me that her uncle William Randolph Allen had cornered the market on yellow journalism by buying old newspapers, I'd tell her to "Say good night, Gracie."

And that's exactly what she said.

In addition to a big opening and bigger closing,

every act needed one more thing—insurance. Insurance didn't mean somebody would pay you if the act didn't go over—who would sell me that kind of policy?—it meant three minutes of surefire material, guaranteed to wake up the audience. It was the stuff you did when the audience seemed to be mistaking your act for the Cherry Sisters. Jolson sang "Mammy." Sophie Tucker did "One of These Days." Blossom Seeley sang "Toddling the Todalo." Cantor did "If You Knew Susie." Jessel picked up the telephone, "Hello, Momma, it's Georgie from the money. . . ." Milton did Jessel picking up the telephone, "Hello, Momma, it's Milton from the money. . . ." And me? I had the best insurance of all. I'd turn to my insurance and ask, "Gracie, how's your brother?"

She never failed. "He was held up by two men last night."

"Your brother? Held up? By two men?" Raise my eyebrows. "Where did they hold him up?"

"All the way home."

Not too long ago I made a video called "The Wit and Wisdom of George Burns." I played George Burns. A small part of it showed me doing my act at Caesars Palace Hotel in Atlantic City. The producers of this video wanted to include a few more minutes of my act and I wouldn't let them. My manager, Irving Fein, wanted me to give them permission. Irving Fein has been a producer and manager for forty years and he hasn't done too well at it. In all that time he's only had two clients. Jack Benny and me. You think I'm going to let a man who's only had two clients in forty years talk me into something? "Irving," I explained to him, "I can't let them use more material. That's my insurance."

Maybe the best thing about vaudeville was the people you met. If you worked in vaudeville long enough, eventually you were on a bill with just about everybody in the business. It was easy to make friendships. We were all young and ambitious and hardworking and the only thing that any of us wanted to do was get up on the stage and entertain. As Jack used to say, "In those days the only thing we knew about life was, 'A guy walked into a bar with a chicken on his head. . . .'" With all the traveling we did and the hours we worked, we were forced to spend most of our time with each other. We just about lived in the theater, and between shows there was nothing to do except sit around talking and playing cards. Edward Albee even installed pool and billiards rooms in his big-time theaters so we'd have someplace to relax between performances. We called them "Green rooms," and I suppose that's why even today the room that performers wait in before going onstage is called the green room. A lot of friendships that began backstage in run-down theaters or fleabag hotels lasted a lifetime. Me and Jack. Cantor and Jessel. Clayton, Jackson and Durante. Blossom and Benny. Flo and Jack Haley. Jolson and himself. . . .

That was some pair, Cantor and Jessel. They were perfectly matched—Georgie was always getting into some kind of trouble and Eddie was always trying to get him to straighten out. Whatever Jessel did, Cantor criticized. That was the basis of their relationship. I remember one night the two of them were working in Houston, Texas. Directly opposite the theater was a huge church, and in front of this church was a big electric sign declaring, JESUS SAVES. When Jessel went on that night he told the audience, "It is a great pleasure to be in your beautiful city, and when I came to the theater tonight I couldn't help but notice that very inspiring sign on the church across the street. But if I may be so bold as to make a suggestion, I think you should add to the words 'Jesus Saves,' . . . 'but not like Cantor.'"

Georgie always had problems with money—he constantly spent just a little more than his friends had. At one time he owed a lot of money in back taxes to the IRS. The IRS sent him a certified letter telling him exactly how much he owed them. I don't remember how much it was, but I know it was a lot of money.

Jessel loved America as much as anyone, and he always believed that one of the greatest things about this country was that the government worked for the people; and he certainly wasn't going to allow someone who worked for him to take all his money away. So he wrote to the IRS, telling them that his attorney had figured out the whole thing and that he didn't owe them that much.

The IRS wrote back again, informing Georgie

that his attorney was completely wrong, and explaining the penalties for nonpayment of taxes.

So, Georgie told them, arrest my attorney.

Eventually the IRS sent an agent on tour with Jessel to collect the money out of his weekly paycheck. Gracie and I were with Georgie on the bill and we were making $700 a week. He had to be making $3,500 a week, and the government wanted $2,500 of that. At the end of the first week Jessel got paid and the agent took $2,500. Georgie couldn't believe it. He asked the agent, "How much is the government paying you?"

One twenty-five a week, the agent said, or something like that.

"Okay," Georgie offered. "I'll give you two hundred fifty dollars a week to go to work for me."

"What do I have to do?"

"Nothing. But you have to do it every week." That was Jessel.

"Don't look at me, I'm not coming to visit you in jail." That was Cantor.

I remember the first time I met Jessel. Actually, it was the first time I almost met him. He was starring on Broadway in the dramatic version of *The Jazz Singer*. It was a big hit, and Georgie was brilliant. *The Jazz Singer* is the story of a cantor who wants his son to become a cantor, while the son wants to go into show business. At the end the father dies and the son quits show business and becomes a cantor. The show ended with Jessel singing the "Kol Nidre," a sacred, very emotional song. *The Jazz Singer* was almost the story of my life and it really affected me. I was sitting in the audience crying. I don't think I'd ever seen anything on a stage that affected me quite so much —if you should see Jolson, please don't tell him. So after the show I went backstage to meet Jessel and tell him how great I thought he was. I figured he'd enjoy hearing his own opinion confirmed. By this time we had some mutual friends, so I mentioned their names and got to his dressing room. But I was stopped outside the door by his cousin, Bob Milford. "You can't go in right now," Bob told me, "he has his clothes off."

The tears were still dripping from my eyes, that's how wonderful Jessel had been. "That won't bother me," I said, "I've seen a naked Jew before. I just want to tell him how much I enjoyed his performance."

"I'm sorry," Bob said, shaking his head, "you really can't go in." He dropped his voice to a whisper. "He's got a girl in there."

I was shocked. Until that moment I'd believed that there was nothing that could follow "Kol Nidre."

I finally did get to meet Jessel, and Cantor, and Jolson, and we became friends. When I started working with Gracie they were great to us; Georgie pushed us in vaudeville and Cantor gave us our first break on the radio. Jolson gave us tickets to his concert.

This was the beginning of the Roaring Twenties and it was an incredibly exciting time to be young and a vaudevillian in New York. Jessel would often invite me to tag along with him, and he always seemed to have somebody important with him. Maybe it would be "Gentleman Jimmy" Walker, the dapper Mayor of New York, or Pola Negri, with whom he was having a fling, or Irving Berlin or George M. Cohan. It was hard for me to believe I was there; just a few years earlier I'd been playing stooge to a seal, now I was having dinner with George M. Cohan. Jessel only gave me two words of advice: "Don't sing."

There was something great to do every night. Sometimes a group of us who stayed at the Forrest Hotel on 49th Street would get together and go to a show or to one of the hundreds of speakeasies in the city to see performers like Lou Clayton, who was then working with Ukulele Ike, or "Rag-time Jimmy" Durante, who was starting to make a name for himself.

A lot of nights we wouldn't go out at all; after the theaters had closed we'd meet in somebody's room and send out to the Gaiety Delicatessen for sandwiches and sodas while we played cards or charades all night long.

When we had enough people, we'd even put on our own show. We'd all gather in Jack's room and hang a sheet right across the middle of the room. That was our curtain. Then Jack and me and Benny Fields and Ted Lewis and Jack Pearl and maybe Jesse Block and Eddie Cantor and whoever else was there would go behind the sheet and fight about who would get to sing first. That was our cast. The girls, Gracie and Mary Kelly and Ida Cantor and Winnie Pearl and whoever, would sit on the bed and on the floor. That was our audience. It was a tough audience too; they'd heckle the cast, the sandwiches, they'd even heckle the sheet. And always, just before we started, I'd peek over the top of the sheet and announce, loudly, "Hey, fellows, we got a full house tonight."

Our little group played a lot of cards. Cards were the best timekiller in vaudeville. We played gin and bridge and casino and, one night, we played panoochi. Panoochi was invented by Zeppo Marx and Benny Rubin. The rules were pretty simple: there were no rules. Panoochi was to card games what the Marx Brothers were to a script. A panoochi player could do anything, say anything, and play anything, so long as it made no sense.

Actually, there was one rule: you weren't allowed to tell people who didn't know that there weren't any rules that there weren't any rules. They had to figure it out for themselves. That made it great fun to play with them. And often very profitable, too. Benny Rubin used to love to tell about the night he taught Jack Pearl how to play panoochi at Eddie Cantor's apartment in the Pierre Hotel. Cantor and Eve Sully played against Pearl and Benny Rubin.

They started by drawing for the deal. High card dealt. Eve pulled a two, she dealt. "Okay," she said, giving four cards to Cantor, five cards to herself, six cards to Jack and two cards to Benny

Rubin, "let's play garner on the nines, blues everlasting seven."

"Not again," Cantor complained. "Oh, all right, go ahead and get your points, but don't krivet my nines." He threw two dollar bills into the pot. "Just bury me a card and call on elevens." He turned to Jack Pearl. "That's thirteen points, please."

"Up and down the ladder," Rubin said happily, picking up Cantor's two dollar bills and replacing them with two other dollar bills. Then he laid down his two cards. "Give me five cards, please." Eve dealt him five cards. He picked up four and left one lying facedown on the table.

Eventually, Jack Pearl figured out the no rules. Then he thought he'd outsmart everybody. "Panoochi!" he screamed, laying down his cards and reaching for the pot.

"Just a minute," Benny Rubin said, looking at Pearl's cards as if they meant something. "I'll dribble."

Eve Sully was a great panoochi player. "You sure, Benny?" she asked.

Benny nodded. "I think so." He laid down his own cards.

"Too bad, Jack," Eve told Pearl. "If he meets your panoochi with a dribble, you have to pay him triple." She counted the pot. "There's four dollars there, you owe him eight seventy-five." I think panoochi was one of Gracie's favorite games, right after frontgammon.

I'll tell you who everybody hated to play cards

with, Fanny Brice. Fanny was the world's slowest gin player. She would take forever to decide what cards to discard. One day Cantor was playing with her and he got so frustrated with her slow play that he got up and left. Two days later he sent her a telegram reading, WELL FANNY?

A lot of us were still single at that time and I admit it, we went out with girls. And sometimes, if we were very lucky, we stayed home with girls. What's wrong with liking women? They're better than sliced tomatoes. We were young, we dressed snappy, we knew all the hot places in every city, we had a little money, and we were in show business.

We did pretty good with the women too. I suppose you want to know all about it and, believe me, I'd really like to tell you. But all this took place at a time when gentlemen did not discuss their relationships with women in public. And I was a gentleman; I could tell I was a gentlemen because whenever I went out I wore my spats.

Fortunately, times change. Before I knew it, years had passed and it was already Chapter 9 of this book, and by that time a gentleman could discuss anything he wanted to. And I was still a gentleman; I could tell because whenever I went out I wore my toupee. Times change. So wait until you're about 150 pages older and I'll tell you everything.

We didn't spend all of our time offstage playing cards and going out with girls, we wasted some time too. And a lot of that wasted time was spent drinking. The man with the biggest reputation as a drinking man was W. C. Fields. Drinking was part of the character he created—Jessel got the girls, Fields got the booze, I got the cigars—but it was also part of his life. "I once donated a pint of my finest red corpuscles to the great American Red Cross," he claimed, "and the doctor opined my blood was very helpful. Contained so much alcohol they could use it to sterilize their instruments."

Cantor was always trying to reform Fields—Eddie Saves—warning him that his drinking was going to ruin his constitution. "What constitution?" Fields told him. "It's long gone. I've been living on the bylaws for years." I got to know Bill pretty well after Gracie and I worked with him in the movie *Six of a Kind*, and I've never met anyone who could hold as much liquor as he could. Ahhh, yes, as he would say, he used to wear a specially made vest that had pockets in which he could hold four of those small bottles of liquor.

Once, I remember, the story went around Hollywood that Bill's doctor had ordered him to stop drinking. I ran into him at Chasen's and asked him if it was true that he wasn't drinking anymore. "Well, George, my dear friend, your source is impeccable. It's quite true I'm not drinking anymore," he said. "However, I'm not drinking any less either."

Fields probably wasn't the biggest drinker in vaudeville, he just had the biggest reputation. Comedian Jim Thornton could hold his own with

Fields and with a lot of other people too. Thornton used to tell people, "I like the idea of being drunk continuously. It eliminates hangovers."

They used to tell a great story about Jim Duffy and Fred Sweeney. I did not know either of these two gentleman, so I wouldn't want to risk my reputation for telling the truth on the accuracy of this story. But supposedly the two of them had been standing at a bar for several hours, drinking continuously. Finally Sweeney downed another shot and then, without a word, fell over backwards onto the floor, out cold. Duffy looked down at him then hoisted his own glass in salute, saying, "I like a man who knows when to stop."

Bert Fitzgibbons liked to drink his whiskey out of a water glass. Bert could put it away pretty good too. One day, while he was pouring himself a drink, somebody pointed out to him that he was putting whiskey in the big glass, not water. Bert looked at him as if he were crazy, and asked, "Do I really look like the kind of guy who would drink that much water?"

Drinking almost killed Jessel. Georgie always claimed to have invented the Bloody Mary. That was a big surprise to everybody, normally he would have claimed to have slept with her. I think this story is true, though. He was in Palm Beach one winter and he needed a drink to cure his hangover. He tried a lot of different things, but nothing worked. In fact, his hangover got worse. Then the bartender offered him a bottle of a clear liquor he'd never seen before. "Vodkee, he called it,"

Georgie remembered. "I opened it up and it smelled like rotten potatoes." To kill the smell, Jessel added Worcestershire sauce, tomato juice, a little pepper and lemon, then mixed it all up. The result was a deep red drink that tasted pretty good. Just after he'd brewed this concoction, a socialite named Mary Brown Warburton, her family owned the Wanamaker's department stores, walked into the bar. Georgie offered her a taste, and when she sipped it, she spilled some of it on her white dress.

"Well," she said, trying to wipe it up, "I guess you can call me Bloody Mary."

Maybe a year later Jessel was in a hotel room with comedian Ted Healy, and both of them had been doing a little drinking. All right, a lot of drinking. At that time Healy happened to be going out with Mary Brown Warburton. Healy started reading Walter Winchell's column and saw an item telling the story of how Jessel created and named the Bloody Mary. And he got very angry. "What the hell were you doing making a pass at my girlfriend?"

Healy pulled out a pistol and fired. Luckily he missed, but that's how drinking almost killed Georgie Jessel.

As I explained before, every act needs a big finish, something the audience will remember for a long time. Some performers would even beg, but if I got down on my knees it would take me two weeks to get up. Besides, I have too much respect for you to do something like that. I admit that I had considered showing you a picture of an American flag right here, and maybe writing a few bars of "It's a Grand Old Flag," but I don't believe that such an intelligent, witty, nice reader such as you are would appreciate that kind of cheap theatrics. Instead, because I recognize your incredible talent, and I know that you're just waiting for that big break, before I bring on the next chapter I'd like you to help me get offpage. I think you probably know how to do this. Just do exactly what I tell you. Now, please, say, "Goodnight, Gracie."

"   ," you say.

You ever thought about going into show business?

4

After seeing me work onstage, people sometimes gave me more credit than I really deserved. It was performers like George Burns, they said, who killed vaudeville. That's just not true. I was just a mere vaudevillian—in fact, as Gracie always said when she was defending me, "No one was merer." Okay, maybe I inflicted a few wounds, but it took a power much bigger than mine to kill vaudeville. Electricity.

Vaudeville really started dying when people were able to have radios in their own homes. Before that happened in the late 1920s, every few years something new would come along that was supposed to replace vaudeville. For a while roller-skating really hurt the box office, and thousands of huge roller-skating palaces were built all over the country. So people skated around in a circle for a couple of years, and when they got bored doing that they skated in the other direction for a couple of years. Then they went home. Then it was dancing that was supposed to end vaudeville, and a lot of the deserted roller-skating palaces got turned into huge dance halls. The men swung their girls to the right for a couple of years, then they swung them to the left, then everybody went home. Finally, the moving pictures were supposed to end vaudeville, but vaudeville had shared the bill with the movies for years. In fact, in the early days of movies, instead of advertising the name of the film, theater owners advertised how many feet of film they were showing. And if the theater owners thought they could draw an audience for an extra show, they cut the film, not the vaudeville acts.

But radio was different. Until radio came along home entertainment consisted of listening to a relative play the piano or violin, dropping a stray cat on top of the sleeping pet dog, or slipping a whoopee cushion under the old man's chair.

Radio allowed people to bring outside entertainment into their own homes for the first time. In most cases people didn't even care what they listened to, the radio set was the star. I remember when Gracie and I were just getting started in radio we were walking down Broadway and a woman recognized Gracie's voice—she didn't recognize Gracie, she recognized her voice—and she told us, "I heard you on the radio last night . . ."

I got ready to be modest.

". . . and my sister who lives in St. Louis heard the same thing at the same time! Isn't that wonderful?" It didn't matter how good or bad we were, just how far our voices went.

There had never been anything like radio before. It was so new, so exciting, that there were all kinds of rumors about it: the invisible radio waves coming into your home were supposed to be dangerous, the sound was supposed to damage your ears, the tubes in the radio set were supposed to explode and cause fires. Nobody cared. The radio brought famous people right into the living room, it let people hear the news the same day it happened, and when the rural areas were electrified it put the farmer in touch with the city slickers. Once it took a new song six years to become known nationally, radio made it happen in two weeks. In those days the whole "family entertainment center" consisted of the radio set. That was it. At night the family would gather around the set not just to listen, but to look at it. Radio was magic.

Vaudeville didn't just drop dead, it faded away slowly, like applause after a second encore.

It managed to last through the 1930s, but it was never the same as it had been. Even the big-time bills consisted of a few acts and a talking picture. Salaries were cut to almost nothing. Things got so bad that a strong man would bend a spike in half in one show, then straighten it out in his next show. Acrobats were reduced to throwing one Indian club. Comedy teams had to split up, leaving the straight man with his half of the act. "How's your brother?" he'd say. "Really? Down two flights of steps? Did he drop it?" My old partner, the seal, had to get a job as a public notary. Okay, maybe I'm exaggerating, but for everybody except the really big stars, vaudeville had ended.

A vaudevillian didn't have to be a genius to figure out that radio was the soundwave of the future. I mean, I did. Obviously, some acts couldn't make the transition: what could an elephant do on the radio? The only trick a magician could do was make the radio disappear. All the dumb acts were out of business; there was nothing they could do but go home and wait for someone to invent television.

But radio was made for performers who talked or sang. It didn't matter what you looked like, or how you dressed—there was no costume budget in radio—only what your voice sounded like. Radio allowed performers to create any fantasy they wanted to: think of it this way, among the biggest stars on radio were Amos 'n' Andy, two black men played by two white men; Baby Snooks, a six-year-old child played by a fifty-year-old woman; and the team of Edgar Bergen and Charlie McCarthy, a ventriloquist and his dummy, played by Edgar Bergen. How does a ventriloquist work on radio? Very easily. What was the audience going to say, he moved his tubes?

So Gracie and I were perfect for radio. Both of us could stand still in front of a microphone and read out loud. Gracie had a terrific voice, and I had Gracie. And that's all it took. We were on the air for almost twenty years. I think I loved being in radio more than any other part of my career. Radio meant show business, and I wanted to be in show business. Radio was that place where performers who couldn't do anything except talk, could talk.

The first real radio station went on the air in

Pittsburgh, Pennsylvania, in 1920. For a long time most of the programming on radio consisted of music and practical information. Every band and orchestra and piano player and violinist played on the radio. The practical information consisted of important tips like: Never go to a barber nick-named "Cueball." Never accept a blind date with a woman named Goldie Burns.

There were no regularly scheduled comedy shows on early radio, but sometimes, to break up the music, the announcer or members of the band would tell a few jokes between songs. Most of their material came from the same writers who were doing my material, the editors of *College Humor* and *Whiz Bang*. For example, the band leader would say, "Before we do our next number I'd like to tell you about a friend of mine who made a fortune renting rowboats. Business wasn't too good until he put up a big sign that read, RIDES ON THE LAKE, TEN CENTS FOR MARRIED MEN, WIVES THROWN IN FREE. Now we'd like to do a sweet tune for you. . . ."

Eddie Cantor was the first big vaudeville star to go on the radio, broadcasting for the first time in 1921. Ed Wynn almost became the first national radio star. He just missed it by about forty-six states. He would have missed it by more, but there were only forty-eight states. In 1922 the government built a huge transmitter-receiver in Los Angeles and they wanted to attempt a coast-to-coast broadcast. They asked Ed Wynn to do his stage show, *The Perfect Fool,* from a station in New

Jersey to see if people in Los Angeles could hear him. They barely heard him in New York. And Wynn hated radio, by the way. When he went on the air he stood in front of the microphone and told his first joke and waited for the laugh. He could still be waiting there. That was when Wynn discovered one of the most important things about radio comedy—microphones don't laugh. Without an audience to help his timing, Wynn didn't know what to do. The station staff got everybody working in the place, from the owner to the cleaning lady, into the studio so Wynn would continue the broadcast.

Gracie and I went on the radio for the first time while we were touring England with our stage act in 1929. In those days radio stations would use five minutes of comedy to break up the orchestra music. So one day we did five minutes in London, the next day we did the same five minutes in Liverpool, the day after that we did the same five minutes in Southampton. We were always smart enough to stay one day ahead of our reviews.

In 1931 Cantor became the first vaudeville comedian to make it in radio. Radio allowed Eddie to be what he always wanted to be—the whole cast of the show. Sometimes Eddie would play both the straight man and the comedian, asking himself a question in one dialect then answering it in his own voice. It was on that show that Eddie became the first person to use his orchestra leader as a straight man—and, in fact, Eddie played the orchestra leader too.

On "The Chase and Sanborn Hour" Eddie would tell a few jokes, do a skit, sing a song, then the orchestra would play a song, then Eddie would tell a few more jokes and sing another song. There was no continuity to Eddie's character. In his first joke, he'd claim to be so cheap that when he lost a one-dollar bill he tried to have George Washington declared a missing person; in his next joke, he was so generous that when he got mad at somebody, instead of giving them a piece of his mind he gave them the whole thing.

Whatever Eddie did, it worked. For almost three years he had the highest-rated show on radio. His Crossley rating, which they figured out by calling up people and asking them what programs they'd listened to the day before, was usually over 50, meaning more than one out of two people listening to the radio were listening to him.

It was Eddie who gave me and Gracie our first break on radio. After working with us for nine weeks at the Palace he asked Gracie to appear on his show. We agreed—as long as he let me write her material. The bit I wrote was a combination of old and new stuff—like everybody else on radio, I just rewrote part of our stage act; then I added some new material about the one thing everybody on radio liked to talk about—being on radio.

After being introduced, Gracie told Eddie that she wanted to interview him for a newspaper. During the interview Eddie mentioned that his show was being sponsored by Chase and Sanborn, and

Gracie told him that she drank a lot of coffee. "You like coffee?" Eddie asked.

"Oh yeah," Gracie said. "But I like it best when I make it with tea."

"You make coffee with tea?" he asked.

Obviously another character Eddie could play very well was George Burns.

"Well," Gracie answered, "not all the time. Sometimes I make it with cocoa." In just those few lines of dialogue Gracie had established her character with the radio audience: Gracie Allen, the lovable, dizzy lady, whose illogical-logic raised confusion to a new height. About 5'2" in high heels.

The response to Gracie's first appearance on American radio was overwhelming. The phone call came pouring in. It came from the advertising agency man in charge of Rudy Vallee's "Fleischmann's Yeast Hour," and he wanted us to make several appearances on the Rudy Vallee show. On that show Gracie told me she'd been up in an airplane for nine straight months and I asked her if she'd ever heard of the law of gravity. "Oh yes," she said, "but you see, I went up before the law was passed."

We were a big hit. And when we left the studio that day there was only one thing bothering me: we had about another two hours' worth of tested material left, and somehow I had to figure out how to stretch it out over about twenty years.

With vaudeville dying, radio was the only way a lot of performers could stay in show business.

But not Jack Benny. Jack was more successful than he'd ever been, starring in Earl Carroll's Vanities for $1,500 a week. Jack was so smart though, he knew how important radio was going to be, and asked Earl Carroll to let him out of his contract. Just imagine that, the man who was going to give greed a good name was willing to give up $1,500 a week just so he could try to get into the radio business.

Actually, Jack's first experience in radio was as a writer for Benny Rubin. Benny was hired to do a local show in New York and Jack wrote a few jokes for him. His big contribution was the joke that started with a stooge asking Benny Rubin, "Where you from?"

"Ireland," Rubin answered, "I mean, Coney Ireland." With jokes like that, Benny Rubin didn't need an audience in the studio not to laugh.

Jack made his own debut on radio on a local Chicago station in 1931, while he was still starring for Earl Carroll. The station gave Jack fifteen minutes to fill; he planned to do eleven minutes' worth of material then have Harry Stockwell sing for the last four minutes. There was a huge blizzard that day and Stockwell was afraid of getting a cold so he didn't show up. Fortunately, Benny Rubin, who was in Chicago starring in the show *Girl Crazy*, had come to the studio with Jack. To fill the last four minutes, Jack told his listeners that he was going to do his imitation of the well-known vaudeville and musical comedy star, Benny

Rubin. Then Benny Rubin did four minutes of his best stuff.

The next day the newspaper reviewers wrote that Jack had been very funny—until he tried to do that awful imitation of Benny Rubin. So I called up Jack and gave him some very good advice. "Jack," I told him, "don't ever go out of your house without your writers again." Then I hung up on him.

Jack always started laughing hysterically when I hung up.

No one was better suited for radio than Jack. Radio consisted of sound and silence. That was it. And while the rest of us were trying to figure out ways of using sound, Jack was smart enough to figure out how to use the silence. No one ever got more out of nothing than he did. He did such a great job that his show was on the air for twenty-five straight years, and he was voted the Greatest Personality in Radio History. That's not bad for the man who actually took credit for writing the punch line "Coney Ireland."

Jack made his first major radio appearance on newspaper columnist Ed Sullivan's New York program. Jack had run into him in Lindy's and Ed had asked him to appear on his show. "But I don't know anything about radio," Jack told him.

"Nobody does," Ed said. The fact that Ed had his own show was certainly proof of that.

Fred Allen once said, "Ed Sullivan will last as long as someone else has talent." That really wasn't fair. Ed's talent was . . . Ed was really . . .

Ed could . . . Ed did really, really big introductions. And he cracked his knuckles great. Look, whatever it was that he did, he must have done it very well because he was one of the pioneers of both radio and television. Think of him this way: Ed Sullivan was the man who introduced both Jack Benny and The Beatles to American audiences. His first radio shew, as he would have said, was broadcast in 1932. It was sort of a newspaper column on the air, a combination of entertainment news and short bits. Years later, on his television show, Ed would introduce guests sitting in his audience, just like they used to do at the Palace Sunday-night concerts. Now, if Ed had been really, really smart, he would have done something like this on his radio show. "Ladies and gentlemen, we're absolutely delighted to have with us in our audience tonight the wonderful statesman and author . . . Winston Churchill. Winston, would you stand up and take a bow please. Winston Churchill, ladies and gentlemen, let's give him a big hand." In radio we could do things like that.

Don't you love it when I do impersonations?

After being introduced by Sullivan, Jack said in his usual enthusiastic, energetic tone, "Hello, folks, this is Jack Benny. There will be a slight pause while everyone says, 'Who cares?' "

A couple of months later Jack finally got his own show, sponsored by Canada Dry. I guess they felt his kind of humor best represented their product. They signed Jack for seventeen weeks, and as soon as the deal was made, Jack started worrying. You know, one of the most surprising things about Jack was that the character he created and played was always so calm, so controlled, while offstage Jack was incredibly nervous before every performance. That was true his whole life. And naturally, as his best friend, I tried to calm him down about doing the radio show. "Jack," I said, putting my arm around his shoulders, "Jack, there's absolutely nothing to worry about. Nothing at all. Just forget all about the fact that more people are going to hear you on the radio than heard you during your entire career in vaudeville, and that if they don't like you, your career is probably over." No, that's not true. What I did tell him was, "Hire a writer."

On May 2, 1932, announcer Ed Thorgerson introduced "That suave comedian, dry humorist and famous master of ceremonies, Jack Benny." In vaudeville, Jack would have then walked onstage to nice applause, in radio there was no stage, just microphones standing on the floor, and no applause.

"Thank you, Mr. Thorgerson," Jack began. "That's pretty good coming from a man who doesn't even know me. Ladies and gentlemen, this is Jack Benny, and I'm happy to be making my first appearance on the air professionally. By that I mean I'm finally getting paid, which I know will be a great relief to my creditors."

It was on that first show that Jack told his first joke on radio about being cheap. The big surprise though, was that he wasn't talking about himself. "My orchestra leader, George Olsen, invited me to dinner the other night," Jack explained, "and he paid with a five-dollar bill that had been in his pocket so long that Lincoln's eyes were bloodshot." Jack's character, the cheap, vain, egotistical, stuffy, stubborn, pompous boob, the bragging show-off who couldn't get a date, the balding, untalented thirty-nine-year-old violinist hadn't been born yet.

The first year Jack was on the air his show was pretty much like every other comedy-variety show. Jack did all kinds of question-and-answer gags, the orchestra played a few songs, Jack would do a bit with his guest. One week the guest was a character created by Jack's writers, a fan supposedly from Plainfield, New Jersey, named Mary Livingstone. Jack asked his wife, Sadie, to play the role and she did—for about the next forty-five years. Talk about a continuing role. And the money was good too—everything Jack earned.

Jack was not an instant success on radio. Jack wasn't even a slow success on radio. After his first season Canada Dry dropped the show and General Motors picked it up for Chevrolet. Chevrolet sponsored the show for the following season, then dropped it. When Jack asked the agency representative why they weren't renewing their contract, the man told him that he didn't like the kind of comedy Jack did. "When I asked him what he meant by that," Jack told me. He said he couldn't really describe what he didn't like about it, but it wasn't high class enough for his car. I reminded him that my ratings were good, then told him that Chevrolet shouldn't try to sell pink automobiles when people wanted to drive black and blue or brown cars. 'There,' he said, 'that's exactly the kind of humor I don't like.'"

At that time it was easy to find sponsors, every manufacturer was trying to get on radio, and Jack signed with General Tire. Jack had been reduced from a whole car to just the tires, but his format was beginning to change. Instead of the endless question-and-answer gags, he started developing his own character. "It's not that I'm cheap," he told his listeners, "I'm actually pretty smart. When I was down in Florida I went to the dog races. And I bet on the rabbit—to show." I don't think Jack ever planned to be cheap or vain or egotistical, I know he didn't plan on being a bad violinist; the audience found his character. But Jack was smart enough to listen. He told a joke about being cheap and the audience laughed, so Jack got cheaper. In real life Jack wasn't actually very much like the character he played on radio and later on television. I mean, in real life, for example, Jack was thirty-nine years old for only three or four years.

Most of the popular comedy shows were a combination of gags and music, standing gags I guess you could call them, because there were no running gags from week to week. Most of the time there wasn't even continuity from joke to joke. The biggest comedy stars on early radio were people like Cantor and Will Rogers and Ed Wynn, Joe Penner, Jack Pearl, and they were really doing vaudeville acts on the air.

Eddie Cantor did something that almost nobody else was doing on radio—visual jokes. Eddie would do slapstick bits and wear funny costumes. Believe me, it's tough to get big laughs out of a costume on radio. Eddie's announcer would describe what Eddie was wearing, saying things like "Oh, Eddie is really wearing something funny tonight." After he'd describe the costume, Eddie would tell jokes about how silly he looked. During his "Chase and Sanborn Hour" Eddie would do things like break an egg over somebody's head or jump into somebody's arms. The people in the studio audience would laugh and the people listening at home would look at the radio to see what was so funny. But radio was still so new and the audience at home was so happy to be listening to Eddie Cantor in their own home that they didn't care.

Ed Wynn was "Texaco's Fire Chief." The Fire Chief wasn't a character that Ed created, it was the costume he dressed in. As far as Ed was concerned, radio was just a stage show being broadcast. He played to the studio audience. The story was that Ed got his show after executives from Texaco and its advertising agency sat through four performances of a Broadway show he was starring in with their backs to the stage and their eyes closed to hear if Ed's material would work on radio. They decided it would. So that's what Ed

Wynn's radio show was like—like being at his stage show and sitting with your back to the stage and your eyes closed. After Wynn's experience trying to do "The Perfect Fool" on radio, he agreed to do the Texaco show only if they let him do it in front of a live audience. Most sponsors didn't want an audience in the studio when the show was being broadcast because they thought their laughter would bother the people listening at home. Ed played to the studio audience, his show was even broadcast from the stage of a theater. During the broadcast he wore makeup and even changed his costume as many as six or seven times.

At the beginning of the show Ed would tell his announcer, Graham McNamee, "I'm the chief, Graham, and tonight the program's going to be different." I think what he meant was that his jokes were going to be different than Cantor's. And a lot of the time they were. But like Cantor, Wynn got most of his material from a file containing 100,000 jokes and 14,000 joke books he'd collected during his career. Ed spoke with a lisp, and he always giggled before he told a joke. I guess the reason he giggled was that he knew the punchline before the audience did. And if the audience didn't laugh at his joke, he was left with his giggle hanging out.

Wynn did the usual question-and-answer bits with McNamee, and he also had a weekly spot in which he'd make fun of a popular book, children's story or opera. "The opera tonight, Graham, is very unusual," he'd begin. "The title of it is *When You Were Eight and I Was Nine and We Were Seventeen.* It's about a boy and a girl, the boy's name is J. Weatherstrip Reilly. He was born during the World War and they called him Weatherstrip because he kept his father out of the draft. Soooo . . ."

Soooooo . . . was Wynn's most famous line and people all over the country started imitating him. Radio made catchphrases, the sayings used by the most popular performers, instantly well known across the country. When Gracie said, "Take my little nephoo . . . if you can use a little nephoo," everybody tried to give away their nephoos. But the best known catchphrase of early radio was created by Joe Penner. Joe Penner had been a small-time burlesque comedian before radio. In burlesque he'd done a nut act in which he was constantly shouting silly questions at the audience like "Wanna buy a flat tire?" or "Wanna buy a rhinoceros?" or the question that made him famous, "Wanna buy a duck?"

Rudy Vallee gave Penner his first break on the Fleischmann's show. After Rudy introduced him, Joe said, "Hi, Rudy, wanna buy a duck?"

Rudy told him that he most certainly did not want to buy a duck.

"Oh," Penner said, introducing his second-most famous line, "you nahhh-sty man!"

That one line, wanna buy a duck, made Penner a star. After appearing with Rudy a few more times, Penner got his own show. Within a year the show was the second-highest-rated comedy show on the air and Penner was voted radio's most popular comedian. He even had a real duck, named Goo-Goo, who became the most popular duck in America. As bad as I felt about Penner being the most popular comedian, imagine how poor Donald must have felt.

I got to know Joe Penner a little and I liked him. One summer Gracie and I were in Honolulu, and we were staying at the same hotel as he was. Now, you may not believe this, but when I'm not getting paid I'm really very funny. When I wasn't on the air, people loved to laugh at me. So I was on the beach making people laugh and I guess that made Joe Penner a little insecure. Because when we all got into the elevator together he said to me, "You know, I always rest my brain in the summer. I never get laughs in the summertime."

"That's good," I told him. "I'll take them anytime I can get them."

The problem with relying on catchphrases is that they get very old while they're still new. A year after Penner had been named the most popular comedian on radio his show was canceled because of poor ratings. Gracie and Jack were smart enough to stop using a catchphrase very soon after it caught on, then they'd use it once in a while, so that every time they did the audience was surprised and the line got a good reaction. Jack Pearl didn't learn that lesson until it was too late.

Jack was born on Rivington Street on the Lower

East Side and started in vaudeville with Cantor and Jessel and Winchell in Gus Edwards' show. He was just like me, he would do anything to stay in show business; he worked as a song plugger, he worked in small-time, he was a burlesque comedian and a good actor. Eventually he became a very famous musical comedy star on Broadway. He was in a dozen of the big Shubert shows, co-starring with everybody from Mae West to Gertrude Lawrence, and finally became the lead comedian in Flo Ziegfeld's Follies.

Jack was also the most superstitious man I've ever known. In one of his pockets he carried two dimes, two nickels and four pennies, the thirty-four cents that somebody had given him on his thirty-fourth birthday, and in another pocket he carried the stub of a pencil he'd used at PS 171. He had some sort of good luck charm in every other pocket. If someone touched his earlobe, he'd stop whatever he was doing until he'd touched that person's earlobe. Naturally, as soon as we found out about Jack's superstition we were very sympathetic—we told everybody we knew. Jack couldn't go anywhere or do anything without somebody touching his earlobe. Once he was sitting in the barber chair, lathered up, when somebody snuck up on him and touched his earlobe. Jack leaped out of the chair and raced four blocks until he caught that person and touched his earlobe. Would I make something like that up? Well, sure I would, but that happens to be true. Before Jack would leave his dressing room to go onstage he'd tear a tiny piece of toilet paper off the roll and drop it in the toilet—but he wouldn't flush, then he'd go through all the motions of combing his hair with a comb and brush, but he would never touch his hair with either the comb or the brush.

Other than that the man was not superstitious at all.

Let me tell you something, superstitions are very important to a performer—as long as he has talent. And Jack had talent. When "The Ziegfeld Follies of the Air" went on radio in 1932, Will Rogers hosted the first week and Jack hosted the second week. George Washington Hill, President of the American Tobacco Company, heard him on the Ziegfeld show and hired him to star on "The Lucky Strike Program." In those days you could smoke on radio, in fact, on radio, you didn't even have to smoke to be smoking on radio. On the show Jack played a character named Baron von Munchausen, who spoke in a thick German accent that came from the vaudeville region of Germany. Cliff Hall played his straight man, Charlie. The Baron was probably the biggest liar in history who never worked with Captain Betts' seal. He would tell the most outrageous stories and when Charlie said he didn't believe him, the Baron would ask in a very offended voice, "Vus you dere, Sharlie?"

"Vus you dere, Sharlie" became the most popular saying in the country. Anytime anybody

121

doubted anything, the other person would ask, "Vus you dere, Sharlie?"

"Zere I was in the frozen North," the Baron would tell Charlie, "having one terrible argument vit one of ze eskimos. It vus so cold zat the words froze before they left my mouth."

"Well then, Baron," Charlie asked, "how'd you know what they were saying?"

"We took ze conversation with us inside ze igloo and thawed it out."

"Boy, Baron, that's pretty hard to believe."

"Vus you dere, Sharlie?"

The Baron's Crossley rating topped 75, and Jack Pearl became one of the biggest stars in the country. One day, when he was at the absolute top of his popularity, he was out playing golf with Jack Benny—what other sport would the greatest liar in show business play?—and Jack said to him, "I think your 'Vus you dere, Sharlie' is sensational, but let me make a suggestion. I think you're overusing it. I think you'd do much better with it if you skipped it for a week or two. That way, when you hit the audience with it, it'll be even funnier."

Pearl shook his head. "That saying's the biggest thing on the show. My listeners can't wait for it. If I don't do it every week they'll be disappointed. Uh, what'd you get on that last hole?"

"One," Jack said. "You?"

"None," Pearl said. Then the caddy said, "Vus you dere, Sharlie?"

Of course Jack Benny was right. When listeners

finally began getting tired of the line Jack Pearl had no insurance. After two successful seasons the show lost its popularity. Jack Pearl told me once that "Vus you dere, Sharlie" became "The Frankenstein of lines." The Baron had become bigger than his creator. Jack couldn't get away from him; he was so well known as the Baron that no one would hire him to do anything else.

After a while Jack Pearl just didn't want to be the Baron anymore. "Maybe I'm sadistically inclined," he told me one day when we weren't on the golf course, "but I love to see people cry." That's when I thought he was going to ask me to sing, but it turned out he was telling me he wanted to be a serious actor.

That reminded me of a story about Durante. "Jack," I said to Pearl, "somebody once told Jimmy that every comedian, at some time in their life, wants to play Hamlet. 'Nah, not me,' Jimmy said, 'I don't care if I never play one a dem small towns ever again.'"

But Pearl really wanted to be an actor. Radio sponsors kept asking him to bring back the Baron, but he wouldn't do it. "I'm stubborn," he'd say, "I'm not going to do it. I'm like the guy who has a bad toothache and goes to the dentist to have it pulled. When the dentist asked him which tooth hurts, he won't tell him. 'You're the one with the license, you figure it out.' That's how I feel about doing the Baron again."

But Jack finally changed his mind during World War II. Maybe he did it because he needed the money—with inflation his thirty-four cents was probably only worth twenty-eight cents. Who knows, but he went back on the air as the Baron. Of course, during World War II was probably not the best time to be a German-dialect comedian, so the Baron admitted that he'd been lying about his ancestry, then claimed he was really from Holland. From the vaudeville region of Holland.

But radio had changed and the Baron's question-and-answer format and his dialect comedy just weren't popular anymore. A lot of actors have killed off their characters, but this was probably the first time that the character had killed the actor's career.

After working with Rudy Vallee, Gracie and I were hired to do brief comedy bits on the "Robert Burns Panatella Hour," no relation—he was from the Scottish Birnbaums—starring Guy Lombardo and the Royal Canadians. I don't know if it was something we said, but after a few months Guy and his band left the show and signed with a new sponsor. So, after about three months of struggling our way up from just below the top, Gracie and I had our own show. That's how easy radio was.

Our format was pretty much the same as everybody else's on the "ether," we just did an expanded vaudeville routine. The only thing that was the same from week to week was Gracie's character, the woman I once told, "You'd better not let your mind wander, I think it's too weak to be out alone."

On one of our early shows, for example, she told me that she had a garden. I asked her what was the first thing she'd planted. "My right foot," she said.

"Well," I asked her, "what have you got in those little envelopes?"

"Seeds."

"And what have you got in that big bag?"

"The rolls the seeds came off."

The next week we did a routine about a policeman who gave Gracie a ticket—and when he did she asked him for another one so I could go with her. And every week Gracie's family got bigger—she had a brother who could hold his breath so long that when he picked up the trumpet he played "Stars and Stripes Forever," and another brother who thought he was a ghost because he walked around the house all day singing "I Ain't Got Nobody," and another brother who was hiding out in a nudist camp because the police were looking for him in a blue serge suit and an uncle who invented the rubber radio tube, it didn't work but it never broke. Gracie would add another relative every time we needed another joke. In radio, that was known as family planning.

Jack Benny changed all that. Jack changed radio. In fact, Jack was so smart that he changed commercial television and that wouldn't even be started for another fifteen years. He did something that no comedian had ever done before—he eliminated most of the jokes. Jack's shows got plenty of laughs, but the humor came from familiar characters and their relationships with each other. The audience knew the characters on his show and because of that lines that weren't the slightest bit funny became hysterical. Let me give you an example: Oh, shut up. Nothing, right? I could have written that line. In fact, I just did. Maybe you noticed though, that when I wrote it, it wasn't funny. But Jack always claimed that that line got the longest laugh in the show's history. And it wasn't even his line.

His wife, Mary Livingstone, played his girlfriend, Mary Livingstone, on the show. Her character was always deflating his big ego. When Jack and Mary were supposed to be going to the racetrack, for instance, he said, "I sure hope I win. I can use the money." And Mary told him, "Why? You've never used any before."

So on the show one Sunday night Jack's announcer, Don Wilson, was having a long conversation about opera with the famous opera singer Dorothy Kirsten. I mean, a long conversation. They discussed *Madama Butterfly*, Puccini, bel canto, allegro, *Aïda*, sopranos . . . and as this conversation was going on, the audience was aware that Jack didn't know the slightest thing about opera, but they also knew that at some point that wasn't going to stop him.

Finally, finally, Jack couldn't take it anymore. "Well," he said, "I think—"

"Oh, shut up," Mary snapped.

That joke only worked if you knew the characters. It wouldn't have worked for Eddie Cantor, for example, who would have played both Jack and Mary. Jack used to say his best jokes took five years to write, because that's how long it took for the audience to really get to know a character.

Besides Mary, there was always a young, naive tenor, played by Frank Parker, then Kenny Baker and finally Dennis Day. Dennis Day was played by Eugene McNulty. The tenor would say silly things like "I was out in the phone booth talking to my girlfriend, but then somebody wanted to use the phone so we had to get out."

Bandleader Phil Harris played the brash, aggressive, confident bandleader Phil Harris, the kind of guy who would tell Jack, "Listen to me, Jackson. Without me your program is like a Persian rug. It looks good, but it just lays there."

Don Wilson was the big, happy, jovial announcer who did the commercials and played straight man for Jack. Let me describe him this way: if Don Wilson hadn't created the character, Ed McMahon might have had a nice career as a mall Santa Claus.

Maybe the most popular character was Rochester, Jack's black valet and chauffeur, played by vaudevillian Eddie Anderson. The gravelly voiced Anderson created the role of the wisecracking servant. On one show, for example, Rochester wanted to install his own telephone in the house, but Jack told him it wasn't necessary, that he could always use the house phone. "Oh, thank you, boss," Rochester said, "but what if the house was burning down and I didn't have any change?"

There were also several characters who appeared every once in a while. They were played by different actors—the difference between a radio star and a radio actor was that when you mentioned a star's name you didn't have to tell what role he played. On Jack's show Ed, the guardian of the vault, was played by an actor who appeared on the show two or three times a season. Ed was a character who had been guarding the vault in the basement of Jack's Beverly Hills house for so long that when Jack asked him if he wanted a radio, he said, "I don't know what it is, but send it down. If I like it, I'll eat it."

Mel Blanc, the greatest sound mimic who ever lived, played several different characters, including a train announcer, a French violin teacher and, on occasion, himself, a character on Jack's show who played several different characters, including a train announcer, a French violin teacher and, on occasion, himself, a character . . .

Fred Allen played Fred Allen on Jack's show, the star of his own radio show, "Allen's Alley," and Jack's worst enemy in the world, in the longest-running, most famous feud in show business history. Jack and Fred didn't plan to have the feud, it just started one night when Fred had an eight-year-old violinist on his own show. After the child had played beautifully, Fred said, "Only eight years old . . . Why, Jack Benny should be ashamed of himself." Jack answered on his show the following Sunday night and they traded insults, often appearing on each other's shows for the next eight years. "When Jack Benny plays the violin," Fred said, "it sounds as if the strings are back in the cat."

"Listening to Fred is like listening to two Abbotts and no Costello."

"They planted a tree in the courthouse square in Waukegan to honor Jack and, you know, the tree died. That didn't surprise me, how could a tree live in Waukegan with the sap out in Hollywood?"

"With those bags under his eyes Fred looks like an old pair of pants with the pockets turned inside out."

"That joke was first told at the Ford Theatre in 1865 and the shot that killed Lincoln was intended for the actor who told it."

"You wouldn't dare say that if my writers were here."

But the whole show was built around Jack's character. I'll tell you how good Jack's character was. When we were all starting out every cheap joke was told about Scotsmen. By the late 1930s they were all told about Jack Benny. So in about eight years that character was so successful that he succeeded in wiping out the entire country of Scotland.

The audience knew Jack's character so well that they would laugh in anticipation of his response. That's why Jack could get laughs from silence. When he was held up by a robber who demanded,

"Your money or your life?" Jack's silence while he thought it over was the funniest thing never said on radio. Maybe a minute passed before the robber started to repeat his demand, but Jack interrupted and told him, "I'm thinking it over, I'm thinking it over."

Nobody had as much courage on the air as Jack did. When it came to doing something new, everybody else wanted to be the first person to do it second. Not Jack. Jack was willing to take risks that nobody else would take. Fred Allen used to say, "There are two kinds of jokes, funny jokes and Jack Benny jokes." But Jack never cared who got the laughs—as long as they were getting them on "The Jack Benny Show."

Once, for example, Jack supposedly went to the train station to buy a ticket from Los Angeles to New York. The ticket clerk, played by Gale Gordon, asked him if he wanted a round-trip ticket. "No," Jack told him, "one way."

"Good," Gordon said.

Let me tell you a little story. Goodman Ace, one of the great comedy writers and later the host of his own show, "Easy Aces," was head writer on Danny Kaye's radio program. Every Monday morning Danny's cast and writers would meet to read through the rough draft of the script for their next show. One week Danny didn't like the script at all. When the read-through was finished he calmly laid his script down on the table, looked at Goody and said coldly, "Nice going. I guess this script makes me the highest-paid straight man in show business."

The room was absolutely silent for about a minute. Then Goody, looking down at the floor, said softly, "Jack Benny makes three times the money you do."

If there's one thing I've learned, it's how to be a straight man. There are three things a straight man has to always remember: make the straight lines sound believable because they set up the punch line, never start speaking until the audience has stopped laughing, and don't step on the seal's wing. Jack was a master of the first two. He knew how to protect a joke. Most of the time, after someone else had gotten a laugh, Jack made sure he had the next line. For example, Phil Harris said, "Gee, Jackson, that's a nice suit. You think that style'll ever come back?" The next line could have been Mary's, who would have defended Jack. But Jack would always put a line in for himself, even if it was "hmmmmm," or "Cut that out!" and Mary wouldn't speak until he'd done his line. That was his way of making sure Phil Harris got as much laughter out of that line as Jack got out of that suit.

Jack's show was avant-garde long before everybody else. He was always trying something a little different. When practically every other show on the air was running a contest, for instance, asking listeners to send in box tops and describe something in fifty words or less, Jack ran the "Why I Can't Stand Jack Benny" contest. Like a lot of running gags we all did, this one started as a bit on one show, but became a real contest when Jack discovered how many listeners couldn't stand him. He figured out that based on the number of responses contests run by other shows had received, he could expect to get about 15,000 entries a week for the three weeks the contest was scheduled to last. He got 277,000 entries. The winning entry was a poem, and read . . . hmmmrmp, excuse me:

> *He fills the air with boasts and brags,*
> *And obsolete obnoxious gags.*
> *The way he plays the violin,*
> *Is music's most obnoxious sin.*
> *His cowardice alone, indeed,*
> *Is matched by his obnoxious greed.*
> *And all the things that he portrays,*
> *Show up my own obnoxious ways.*

The winner was a young man from New York City named Edward Cantor.

All right, I admit it, Eddie Cantor really didn't win the "Why I Can't Stand Jack Benny" contest. I made that up. Actually, Eddie finished tied for third.

Jack's shows were often based on real life. If Jack was really being honored at a dinner in New York, that fact would be the basis of a story. If the cast was really going cross-country on a Pullman, the show would take place on the train. Another week the show would be about Jack dreaming he was a ladies' man and that was real too, because by the time he became a radio star the only way he could have been a ladies' man was to dream about it. On the show Jack's Beverly Hills house had a vault deep in the basement, surrounded by a moat and guarded by wild animals and Ed, in real life . . . well, some of the things were true, of course.

"The Jack Benny Program" was so popular that NBC gave Jack a lifetime option on his time slot, Sunday night from seven to seven-thirty, as long as he had a network-approved sponsor. That was the perfect gift for Jack—most companies, when they want to honor an employee, give him an expensive watch. Instead, NBC gave Jack the time.

Actually, that only lasted a few years. Anybody could change stations on the dial, but when Jack decided to change stations, he really changed stations. In the biggest deal ever made in radio history, Jack left NBC and signed with Bill Paley at CBS for more than two million dollars. Almost everybody followed him to CBS; why not, we'd all been following him in the ratings for years. Within one season CBS became the most popular radio network.

Jack's success really caused the end of vaudeville-format shows on radio. Cantor stayed on the air for a long time, but never had the kind of success he had at the beginning. By 1952 Eddie was doing some television and working as a disc jockey on a network radio show, still doing a lot of old bits he got from his basement files. But instead of doing them between orchestra numbers, he did them between recordings of orchestra numbers.

Ed Wynn had the same problem as Eddie. He tried to solve it with a situation comedy called "Happy Island." He played the King of Happy Island, a place that probably would have been a lot happier if its ratings had been better. It probably should have been called something like, Mildly Amusing Island. Ed was still performing for the studio audience, and "Happy Island" was done onstage with expensive sets and actors in full makeup and costumes. Big sets and fancy costumes on radio made about as much sense as taking Charlie McCarthy out for an expensive dinner. The show was canceled after one season and Ed tried a comeback as the Fire Chief on "The Texaco Star Theatre," but after a year the Chief was fired.

Go ahead, Milton; take my joke, please. Sorry, Henny.

Edgar Bergen and Charlie, Fanny Brice and Fred Allen, were also able to make the transition from vaudeville to radio. It took Bergen a long time to convince a sponsor that a ventriloquist could be successful on the air. Supposedly, one advertising executive said, "A ventriloquist, huh? Well, they'd better be funny." In any other business a person who had long conversations with himself might be put away, on radio Bergen became a big star. It was Rudy Vallee who finally put Edgar and Charlie on his "Fleischmann's Hour" and they—he—was so funny that Edgar Bergen was given his own show, "The Charlie

McCarthy Show." On the show Charlie was a wisecracking kid, and Bergen was always trying to teach him proper behavior, respect for other people and good moral values. "Charlie," Edgar would ask, "do you know how to make people look up to you?"

"Live up on a hill?" Edgar would answer.

One week, in one of the funniest stunts ever done on radio, Charlie and Marilyn Monroe were going to get married. This was a marriage that all of America tried to stop. In the middle of the show, for example, the announcer said, "And now a word from our sponsor—Don't do it Marilyn!"

Charlie was determined. "Will your marriage be an afternoon or evening affair?" Edgar asked himself.

"Oh," he answered, "we expect it to last longer than that." Because Charlie was a dummy, and he was supposed to be a child, Bergen could get away with the kind of risqué, or "blue" material that probably would have been censored if a real person had said the same thing. One thing for sure, Bergen was no dummy.

Marilyn Monroe played herself on that show. Never was there better argument for the invention of television. "I'm just a woman," she told Charlie.

Charlie said, "I know, but you're so good at it."

Could you see my page move when you read that? If you think doing ventriloquism on radio is easy, that's how simple it is in a book.

Edgar loved playing straight man to a dummy. On the air Charlie would tease him about being cheap, getting bald, moving his lips. And just like Jack and Fred Allen, Charlie McCarthy had his own feud—with W. C. Fields, who became a regular on the show, playing himself. "You termites' flophouse," Fields would sneer at Charlie, "is it true that when you slide down a banister the banister gets more splinters than you do?"

"Why, you barfly," Charlie answered, "watch out or I'll stick a wick in your mouth and use you for an alcohol lamp."

Finally, Fields sawed Charlie in half. This wasn't a magic trick, I mean Fields sawed Charlie in half. That was terrible, the worst thing Fred Allen ever did to Jack was have several men pull his pants off during a skit—during which Jack warned, "You haven't seen the end of me, Allen!"

Bergen and Charlie were on the air for more than twenty years, usually ranking in the top five comedy shows. After that, I think, Charlie retired and went to live in a suitcase in Florida.

Unlike Ed Wynn, who tried to make radio a visual medium, Fanny Brice took advantage of radio. Oh, I loved Fanny. She was such a great torch singer that people sometimes forgot that she was also a very talented comic. After a lot of our friends from the vaudeville days had settled in Los Angeles we'd get together for big parties. And at these parties we'd all get up and do the things we didn't get to do professionally. I'd sing and make people laugh. Milton would tell original jokes. No, that's not true, Milton wouldn't do that. And Fanny would do the character she'd been playing for friends for years, a whiny little girl named Baby Snooks, or Schnooks, as Fanny called her. She'd speak in a goo-googley voice, scrunch up her face, pout, and somehow this mature woman who could make you cry singing about her lost love would become a little girl. When she sang a song like "Dainty Me," she was so good that you'd think Shirley Temple had to be imitating her.

She first did Snooks onstage in the Ziegfeld Follies in 1934. Two years later Snooks appeared on radio on "The Maxwell House Program." Baby Snooks was everybody's neighbor's kid. She was the kind of little girl Gracie's character would have been, if Gracie's character had ever been a little girl. For example, when her father, Daddy Higgins, warned her that if she did one more bad thing, "I'll have to take my belt off and then you know what'll happen . . ."

She told him, "Your pants will fall down."

Snooks was tough to play. When Jack was being cheap or vain, he was still playing a man about his own age. Gracie was always a lady. But Fanny had to become a little girl. And she was so good at it that when she whined, "Why, Daddy?" for about the sixth time you'd want to smack her posterior just like she was your very own. Fanny always claimed, "I could do Snooks blind. I don't have to work at it, it's part of me. It's like stealin' money," but that was just Fanny. During a broadcast she'd become Snooks; squirming, squinting, mugging, jumping up and down—they even had to print her script in type three times the regular size because she wouldn't wear glasses when she was playing Snooks. And when the show ended she stayed in character, not her voice, but her mannerisms, for maybe an hour afterward.

Maybe Fanny was playing a six-year-old, but she could be very tough. She was represented by Abe Lastfogel of the William Morris Agency, who convinced her to hire his new client, a young comedian named Danny Thomas. Thomas had started in show business selling candy in the balcony of a burlesque hall in Toledo, Ohio, and for years he'd been watching small-time performers doing Fanny Brice impersonations. So when he met her for the first time, he was in awe. "Oh, Miss Brice," he told her, "it's such an honor to meet you. I never thought the day would come when I'd be privileged enough to work with you."

Like most vaudevillians, Fanny was a very sentimental woman. "Don't give me that crap, kid," she told him, "you'd just better be funny."

Like a lot of great comic characters, Charlie McCarthy and Jack Benny, for example, Snooks never got any older. Fanny was Snooks for fifteen years, and by the time she died in 1951 she had three grandchildren—making her the only six-year-old grandmother in the world.

Now, Fred Allen. Fred Allen played a sarcastic, bitter, sometimes morbid, miserable, dejected unhappy, sad comedian named Fred Allen. He was perfect for the part. The thing I always noticed about Fred was that he just wasn't happy unless he wasn't happy. Then, he was happy. Fred hadn't been as successful in vaudeville as Cantor or Jack or me and Gracie and Fanny, but radio was perfect for him.

He claimed he went into radio because "The show wouldn't close if there was no one in the balcony, and there was no travel." But the real reason was the same as all the rest of us—it was show business and he couldn't stay out of it.

Fred Allen was radio's most popular pessimist. His outlook on life was very simple: "The world is a grindstone. Life is your nose." He was the kind of person who would look for the dark cloud inside the silver lining.

Fred knew from the very beginning that his vaudeville act wouldn't work on radio—it hadn't even worked in vaudeville. So he needed to find a format that was loose enough to allow him to do what he did best—heckle the world. Fred and I did very different types of humor, the only points I tried to make on the radio were the ones counted by the Crossley people. A lot of people warned Fred that his dry wit wouldn't work on radio, and they kept warning him for the whole seventeen years his shows were on the air.

Fred first went on the air on "The Linit Bath Club Revue" in 1932. I don't think that sponsor really understood Fred's type of humor—for the first show they wanted him to dress up like a Keystone Kop. When he refused to do that, the sponsor packed the studio with orphans brought in from a home and told them to laugh whenever the announcer gave them the signal. Orphans? The show was a series of sketches in which Fred played everything from a department store owner who was always getting into fights with complaining customers to a hotel manager who was always getting into fights with complaining guests. You beginning to see a pattern here? After that show he hosted. "The Salad Bowl Revue," "The Sal Hepatica Revue," "The Hour of Smiles," isn't that a great name for a show, and his most famous programs, "Town Hall Tonight" and "Allen's Alley."

On "Town Hall Tonight," Fred created a format that really suited his talents. The hour was divided into four segments; the first spot, Town Hall News, gave Fred the chance to talk about current events. "There's an old saying," he explained one night, "that if all the politicians in the world were laid end to end, they'd still be lying."

The second segment was an interview with a real person who did something silly. One night it was a worm salesman, another night it would be a sausage stuffer. He told the world's foremost authority on eagles that "I am a man who hears no eagle, sees no eagle, speaks no eagle." He also had on a talking mynah bird who suffered from mike fright and didn't speak on several shows.

In the third segment he did a routine with his wife, Portland Hoffa, who played a dizzy dame just like Gracie—she didn't play it like Gracie, nobody could, but the dame was dizzy like Gracie.

140

For example she'd bring him the last ten pages of *Gone With the Wind* and the last twenty pages of *Anthony Adverse* because he said he wanted some bookends.

The final segment was a skit performed by the Mighty Allen Art Players, in which Fred played a judge who always got into a fight with lawyers, a boxer who always got into fights . . .

Fred was always getting into trouble with somebody. On the Sal Hepatica show—Sal Hepatica was a remedy for stomach distress—he told a cheap Scotsman joke and 200 Scots wrote in threatening never to use the product again unless he apologized. So he did, explaining, "The prospect that they would go through life constipated so frightened the agency that they made me apologize."

His whole career on radio was one long fight with network executives, who were always complaining about something he said, or that his audience laughed too long and his program ran over its time slot, or something they thought he would have said if he could have gotten away with it. But mostly they didn't like the fact that he made fun of network executives, creating jobs like the Vice-President in Charge of Don't You Dare Raise That Window Another Inch, the Vice-President in Charge of Ah Ha! Your Show Is Running Too Long, and the Vice-President in Charge of Leaky Dixie Cups.

On "Allen's Alley" every week he'd visit the people who lived in the Alley to talk about current events. Some of the best-known characters on radio lived there, including Senator Claghorn, a very Southern senator. Claghorn was so Southern, in fact, that when he visited New York he wouldn't go to Yankee Stadium, he wouldn't go into a room unless it had a Southern exposure and the only container he'd drink from was a Dixie cup.

The crusty New Englander, Titus Moody, also lived in the Alley. Moody once complained that machines do all the work on farms. "'Bout all a man can do with his hands on a farm today is scratch hisself." I think as long as he was scratching hisself on the farm the censors couldn't object. But if he tried to scratch hisself anyplace else he'd still be itching.

"Allen's Alley" was a top-rated show until the radio quiz shows started giving away big prizes. "Stop the Music," which was on opposite Fred, offered a jackpot to anyone listening at home who could identify the "Mystery Melody" if the show called them. Fred parodied that show with a skit called "Cease the Music." On his show they gave away 4,000 yards of used dental floss, twelve miles of railroad track and the grand prize—your own human being. When the Alley's ratings continued dropping, Fred took out an insurance policy giving $5,000 to anyone who was listening to his show when "Stop the Music" called them. Great idea. The bad news was that nobody collected. Eventually Allen's Alley was torn down and replaced by a parking lot. Then they put up a bowling alley, but that didn't last long, and a few years ago they knocked down that building and put up a huge mall. So I guess you could say "Allen's Alley" got mauled in the ratings.

That's a lot of trouble to go to for one bad joke. I probably should have forgotten the joke and left the bowling alley up.

I'd better mention Bob Hope right here because if I don't people might say this chapter is hopeless. Maybe that's a terrible joke, but at least I didn't have to tear down a bowling alley to get to the punch line. Hope was born on the Lower East Side—of London. He did as many different types of acts in vaudeville as I did; in fact, I think he was Williams of "Brown and Williams" when it was a British-Yiddish sketch act. He went on the radio with his own show for Pepsodent toothpaste in 1938. Unlike almost everybody else at that time, instead of using continuing characters or a situation-comedy format, Bob opened his variety show with a monologue consisting of as many jokes as he could tell in three or four minutes. In Bob's case, it really was "A funny thing happened to me on the way to World War II."

He told so many jokes so quickly that it didn't matter if some of them bombed. And speaking of bombs, ladies and gentlemen, it was during World War II, when he started broadcasting from military bases all over the world, that his show really took off. And speaking of taking off, nobody visited soldiers in more remote places than he did. Maybe he hadn't been such a big star in vaudeville, but after that he played the biggest theaters in the world—the Far East, the South Pacific, Korea, Vietnam. "I wanted to mail a letter home," he said during a broadcast from the Sahara Desert, "but it's so hot here I had no spit to use on the letter. So I pinned it to the envelope."

"They don't have marriage ceremonies here," he said on a show coming from a weather station in Greenland, "it's so cold that if you wet your lips before you kiss your girl it really is till death do you part."

Hope became the biggest star on radio by leaving the country. There's a message there for me somewhere. He traveled everywhere in the world just to bring a little cheer to lonely Americans serving their country far away from home. It was a terrible struggle for poor Bob, all alone except for a few members of his crew, and people like Marilyn Monroe, Jayne Mansfield, Ann-Margret, Brooke Shields, all the Miss Americas, Ann Sheridan, Carole Landis . . . year after year, Hope and some of the most beautiful women in the world went off to isolated outposts of civilization where they huddled together to keep warm.

So I think you can imagine how much sympathy I have for him. I mean, alone with just these women to keep him company. And Bob never took advantage of it either, although he is the only man I know who told one of the girls that he'd run out of gas—while they were on an aircraft carrier. In the 1940s Bob became one of the biggest stars on radio. I'll tell you how talented he was—he made people want to *listen* to Rita Hayworth.

Milton used to tell people that when they were both in radio Bob once accused him of stealing material from him, and Sarah Berle got very upset at that. "My son would never stoop so low," she said. "My son stoops high!"

In radio, and later in television, Bob and I would exchange visits on each others' shows. But since neither of us do more than a few specials every years, we've agreed to exchange plugs. So here it is: Bob has written almost as many books as I have. He has a new book coming out soon. Believe me, whenever you're reading this, Bob has a new book coming out soon. So read it, it'll make you feel good. I'll tell you the part I like best in his new book—the part where he quotes this book. It's hysterical. Buy it, you'll see for yourself.

The fact that Bob's books sell very well proves how talented he still is—people buy his books to *read* about Loni Anderson.

A lot of very talented vaudevillians tried to make it in radio. I was very lucky, Gracie and I were successful. Let me tell you how popular we were. I've never told this story to anyone before, but at one time I got a call from John D. Rockefeller, inviting me to come up to his office. John D. Rockefeller, pretty impressive. When I got there I saw a scale model of Rockefeller Center sitting on the table. "Young man," he said, "in the middle of this complex there will be a great theater, and as tribute to your talent and all the people who have come before you, I would like your permission to name this theater The George Burns Music Hall."

Well . . . Of course I was flattered. "That's very nice of you," I said, "but I think I have a better idea. Why not name it in tribute to all those brave men and women of the radio industry, those people who keep the tubes burning in homes all across America. Why not call it . . . The Radio City Music Hall!"

"By golly," Rockefeller said, "that's a brilliant idea. I shall do exactly that."

Vus you dere, Reader?

5

The George Burns Music Hall? You know, maybe that wasn't such a terrible idea. But I didn't need something like that to know how lucky I'd been. Making the transition from vaudeville to radio had been very easy for me. All it meant was standing next to Gracie in front of a microphone instead of standing next to her onstage. But there were a lot of talented people who didn't have Gracie to stand next to.

Maybe you noticed that there's no Al Jolson Music Hall either. Jolie had a tough time adjusting to radio. What could he do, black-up the microphone and get down on one dial? He was so used to moving around the whole stage that it was hard for him to get used to standing still in front of the mike. I remember when he broke into radio there were stories that they had to put him in a straitjacket to keep him from moving too far away from the mike. Jolie just never had the kind of success on radio that he had on the stage; of course, that's like saying Columbus didn't do much after discovering America. I mean, he did okay, he went on the air for the first time in 1927, he had four different shows of his own, starred on a lot of specials and made guest appearances on most of the big shows, but he never dominated the airwaves like he had on the stage.

Radio didn't know how to use Jolson. On his first show he was billed as "The Blackface Comedian." The blackface comedian? On radio you needed a sound effect to have a broken leg, who cared if he was in blackface? Then when his ratings weren't very high they began calling him a singer. All they really should have said was, "Here's Jolson."

I don't think he ever felt comfortable on the radio either. "It's a strange thing," he used to say, "that while the radio audience is the only audience that gets in on a free show, it is the most critical audience in the world. . . . Change and diversity is the watchword in radio, and for this reason I don't believe it's a good idea to dally too long in front of the microphone." On two of his shows he didn't even sign a contract, the sponsor just agreed that he'd stay on the show as long as he wanted to, then he could just walk away. I know he hated doing live radio, and at that time there wasn't anything else. "I just don't like going on the air and doing the show direct," he said. "When you go wrong on a song, you can't say, 'Mr. Jones, let's play it over again.' I'd like to do radio just like the pictures—leave the imperfect stuff on the cutting room floor. When I have to stick to a script my hands are tied, my mouth is tied, my kisser is tied."

He was really too big to fit inside a format. His most successful show was "The Lifebuoy Show," that also featured comedians Parkyakarkus and Martha Raye. Parky would wear funny costumes and stand next to Jolson and they'd scream jokes at each other and hit each other over the head with newspapers. Martha Raye was the most dignified person on the show.

When "The Lifebuoy Show" got to be number five in the Hooper ratings—they were supposedly more scientific than the Crossley's—he said, "Think of what this program would be if there was somebody else with class on it." His rating got to be 25.7, which was good, and when somebody congratulated him on that, he'd sort of brush them off by saying something like, "Oh go on now, it ain't nothin'." But if they said, "You should be proud of a twenty-five point six," he'd smile and say evenly, "Twenty-five point seven."

Gracie and I had him on our show three times. He played the world's greatest singer—well, one of us had to do it. And he was his usual humble self in that role, too. On one show, as he arrived at our house our announcer, Bill Goodwin, said, "I was just telling George and Gracie that you're the greatest singer in the world."

"Ah, now, Bill," Jolie said, "you shouldn't tell them that."

"Why not?"

"'Cause they already know it."

It also took Jimmy Durante a long time to make it on radio, and he never really had the kind of success he had in nightclubs or would have in television. Jimmy wasn't really right for radio, the only thing he could throw on the radio was a fit; and there's no such thing as the sound of a big nose. He started as a summer replacement for Cantor, doing bits that allowed him to tell jokes about the size of his nose, "I'm da only man in America who can smoke a cigar in da shower," and mustilate the English language, and sing some of those wonderful old love songs like "A Dissa and a Datta," "Toscanini, Stokowski and Me," "Didja Ever Have a Feeling You Wanted to Go —And Still Have a Feeling You Wanted to Stay," "So I Ups to Him" and "I Know Darn Well I Can Do Without Broadway, But Can Broadway Do Without Me?" Jimmy sang the kind of songs that had such long titles that by the time he announced them he didn't have time to sing them.

Jimmy's problem on radio was that he was so forceful he had a tough time finding someone strong enough to work opposite him. For a while Alan Young played his straight man, but Alan was just too nice. Let me tell you how nice Alan is; when we were casting the "Mr. Ed" television show for my production company I hired him to co-star with Ed because I thought Alan was the type of man that a horse would want to talk to. But he wasn't strong enough to play opposite Jimmy. "I was doing the same character Jimmy was doing," Alan told me, "the lovable bumbler. He kept saying, 'Hit me, Youngey, hit me,' and I'd tell him I just couldn't do it.

"One day he finally got mad at me and lost his temper and shouted something like 'You're not doing it right, Youngey.' For him that was losing his temper. Then he saw that I was really upset and he didn't know what to say. A little while later we were having lunch and, because he had a bad stomach, all he was eating were a few burnt buns. So we were all sitting at the table going over the script and I didn't have anything to eat. Jimmy kept glancing at me and finally he took his burnt bun and broke it in half. 'Here, Youngey,' he said, giving it to me, 'have somethin' to eat.' That was his way of apologizing for losing his temper."

When Garry Moore replaced Alan, Jimmy had somebody strong enough to hit him, and his show became more successful. But the most memorable thing Jimmy did on radio was introduce Mrs. Calabash. Starting in 1946 Jimmy ended every show he did with the loving words, "And good night Mrs. Calabash, wherever you are." Nobody knew who Mrs. Calabash was, and her identity became one of the great mysteries of show business. She became one of the best-known characters on radio, even though she never said one word. A lot of people claimed they knew who Mrs. Calabash really was. But the producer of Jimmy's radio show, Phil Cohan, said that there was no Mrs. Calabash. He said she was supposed to be a joke. Jimmy was supposed to use the line for several weeks to build up the mystery, then reveal that Mrs. Calabash was a racehorse that he'd lost thousands of dollars betting on. "The name came from the kind of pipe Sherlock Holmes smoked," Cohan said, "that was called a calabash because its bowl was made from a calabash gourd."

But a few days before Jimmy was going to go on the air and tell the truth they'd made up, he was visiting some friends at a Catholic monastery and told them the real truth. Real truth is usually very different from show business truth. His friends got very upset, and warned him that his listeners were going to be disappointed because they believed Mrs. Calabash was someone he really loved. Jimmy decided they were right, and kept Mrs. Calabash in his act.

Maybe that's true. Vus I dere? It didn't matter. Mrs. Calabash got him so much publicity that, if I could have found her, I would have paid her twice what he wasn't paying her.

A lot of people thought they knew who she was. Some of Jimmy's best friends told me that she was the widowed mother of a small boy who always listened to the show and wrote him long, loving letters. Some of his other best friends told me that Mrs. Calabash was his pet name for his first wife, who'd died a few months earlier. And still others said that Mrs. Calabash was Jimmy's nickname for his old partner, Lou Clayton, who'd also died a few years earlier.

I don't think that was right. I knew Lou Clayton for a long, long time. Lou was some tough guy. When he died, I knew where he went.

Sometimes Jimmy told people that Mrs. Calabash was his grammar school sweetheart. "We was stuck on each other for a while," he said, "but nuttin' ever came of it." And other times Jimmy told people that she was a girl in grammar school who wouldn't go out with him. Jimmy's second wife, Margie Little, said Mrs. Calabash was the name Jimmy used to mean all the lonely people who were listening to him.

I could probably make up some story about who she really was, but most of you know I don't like to make up things. Except for that last sentence, of course. I think, as Jimmy probably would have said, that Mrs. Calabash really was a frictional person. Because if she had really been a real person, with all the publicity she got, the William Morris Agency would have signed her and she would have gotten her own show. I think Mrs. Calabash was very important to Jimmy, she gave Jimmy one of the most important things any entertainer can have—a great finish. I mean, who would ever boo anybody with a name like Mrs. Calabash?

Jessel claimed he went out with her twice. But knowing Georgie, even if Jimmy had admitted she was a horse, he still would have claimed he'd gone out with her. In Philly, naturally.

I don't know why Jessel didn't make it on radio, but none of the great dialect comedians from vaudeville were very successful on the air. He had his own show for a while, but couldn't get a permanent sponsor. So he became a guest star on other shows. We had him on three times, more often than anyone else except Jolson and Cantor. Georgie was great, whenever I called him and told him we needed him, and it didn't matter whether it was early in the morning or late at night, he responded like a real trouper. "Can I get paid in advance?" he'd ask.

He played himself on our show, and whatever he was doing in real life, that's what he was doing on our show. When Jessel was producing movies in Hollywood, he played a Hollywood producer. "Believe me," he told Gracie, *"The Dolly Sisters* is the greatest picture I've ever made in my life, and I'm hoping my second picture will be even better."

He was good on radio, he did the best Jessel imitation on the air, but his real love was performing in front of a live audience. One night he made a guest appearance on Durante's show and did a nice job. But when the show ended, before the audience got up to leave, he came back onstage and asked them to sit down. Then he did about twenty minutes of his old material and he was great. Durante was sitting up in the control room watching this, and finally he said, just loudly enough for everyone to hear, "Gennelman, you're watchin' an erra."

The whole idea of big stars making special appearances started on radio. Radio was like one big Hammerstein's—if you did something to get your name in the papers and didn't go to jail, somebody would pay you to be on their show. Big names like Jessel, who might boost a Hooper rating a couple of points, could make a lot of money doing guest spots. Shows like Fred Allen, Kate Smith,

Bob Hope, Bing Crosby and Rudy Vallee paid about $1,000 for a single appearance, and the superstars could get as much as $3,500. Some sponsors gave guest stars their product rather than cash. That was great if you were on "The Chevrolet Show," it wasn't so good if you were on "The Sal Hepatica Show."

I'll tell you who was the toughest person Gracie and I ever had to work with—the great film director Cecil B. De Mille. De Mille was so tough that during rehearsals he wouldn't talk to us. How could anybody not talk to Gracie? I'll tell you something, it's tough to do a radio show with a guest who won't talk to you. We were sitting at the conference table, me and brother Willie, who was one of our writers, the comedy writer Paul Henning, De Mille and his secretary. De Mille would speak only to his secretary. I'd say something to him, he would whisper something to his secretary, and she would say, "Mr. De Mille says no." Or, "Mr. De Mille does not like that line." It was incredible, who'd he think he was, Cecil B. DeMille?

I kept wondering what that secretary would do if De Mille burped.

Some stars had difficulty doing radio. When Ronald and Benita Colman were rehearsing to do a Benny show, he was having trouble reading a line. "Jack," he asked, "exactly what is my motivation right here?"

After thinking about it for a few seconds, Jack told him everything anyone needs to know about doing comedy. "I think your motivation is to get the biggest damn laugh you can."

Durante had Greer Garson as a guest on his show one week. This was the very first time she'd done comedy and she was pretty nervous about it. After they'd read the script several times she asked Jimmy, "Do you think it's going to be funny?"

"Yeah, sure," Jimmy said reassuringly, "dis is funny stuff. These writers, they're the best."

"I've never done comedy before," she said. "What happens if we do this and nobody laughs?"

Jimmy then told her everything else anyone needs to know about doing comedy. "Well then, Miss Garson," he said, "we're all gonna be in the terlet together."

There was just no way of figuring out who would be good on the radio. Some people who should have been big stars just never made it. Besides Jessel, that included some talented people like Lou Holtz, Blossom and Benny, Frank Fay, Milton, and Groucho and Chico, who never had the kind of success on radio that they had in other forms of entertainment. Harpo I could understand.

Lou Holtz tried all kinds of different formats, but nothing worked for him. On one of his shows, I remember, he did a maharajah character who spoke in meaningless double-talk—but his sponsor wouldn't let him do it, telling him that if he couldn't understand what the character was saying then the listeners wouldn't understand it either.

Lou told him something like, "But what he says doesn't make any sense."

"I know," the sponsor's representative agreed, "that's what I just said."

Frank Fay didn't understand radio at all. Look, I didn't like Fay. You want me to lie? Okay, I liked Frank Fay. Fay was very different from everybody else on the air—everybody else was nice. When he made his debut with Rudy Vallee in 1936 one of the newspaper critics wrote, "His malicious quality is in contrast to the endless good nature of most radio programs." And that was one of his best reviews. After six weeks with Rudy, Frank got his own program. It really was his show too, he had no writers, no announcer, no singer, no bandleader, no nothing. Just Fay. He wrote the show, announced the show, told the jokes, sang the songs and sold the product. There was no way that was going to work on the radio, no possible way. Nobody wanted to listen to one person do everything for thirty minutes. So naturally, as much as I liked Fay, I told him, "I think it's a great idea. I wouldn't change a single thing."

Well, maybe I didn't, but I probably would've if I thought he would have listened to me. But the Great Fay didn't listen to anybody; it all worked out though, nobody listened to him either.

In the late thirties and forties Milton Berle was the most popular nightclub performer in the business, but he just couldn't make it on radio. I think, like Durante and the Marx Brothers, Milton had to be seen to be enjoyed. But Milton didn't use the language as a prop like Durante did and he didn't have Groucho's quick wit. He depended on telling as many jokes as quickly as he could, and he hoped that some of them would be funny. It worked for Bob Hope, but not for Milton.

Milton tried six different formats and none of them worked. His first show should have been perfect for him. It was a panel show called "Stop Me If—." Gees, I thought, everybody wanted to stop Milton. Now, Milton, if you're reading this, I want you to know I'm kidding. I'm just trying to get a few laughs—and you in particular know how hard that is. Then he did a variety show for Ballantine beer called "The Three Ring Show." Another one of his shows was the memorable "Kiss and Make Up."

Milton's last try was "The Milton Berle Show," which had a variety-show format. A typical bit on that show had Milton trying to borrow a book from the public library, but being turned down because he couldn't fulfill the last of sixteen regulations—no talking in the library. Typecasting. Milton's radio career ended when he got his television show, and there are a lot of people who loved radio who believed that that was the only good thing TV ever did for it.

The Marx Brothers had the same problem Milton did, you had to see them work to really enjoy them, but they were a little more successful than he was. Hey, Mrs. Calabash was more successful than he was and she didn't even exist. Groucho was twice as good on radio as Milton—he only failed with three shows before becoming success-ful on television. Chico worked with Groucho on the first two shows. The fact that Harpo's char-acter didn't speak definitely hurt his radio career. I mean, what could they say, "Harpo is shaking his head"?

The first show Groucho and Chico did was about a funny lawyer and his crazy assistant. I know, there is no such thing as a funny lawyer, but this show, "Beagle, Shyster and Beagle," was written by Nat Perrin and Arthur Sheekman, and everybody in show business knows that two great comedy writers can make one funny lawyer. Groucho played the lawyer, Beagle. Chico, speak-ing in his Italian accent, played his assistant, Ra-velli. After the first show was aired a real attorney named Beagle called up and threatened to sue for libel, so the name of the show was changed to "Flywheel, Shyster and Flywheel." Nobody com-plained, so I guess that proves that there were no Shysters in the legal profession. The dialogue sounded like it had been lifted from a Marx Broth-ers movie. For example, Groucho would ask, "What happened to that ten cents I left in the drawer?"

"Search me," Chico told him.

In another episode Groucho and Chico were supposed to be eating dinner, and Groucho asked, "What are you unbuttoning your shirt for?"

"I justa remember," Chico explained, "da doc-tor, he tell me dat when I eat I shoulda watch my stomach. . . ." In fact, the dialogue sounded so much like it came from a Marx Brothers film that after the show was canceled several of the bits were put into their next film, *Duck Soup*.

Groucho and Chico then tried a show in which they made fun of current events, but that failed too. Groucho really needed a format that would let him ad-lib and those first two shows didn't give him that chance. Groucho really had a quick mind, although sometimes he could be nasty. Once he went to the Plaza Hotel for lunch with the comedy writers Charlie Issacs and Manny Mannheim. Groucho wasn't wearing a necktie and the maître d' stopped them and explained he couldn't come in without one. "Why?" Groucho asked.

"Because those are the rules," the maître d' said.

"Who makes the rules?" Groucho asked, "some guy sitting upstairs in a T-shirt?"

Finally Groucho agreed to wear a clip-on tie and the maître d' escorted them to a table. But just before they got there Groucho stopped and pointed to a bald man sitting several tables away. "Now that's just not fair," he said loudly, "you wouldn't let me in without a tie, but you let him in without hair!"

Groucho finally found the right format when producer John Guedell heard him working with Bob Hope and thought he'd be the perfect host for a quiz show he was planning called "You Bet Your Life." The quiz part of the show was really just an excuse to allow Groucho to interview the contestants. "Tell me, doctor," he once asked a tree surgeon, "did you ever fall out of a patient?" The show was a hit almost immediately and became one of the few programs that was simultaneously taped for radio and filmed for television.

Gracie and I never had Groucho on the show, but one week our guest star was Harpo. I know, I know, with the kind of jokes I tell sometimes it's tough to know when I'm trying to be serious, but we really did have Harpo as a guest. I'll tell you something surprising, the few times Harpo did radio he was great. Strange as it seems, Harpo was a natural for radio. Even if he never said one word. Probably the thing that radio did best was use sound effects, and the biggest part of Harpo's character was the use of sound effects. He honked a horn, he whistled, he smacked his lips together—he did whatever he had to do to make himself understood. I mean, you couldn't have two Harpos talking to each other, people would think they were listening to a traffic jam, but as long as Harpo had a straight man he was wonderful.

On the show Gracie hired him to be a reporter for the gossip column she was doing. The script was terrific. For instance, Gracie asked Harpo, "Where are your brothers?"

He riffled a deck of cards.

"Oh, I see," she said, "playing cards. What are they playing?"

Harpo whistled "How Dry I Am," then hiccuped.

161

Gracie figured that one out too. "Oh, gin."

Harpo was probably the only guest we ever had on the show whose part could have been played by our sound-effects man. Before radio, sound effects were known as noise. Radio is the only business I've ever heard of that could turn slamming a door into an art form. I want you to do me a favor. I want you to hold this page very loosely between your thumb and forefinger and rattle it. Do it right now, I'll wait right here. Dum da dum, dum da dum, dum da dum. Back? You did it? Congratulations, you're now a sound-effects person. You successfully made the sound of a reader rattling a page. In the 1930s you'd be getting $250 a week for that. Look, radio had some limitations. It was very tough to do action on the radio. On the Westerns, for example, when a cowboy good guy like Gene Autry had a showdown with a bad guy, Gene's sidekick Pat Buttram would have to describe the action for the listeners. "Nice shot, Gene," he'd say, "you shot the gun right out of his hand without wounding him seriously." If there was a fight in the script the actors would grunt—and the sound-effects man would punch his fist into his palm, throw chairs, maybe break some glasses, whack a wooden bowling pin with an ax handle and fall down on the floor. Then the actors would grunt again. In radio, when two actors got into a fight, the sound-effects man got bruised.

But the big advantage radio had over everything else was the ability to let the listener use his imagination. When Jack Benny went into his vault, or Harpo was leaving a restaurant dropping a trail of silverware behind him, or Fibber McGee was opening the most overstuffed closet in the radio world, no picture could have been funnier than what the listener was seeing in his own mind.

The story is that the first sound effect on radio was created when an engineer slapped two pieces of wood together to create the sound of a door slamming. But it didn't take long for sound effects to get much more sophisticated—when they wanted to create the sound of a door slamming, they slammed a door. Jack Benny should get the credit for making sound effects an important part of the story. Before Jack started using sound effects everything would have to be explained in the dialogue. When an actor was supposed to be coming, for example, a character would have to say, "Oh, here comes Fenton now." But Jack started using sound effects for effect. For example, the script would say: "Jack goes next door to the Colmans' with a tin cup to borrow a cup of sugar." But when the show was on the air the listener would hear Jack opening and closing his front door, walking down the five steps, walking along the sidewalk, then the clink of a coin dropping into his tin cup and Jack saying, "Oh, thank you," then walking up the Colmans' steps and ringing their doorbell. Once, I remember, Jack was on our show and he was supposed to be proposing marriage to Gracie. "I'd better get down on my knees and propose to you before George gets here," he said. Then listeners heard the creaking sound of an old, rusty door being opened. "Darn it," he continued, "I'm too late, I heard a door open."

"Oh no, Jack," Gracie told him, "that was your knees."

Look, the sound-effects men were the real stars of radio. The producers pointed, the actors read from a script, the sound-effects men did everything else. They really had their own world. I remember after Jack Pearl had done one of his first Baron Munchausen shows I asked his sound-effects man how he'd liked the program. "It was great," he told me. "Wasn't that dish crash wonderful?"

They could create any sound we asked them to do. The crunch of a man walking through packed snow was made by squeezing a box of cornstarch. The sound of a bird flying was really a sound-effects man flapping a leather glove. To make a fire he riffled the straw bristles of a broom. A wire brush scraped across a piece of tin became a speeding train, and ice cubes clinking in a cocktail were just two camera flash bulbs tapped together. If something was too big to fit inside the studio, like an airplane, a car engine or a speedboat, recorded sounds would be used. Vocal specialists, like the great Mel Blanc, were used to create the sound of living things, from an animal growling to a small plant growing.

What does a small plant growing sound like? A lot like a big plant growing, but softer.

When Paul Henning was writing our show he used to love slipping impossible sounds into the script, like "a cat walking on a Persian rug," or "oil dripping on velvet," just to torture our sound-effects man. What does a sound-effects man being tortured sound like? It sounds a lot like Paul Henning pleading for his life.

We even made the sound-effects man a character on the show. He was played by a fine actor named Elliott Lewis, and he was supposed to be a college graduate who hated his job and was very bitter that sound-effects men did not get the recognition they deserved. So I'd leave a room and a door would slam and Elliott would sneer just loudly enough for the audience to hear, "Four years of college and I slam doors for a living." If we complained about a sound effect, the next time he had to close the door he'd really slam it, then ask sarcastically, "Was that loud enough for you?" Sometimes, to show us how important sound-effects men were, he'd intentionally mess up. If Gracie and I were supposed to be leaving the house he wouldn't shut the door. "I've leaving now," I'd say and we'd wait to hear the door slam. All we heard was silence. Then Elliott would ask, "Did you go to college?" I'd tell him I didn't even go to high school. "Then slam it yourself," he'd say.

I'm not kidding when I say the sound-effects man had the hardest job on the show. Believe me, the toughest thing about acting on radio was acting as if it were tough to act on radio. We were all afraid that our sponsors might catch on and stop paying us those big salaries. As Fanny Brice said, acting on radio wasn't exactly like stealing money, it was much easier than stealing money. And much safer too. There was only one thing that was hard about performing on radio—we had to face the most terrifying monster most of us had ever seen—the microphone.

Microphones were still pretty new when we started working in radio. Nobody had liked working with a mike in vaudeville because you had to stand directly in front of it; you couldn't move around the stage. But we didn't have any choice in radio. Instead of playing to the audience, we really had to play to the mike. It didn't matter how much the people in the studio liked you, it was the people on the other end of the mike that made you a success. And it didn't matter how good you were, the microphone wasn't going to applaud, or cheer, or even heckle you—well, sometimes it would whistle, but that just meant you were standing too close.

Almost everybody suffered from mike fright. Ed Wynn admitted, "There isn't a Tuesday that I'm not as nervous as a man who faces the death sentence." Jack Pearl, who was a much bigger star on radio than he'd ever been on stage, still preferred the theater. "In the theater you work every night," he used to say, "in radio I work one night and worry the other six." Jack Benny, supposedly the most relaxed person in the business, used to say that radio was very easy "As long as you don't mind living on a diet of coffee and fingernails." Mary Livingstone hated it, sometimes she'd actually faint just before the show went on the air. It was so tough for her that when Jack started taping his shows she wouldn't even go into the studio. During the taping, Jack's secretary, Jeanette, would read Mary's lines, then a crew would go out to Jack's house and record Mary reading them, and then they would splice Mary's voice onto the broadcast tape.

Even the great Jolson was terrified before going on the air. He'd stay out in the hallway, nervously walking up and down, clearing his throat and singing the first few bars of a song. When he was announced to the studio audience just before the show went on the air, he'd run into the studio from the back and start shaking hands with people as he walked down the aisle. Jolie didn't take any chances—he'd carry a picture of his baby son with him and show it to members of the audience, telling them, "This is my little baby, this is my little baby." Well, one night he had Groucho on his show, and when Jolie ran into the studio Groucho ran right behind him, and when Jolson started shaking hands with people, Groucho was right behind him shaking hands with the same people, and when Jolson showed them the photograph of his son, Groucho showed them the photograph of a partially dressed beautiful woman, and when Jolson told them, "This is my little baby, this is my little baby," Groucho told them, "This is really his little baby, this is really his little baby."

Lou Holtz had absolutely no trouble working in front of 5,000 people at the Palace, but standing alone in front of a mike terrified him. Whenever he was on the radio he'd bring a bottle of sherry or brandy to the studio with him. "Ordinarily, I don't drink at all," he'd tell everybody, "but this radio has me so frightened that I always take a sip about a half hour before the show and another one just before I go on. It's the only way I can lick the radio."

Bill Fields did the same thing when he was working. And when he wasn't working too. Only he took bigger sips. Much bigger sips. And not only would he lick the radio, he'd lick the microphone, he'd lick Charlie McCarthy . . .

Me? I was fine. I didn't have any problems with mike fright. If I had been nervous I probably would have grabbed one of the writers or my brother Willie about twenty minutes before we went on the air, and we would have run across the street to the bar and I would have had one or two martinis to calm me down. But I never did that. I didn't have to—I had the martinis in my dressing room.

For a lot of performers there was really only one way of overcoming mike fright. Television. But that wouldn't be possible until the late 1940s, so we all had to try to find other solutions. One of the things that really helped was having an audience in the studio. As I told you, when radio was just becoming popular the sponsors didn't want an audience in the studio during a broadcast.

They thought hearing a studio audience would ruin the illusion for listeners at home—unless, of course, the illusion we were trying to create was that there was an audience in the studio. But if a show was supposed to be taking place at the North Pole, for example, they knew that everyone would wonder what an entire audience was doing at the North Pole. Besides freezing.

Comedians needed an audience much more than any other performers. H. V. Kaltenborn didn't need to hear people cheering his news. Walter Winchell didn't want people laughing at his gossip. Lowell Thomas didn't care if anybody applauded his animals. "The Inner Sanctum" had its own screams. But comedians needed a live audience. Not just for their egos, but to help their timing. When Gracie and I worked without an audience I had to guess how long our listeners were laughing at her before I said my next line. To me the main difference between oxygen and an audience is that I could see the audience. Of course, that was before I moved to Los Angeles and could see them both. And I needed both of them to be happy.

When Ed Wynn insisted on having an audience in his studio the sponsor compromised—the audience could be in the studio, but they had to sit behind a soundproof glass partition. So radio became the only place where you could find an "audience under glass."

The first studios we broadcast from were very small and had no real seats. Ushers would set up forty or fifty folding chairs in a space big enough for about twenty people and we'd invite people to come in and watch the broadcast. "You couldn't hear them laugh behind that glass," Jack remembered, "so I'd watch them until everybody had their mouth shut, then I'd go on to the next line."

Finally Wynn refused to continue working behind the glass and his sponsor took down the partition—but asked the audience to keep quiet. All the other shows did the same thing. Just before Cantor went on the air, for example, his announcer said, "Ladies and gentlemen, Chase and Sanborn is pleased to welcome you to 'The Eddie Cantor Show.' We ask that you cooperate with us by not applauding or laughing, so that our listening audience can share the illusion of hearing a show without distraction."

Keeping an audience under glass was one thing, but asking them not to react made working in front of them really tough. We would do great material and these people would sit there smiling loudly.

It was silly and it didn't last long. One night while Cantor was on the air he ran into the audience and put on Ida's hat and wrapped her fur boa around his shoulders and started prancing around. Jimmy Wallington, his announcer, did the same thing with his wife's hat and coat. And the audience started laughing. Out loud. Naturally, the Chase and Sanborn people were very upset that an audience laughed during a comedy show, but there was nothing they could do about it. But the next day they discovered that the laughter hadn't left any scars. Cantor's listeners didn't seem to to have been bothered by it. Bothered by it? They actually liked it. I think it made it easier for them to pick out the funny parts.

Of course, not every comedian wanted an audience in the studio. I think Fred Allen didn't even want people listening. Fred said he had nothing against the people in his audience individually, it was just when they gathered in a radio studio that he didn't like them. Fred also did not believe that his listeners benefited from hearing the studio audience react. "Did you ever hear a phonograph record with applause on it?" he asked.

I think as soon as the sponsors began allowing people to come into the studio to watch the broadcast, radio began changing. Instead of working in small rooms, we began broadcasting from theaters. Going to a radio show being broadcast became an event, like going to see big-time vaudeville on Saturday night. On a few occasions we even broadcast from the stage of a vaudeville house we'd played in a few years earlier. Tickets were usually given away, but every once in a while we'd use some gimmick. In the early 1930s, for example, when we were still doing stage shows as well as radio, we'd give anybody who bought a ticket to the live show a ticket to the radio broadcast. That way we packed two houses. During World War II, Jack once broadcast his show from St. Joseph, Missouri, and charged a pint of blood admission. Ten thousand people each donated a pint of blood to the Red Cross for our servicemen overseas.

Jack had one problem. After the show someone who didn't think Jack had been very funny asked for his blood back.

Don't you feel sort of silly heckling a book?

I guess the biggest adjustment we all had to make between vaudeville and radio was that in vaudeville seventeen minutes of good material could last for years, while on radio seventeen minutes of good material would last seventeen minutes. Believe me, nobody who had been in vaudeville ever had a problem doing their first seventeen minutes. It was that eighteenth minute that was tough. When we all went into radio I don't think any of us realized how much material we would need. Even with all my back issues of *College Humor* and *Whiz Bang,* by the end of the third or fourth week we were out of new material. So we began hiring writers to work for us full-time.

Writers came from everywhere. After a show in Buffalo a young kid handed me some original material. A week later he was writing for us. Cantor got into a taxi and the driver told him a few jokes. By the time Cantor reached his destination he'd hired the driver. Writers came from college, they came from newspapers, from advertising agencies; there was really only one place radio writers didn't come from—radio.

When we went into radio there was no such thing as a radio comedy writer. The stars of the very few comedy shows on the air, like "Amos 'n' Andy," "Stoopnagle & Budd," "Burns and Allen," wrote almost all of their own material. Most of the shows on the air starred an orchestra, and the only written material they needed was lines like "For our next song we'd like to . . ."

When we were able to hire a good writer we tried very hard to keep him. Several of Jack's writers were with him almost as long as Mary. The great John P. Medbury worked for me for a long time. Medbury was a very funny fellow. When he was working for me he had a round table with three chairs in his office. Sitting in one of those chairs was a life-sized Indian dummy dressed in a headdress and buckskin suit and pants. This was the Chief. And Medbury never did anything without first talking to the Chief. Each year, when we'd finished our shows for the season, I'd go into Medbury's office and sit down with him and the Chief to talk about renewing his contract. After I told him what my offer was he'd tell me, "Let's see what the Chief has to say about that." Then he'd turn and face the dum—the Chief. "So, Chief, whattya think?" he'd ask. "Should we go along with him?" The Chief was a tough negotiator. Medbury and I would sit there for a little while, waiting, and finally he would whisper to me, "Don't rush him, George. Let him think."

Now, I don't know if Medbury was really crazy or just a writer, so I'd sit there for a few minutes, then I'd ask, "So? What does the Chief think?"

Medbury was such a good writer that if I had to wait for a dummy to talk to me to keep him happy. I waited.

Eventually Medbury would sigh and tell me, "The Chief doesn't know if you're offering enough money. We're gonna have to talk about it and let you know." Sometime during the next few days he'd call me and tell me, "The Chief said it was okay, we're with you for next season."

I'll tell you how valuable a good writer was. During World War II there was such a shortage of good comedy writers that we tried to convince the government to ration them, but the government insisted that a sense of humor was not grounds for a deferment. That made Paul Henning one of the most valuable comedy writers in America because he had something even more important than talent—a 4F classification. He didn't go until everybody in the neighborhood was talking like Baron Munchausen. Now, Eddie Cantor really was my friend. He gave me and Gracie our start. He was on our show many times and we were on his show. There are very few things I wouldn't have done for Eddie Cantor—and giving him Paul Henning was one of them. Friendship, love, respect, gratitude; they're all pretty important, but we're talking about a very talented writer with a deferment here. So one day Eddie called Paul and asked, "Are you happy with George?"

Paul told him that he had been working with me and Gracie for a long time and that we all got along very well and that he was happy and that he had a contract.

"Oh, that's great," Eddie told him, "I'm happy to hear that." Then he paused for a few seconds and asked, "But, are you . . . really happy?"

We were all tough on our writers. I think a lot of that came from fear. Most of us had become successful by writing our own material, and it was hard for us to trust our careers to other people. All right, here's another confession: on a very few, isolated occasions, I may have raised my voice to my writers. Let me explain it this way: Once, when a sound-effects man was trying to figure out what the atom bomb exploding sounded like, somebody suggested, "I think it sounds a little like George Burns in a writers meeting."

And I was the easy one. Cantor was tough. Ed Wynn was tough. Berle was tough. Jack was . . . no, Jack wasn't. Maybe Cantor was the toughest one of all. His show was broadcast Sunday nights, and first thing Monday morning he'd meet with his writers to go over the first draft of the script for his next show. He'd meet with his writers every day to work on the script, and by Saturday he'd be complaining that the jokes were stale, that he'd heard them before. Well, of course he had: on Monday, Tuesday, Wednesday, Thursday and Friday. "Boys," he'd shout, "every week I pay you fresh money. And for that I want fresh material." Even when he was satisfied with the script he'd find something to criticize. "Boys," he'd say, "this is very clever. But from me they expect hilarity."

Eddie just didn't feel comfortable with new material. He had thousands of old jokes in boxes in his basement, and every Thursday or Friday he'd take the new script and go downstairs and punch it up with jokes from those files. He'd even use jokes he'd borrowed from other performers. As far as he was concerned they were new jokes—he'd never told them before.

Cantor never had a good relationship with his writers. In the early 1950s he had a serious heart attack and spent a lot of time in the hospital. One of the writers who'd worked for him for a long time went to visit him. When he came back from the hospital another writer asked him how Cantor was. "You know something?" he said. "He's a whole new man. And I'm not sure I like this one any better than the old one."

Berle and Wynn also depended on their joke files. Wynn claimed he had 14,000 joke books in his collection. Milton says he has compiled the largest collection of humor material in the world: 6,000,000 jokes, thousands of radio and television scripts and vaudeville routines all indexed on a computer. Eleven of them were originally his.

Maybe the two easiest people to write for were Harpo and Jack. That figures. I could have written for Harpo. Here's a great line for him: "Harpo blows horn." Writing for Harpo was like trying to design clouds. Nobody could do it better than the creator, so they didn't even try.

Jack was just the opposite. Jack depended on his writers completely. And trusted them. And paid them very well. So his writers stayed with him for so long that even after twenty years he was still referring to the youngest of his two writing teams, Hal Goldman and Al Gordon, as "the new writers." Let me tell you how much Jack depended on his writers. One day Jack stopped a rehearsal and asked his whole writing staff to join him in a conference. "Look," he said when the four writers had gathered around. "I want to give Mel Blanc credit. I want a line for the tag of the show that says the part of the violin teacher was played by Mel Blanc." One of the writers took Jack's script and wrote on it, "The part of the violin teacher was played by Mel Blanc."

Jack read it over. "This is great," he said, "this is exactly what I wanted to say. Gees, thanks guys."

That was the end of the conference. As the writers went back to their seats one of them said casually, "You know, Jack, I think two of us probably could have handled that job."

A lot of great comedy writers started in radio. For some reason, a lot of them were Jewish. Now I don't know if this is true, but one day an advertising agency sent a memo to the producer of one of their radio shows, telling him, "We suggest you hire several young writers to work on the show." The producer sent a memo right back, "I'll be glad to hire as many young writers as you like," he wrote, "but if you want the scripts done on time, I also need two old Jews and a type-writer."

There was one other thing that was introduced on radio: commercials. As far as I know, nobody advertised on the telegraph. What were they going to advertise, "This distress call brought to you by Jell-O"? Advertising and radio was as good a match as me and Gracie. Salesmen had dreamed of selling air at a profit for a long time, and within a few months the advertising agencies controlled the airwaves. Radio didn't operate like television does today, where sponsors buy fifteen-, thirty-, forty-five-, or sixty-second spots during the show to promote their product. In radio the advertising agency bought thirty minutes or an hour for a client, then produced a show to fill that time. Most of the shows were named after the sponsor, not the performer. So it was "The Fleischmann's Yeast Hour," and not the Rudy Vallee show. It was "The Chase and Sanborn Hour," not the Eddie Cantor show or the Burns and Allen show. "The Kraft Music Hall" starred Jolson, then Bing Crosby. Jack had "The Canada Dry Ginger Ale Show," "The Chevrolet Program," "The General Tire Program," "The Jell-O Program," and "The Grape Nuts Program." He'd already been the top-rated comedian on radio for five years before it finally became "The Jack Benny Show."

The sponsors created the shows, hired the production staff and performers and had total approval over the content. Other than that we could do anything we wanted. Before every show we had to submit our script to an agency representative for approval. These people were terrified that we might say something that would upset our listeners so that they wouldn't buy their product. Of course, the people on "The Sal Hepatica Show" didn't have that problem—nobody bought their product until they got upset.

Most agency people had the sense of humor of Attila the Hun. They were so conservative that they made us call it "The Hoover Darn," and we had to say that people flew in heckicopters. Because of the agency people stars like Sophie Tucker hated to go on the radio. "You can't do this, you can't do that," Sophie complained, "I can't even say damn or hell, and nothing, honey, is more expressive than the way I say damn or hell." That, and the fact that she couldn't sell her book and records in the lobby for cash after the broadcast.

The agency people were in total control and that was a terrible thing, because they didn't know anything about show business. Benny Fields was once doing a J. Walter Thompson show and he wanted to sing "Melancholy Baby" the way he'd been singing it onstage his whole career. He called me up and he was really upset. "I don't know what to do, Natty," he said. "This agency guy doesn't like the way I sing the song. He wants me to sing it his way."

I'd had a lot of problems with agency people over exactly the same thing. But I'd learned how to handle it. "Don't argue, Benny," I suggested.

"Just tell him you're going to sing it his way, then get up and do it your own way. He won't even know the difference."

That's exactly what Benny did and the song was a big hit. And after the show the executive came backstage and shook Benny's hand and said, "Didn't I tell you my way was the right way to sing it?"

Well, I guess you can imagine how well Fred Allen got along with these people. Believe me, Jolson was happier watching Eddie Cantor get a standing ovation that Fred Allen was when he had to deal with these people. I remember once, during World War II, Fred wrote a bit making fun of the famous cigarette commercial that featured a bellboy yelling, "Call for Philip Mor-riss . . ." In the sketch someone was going to imitate the bellhop's call, then somebody else would ask, "Who wants him?" and the first person would respond, "The draft board. His number just came up." Cute. Even the agency man assigned to Fred's show liked it. But he had one very small request: the agency represented a different cigarette brand, so he wanted Fred to change the first line to "Call for Lucky Strikes."

Another day Fred sat down with the agency man to go over the script, and the agency man had several changes he wanted made. Fred wrote most of his material by himself and really struggled over his scripts, so he hated being told to make changes. The agency man kept talking and Fred sat there listening, getting angrier and angrier. Finally, the man said, "Now, at the top of page fourteen . . ."

That was it. Fred just couldn't take it anymore. He stood up and screamed, "You no good bald-head sonofabitch, just who do you think you are? Where were you when page fourteen was white?"

Actually, there were some people on radio who could get away with saying almost anything. Kids, like Baby Snooks, could say things that adults, like Fanny Brice, would never have been allowed to say. Dummies like Charlie McCarthy could say things that Bergen couldn't say. And anybody who did country humor could tell almost any story they wanted to—as long as it had an animal in it. On shows like "The National Barn Dance," "The Grand Ole Opry," and "The Uncle Ezra Show," those good ole boys told some stories what would dern near shock the husks off an ear a corn. Pat Buttram started his career as a country humorist, on the radio, tellin' the kinda stories a city slicker like me never could have gotten away with. "We could do anything we wanted to with our animals, crops, fields, outhouses, as long as we stayed out of the bedroom," Pat told me. "Once I told the story about a husband and wife who were invited to a masquerade party. They looked around the farmhouse and found some skins and horns, so she dressed as a cow and he dressed as a bull. On the way to this party their car broke down and they decided to cut across an open pasture. They got halfway across when this old bull started charging down the hill towards them. Well, this husband and wife were really scared, and the wife said, 'What'll we do, what'll we do?'

" 'Well, honey,' the husband said, 'I'm gonna munch grass. You better brace yourself.' "

Gracie and I never really had any serious problems with the agency people about our material. We didn't do anything off-color. I mean, the closest we ever came to doing anything even slightly risqué was Gracie's routine about her little blue hat. Gracie was so sensitive that she once refused to do a gag about a mouse because she thought that people might be eating while they were listening to our show and she was afraid the joke would ruin their appetite. But I'll tell you something, I never liked the idea of someone telling me what kind of material I could do. So after we'd been on the air a few years I told our agency that I wasn't going to submit our scripts for approval anymore. "If that's not all right," I said, "there's plenty of time to cancel the show." I don't think he was very happy about it, but he knew we had the three things that really mattered: a good rating, a good rating, and a good rating.

The only thing that sponsors really cared about was your ratings. Agency people used to claim that a perfect heartbeat was 35.2 beats an hour, depending on the time slot. In radio we used to tell a story about two agency men who were walking down a street when they saw a beautiful girl. The first one said, "Isn't she gorgeous?" and the second one said, "I don't know yet, the ratings aren't in."

But even if you had good ratings, if you did something or said something that upset the sponsor, they canceled you. I'm being serious again—I always like to let you know—because I want to tell you what they did to Eddie Cantor. Whether people liked Cantor or not they had to admire his courage. At the 1939 World's Fair he made a speech criticizing Father Coughlin, a priest who used his own radio show to preach prejudice and hatred. The day after Eddie said out loud what a lot of other people were thinking, his show was canceled. He couldn't get a sponsor. Suddenly Eddie Cantor, one of the most successful radio entertainers, was off the air. Grace and I had him on our show a few times, Jack had him on, but Eddie was very depressed.

Cantor without an audience was like Jessel without a girlfriend. Eddie always needed the attention. Once, I remember, Eddie was doing a benefit in San Francisco and he was walking along with my manager, Irving Fein. The streets were crowded, but nobody recognized Eddie. They walked a little further and Eddie tilted his hat back so people could see his face. Still, nobody recognized him. So they walked a little further and he started clapping his hands in that distinctive style of his and still nobody recognized him. He just couldn't stand it any longer, so out of the side of his mouth, just barely loud enough for everyone in northern California to hear, he sang two choruses of "If you knew Susie, like I know Susie, oh, oh . . ."

"Eddie Cantor!"

"Ah, please," Eddie said shyly, "I was hoping you wouldn't notice me."

So you can imagine how tough it was for Eddie to lose his show. He was off the air for a year. Jack saw how depressed he was, so one night he picked up the phone and called the president of the New York advertising agency that represented his sponsor. The president told him that the business people thought Cantor had become too political, that no one wanted their products associated with controversial things like justice and honesty. Jack finally convinced him to meet with Cantor. Cantor gave his word that he wouldn't talk about politics and a few weeks later he was back on the air. Jack had the power to do something like that because he had the three things that really mattered: good ratings, good ratings, and good ratings.

Considering how sensitive the advertising agencies were about little things like risqué humor and politics, it was surprising that radio commercials were so clever. Today, because TV shows have a lot of different sponsors, only the live talk shows have a member of the cast doing the commercials. But on radio the commercials were often part of the show. And most of the time they were very funny.

Ed Wynn was the first person to make fun of his sponsor's product. Publicly, I mean. In vaudeville Ed had told jokes about his Ford automobile. When Henry Ford heard him, instead of complaining, he said, "I'm perfectly happy just as long as you keep everybody talking about my Tin Lizzie." Wynn convinced the Texaco people that the same approach would sell gasoline on radio and they let him try it. "I'm not going to buy a car, I'm going to stick to my horse," he told his listeners, "because he doesn't have to be repainted every year."

Wynn's commercials were so successful that every agency wanted performers to make fun of its products. Naturally we were happy to do it. "I was driving across the Sahara Desert," Jack said on one of his first shows, "when I came across a party of people who had been stranded in the desert for thirty days without a drop of water. They were ready to perish from lack of liquid. I gave each of them a glass of Canada Dry Ginger Ale, and not one of them said it was a bad drink."

Now there's a ringing endorsement. We always tried to integrate the commercials into our plot. Our announcer, Bill Goodwin, played a real ladies' man, and one week when Jolson was our guest star, Bill supposedly convinced Jolson's secretary to marry him. Jolie was amazed. "Marguerite," he said, "you've turned down bankers, oilmen, movie stars and now in twenty seconds this man got you? What'd he say?"

"Bill, honey," she told Goodwin, "say it once more."

"Okay, baby," Bill said, then took a deep breath and announced, "Are you reducing tooth decay with Amm-i-dent toothpaste . . ."

185

Jolson couldn't believe it. "That's what got you?"

Bill explained, "Al, you ain't heard nothin' yet."

"Oh no. He's not only stealing my secretary, but my material . . ."

"That's right, because more dentists recommend Amm-i-dent than any other . . ."

Not bad, huh? Maybe the sponsors were right when they suggested we spend twenty-six minutes on the commercials and the rest of the half hour on the program.

Eddie Cantor came up with the best advertising gimmick in broadcast history. It created a sensation: truth in advertising. Cantor told his listeners that he didn't even use his sponsor's product. "Ladies and gentlemen," he said, "I do not drink Chase and Sanborn coffee. The people who sponsor this program haven't got enough money to make me say I do, because I don't. . . . But when we have friends over for dinner, they know they'll always finish the meal with Chase and Sanborn coffee. Ida likes it. My girls like it. And I believe if I drank coffee, I'd drink Chase and Sanborn."

I don't remember why Eddie didn't drink coffee, maybe he was afraid it would make him too energetic. That's a joke by the way, Eddie had so much energy he made coffee beans jumpy.

Cantor's commercial was a big success. I guess people felt that if Eddie Cantor didn't drink Chase and Sanborn, it was good enough for them. Sales picked up. The Chase and Sanborn coffee ads were so successful that a group of South American coffee growers wanted to manufacture "Eddie Cantor Coffee" and offered him part ownership in the company if he would admit that he really didn't drink their coffee instead of Chase and Sanborn.

Eddie turned them down. It took more than a few dollars to convince Eddie Cantor not to use a product. And, of course, I feel exactly the same way. And that's why I'm happy to admit that I'm not riding around today in a brand-new cream-colored Cadillac Fleetwood convertible with the Delco-Bose radio.

With the leather interior.

6

I think I loved being in the movies more than any other part of my career. The movies meant show business, and I wanted to be in show business. Movies were that place where performers who never had a good act became actors. Making movies was always easy for me. When I was working with Gracie all I had to do was ask her "How's your brother?" and remember to stay out of her way. When I was working by myself I didn't have to remember anything. If the director said, "Go in," and I went in, I was a good actor. If he said, "Go in," and I stayed out in the hall, I was a bad actor. I always went in—I was a good actor. When I made *The Sunshine Boys*, with Walter Matthau, the director, Herb Ross, told me not to smile at Matthau. I didn't smile at Matthau so well that they gave me an Academy Award. That Matthau must be some funny fellow if all you have to do is not smile at him to get an award. If I had known that was all I had to do to be a big movie star I wouldn't have smiled at him years earlier. So I won the Academy Award and in my next movie I was God. That was some quick promotion.

In *The Sunshine Boys* I played an old vaudevillian. That's what they call typecasting. In *Oh*

God! I played God. That's not what they call type-casting. When Milton Berle was in the classic picture *Can Hieronymus Merkin Ever Forget Mercy Humppe and Find True Happiness?* he played the Devil. I'll let you decide what to call that one.

I remember when the movies were invented. The first movies were called flickers and they were shown in vaudeville houses. Pictures didn't even have names, they were just advertised on the bill as "moving pictures." The first real movie theaters, the nickelodeons, opened in 1904. I remember them as clearly as if it was just eighty years ago. In those days going to the movies was a lot different than it is today. Not only didn't the actors in the movies talk, the people in the audience didn't talk either.

It was in 1911 that Georgie Jessel made one of the first talking pictures, starring in an experimental clip made by Thomas Edison. Twelve years later Lee De Forest, who invented the vacuum tube used in radios, filmed a man dropping pie trays on the floor, then added a soundtrack. So the first big stars of sound movies were George Jessel and a man dropping pie trays.

Jolson starred in the first full-length picture that had sound, *The Jazz Singer*. The sound consisted of Jolson singing a great song, "It All Depends on You," playing the piano, and then saying a few lines of dialogue. At first Jolson and the Warner brothers didn't want to include the dialogue. They thought that it wouldn't sound right following the song, and were afraid the audience might laugh at the movie. So they filmed the scene with and without the spoken dialogue, then decided to leave it in after looking at the finished picture.

The Jazz Singer started a feud between Jolson and Jessel that lasted both of their lifetimes. When Jolson died he insisted in his will that Jessel not give the eulogy at his funeral. What happened was that Jessel had created the role of the cantor's son in *The Jazz Singer* on Broadway and wanted to play it in the movie. To prove that he could carry a talking movie, Jessel made three two-reel shorts with sound for the Warners. Seems to me that was a pretty expensive way to prove that Jessel could talk. Talk? The really impressive thing would have been keeping him quiet.

The shorts were brief, silly stories. In one of them Georgie played a producer who met a beautiful young actress who had run away from home—and Georgie convinced her to go home to her mother. Now who was going to believe that? Another one of these shorts, the filmed version of his vaudeville act entitled "Talking to Mother," was shown at the opening of the first Vitaphone theater in New York. "Vitaphone" was the name of the process they used to add sound to pictures. It really didn't matter what the film was about, the sound was the star of the movie.

Jessel wanted $5,000 to play the part, plus the $7,500 that the Warners owed for the shorts. The brothers wanted him to take his salary out of the movie's profits, but Jessel thought that sound movies were risky, so he wanted to be paid up front. While negotiations were going on, Georgie went to see Jolson to discuss it. The two of them spent half the night talking in Jolson's suite at the Biltmore. Jolson was very supportive of Jessel's decision. He told Georgie that he was doing the right thing by holding out.

Jessel stayed overnight in the suite, and when he woke up the next morning Jolson was on his way out. He was going to play golf, he said, and insisted Jessel go back to sleep. Jolson didn't come back, and the next day Jessel read in *Variety* that Jolson had signed to play the lead in *The Jazz Singer*.

Jolson wanted the part so badly that he gave the Warners a $180,000 loan. In return, they gave Jolson stock in the company that was worth $30 a share.

Jolson apologized to Jessel, telling him he had to star in the picture because it was the story of his life. Of course, a few years later Jessel claimed that Jolson gave him the same reason for wanting to star as "De Lawd" in the movie version of *Green Pastures*.

To make things up to Jessel, the Warners starred him in a low-budget film called *Drive It, Izzy Murphy*. And Jessel never forgave Jolson.

The Jazz Singer turned out to be the most successful movie that had ever been made, although it wasn't nominated for any Academy Awards because talking pictures weren't eligible. Jolson became an even bigger star than he already was, and he made a fortune when the stock the Warner

Brothers had given him went up to $140 a share. But Jessel did get the last word. When Jolson died, the William Morris Agency booked his funeral, William Morris represented Jessel and he warned them that if he didn't play the funeral he'd fire them. So Jessel delivered Jolson's eulogy, which CBS recorded and distributed—and that really was the last word.

You know who else got very angry about *The Jazz Singer?* Cantor. Cantor told me that the Warner brothers had asked him to star in the film too. He said that they'd called him saying that Jessel had demanded too much money, then offered him the lead role. Eddie said he'd turned them down, then promised to talk Jessel into taking less money to play the part. Before he could do that, though, they signed Jolson. Maybe that's true, maybe Eddie Cantor did turn down the chance to star in the first talking picture because of his friendship with Jessel. And maybe they offered the part to him right after they offered it to me.

The only thing I knew about the movies was that if you could convince somebody to open the exit door for you, you could get in free. Berle had started his career in the movies, Jessel had made some shorts, but until *The Jazz Singer* changed the movie business, vaudevillians just didn't treat it seriously. Eventually though, everybody who could talk and move at the same time tried to get into the movies. Durante made thirty-two pictures, Jack Benny made two great films—and two out of twenty-one isn't bad. Bob Hope teamed

with Bing Crosby and made a series of *Road to
. . .* pictures that were very successful. Cantor made a lot of pictures, Frank Fay made pictures, and Fanny Brice and Jack Pearl and Jessel and Berle and Jack Haley and Gracie and I all made pictures. I didn't say we made good pictures, but nobody got hurt while we were making them, and that's good.

Of the people I worked with in show business only the Marx Brothers, Bill Fields, Cary Grant and Jack Haley were really movie stars. The rest of us were much better known for our work in other areas of show business. Making movies was just something we did for fun and money—the fun part was making the money.

The Marx Brothers fit into the new movie-business just as easily as somebody else's material fit into Milton's mouth. They made fourteen pictures together, Groucho made five more by himself and Harpo made one by himself. The Marx Brothers were very important people in motion picture history. I'm being serious now, you can tell that because I called them "motion pictures" instead of "the movies." In the silent films, comedians like Charlie Chaplin, Buster Keaton, Joe E. Brown and the Keystone Kops depended completely on sight gags for laughs. A complicated storyline had people throwing both whipped cream and cherry pies into each others' faces, instead of just whipped cream. The first comedians in talking pictures, like Jessel, stood in front of the camera and did their vaudeville acts. The Marx

Brothers were the first people to take advantage of both sight and sound—Harpo did the sight gags and Groucho told the jokes. Harpo and Groucho were really the whole act. Chico just wanted to have enough lines so that he'd look like he was doing something, and get to his card games on time. Zeppo played the romantic interest in the Marx Brothers' first five films, then retired to become a talent agent.

It was typical of the movie business that Harpo, who wore a bright-red wig and a raincoat and never said one word, would become famous for not talking as soon as they started making talking movies. Harpo had tried very hard, with no success, to get into silent films. I don't know, I guess they wanted actors who looked like they were talking in silent movies. But when they added sound, he didn't say a word and he became a big star. In fact, he was so famous for not talking that a producer offered him $55,000 to say one word in *A Night in Casablanca*. Gees, $55,000 for one word—for that price Jack would have read the whole dictionary.

The Marx Brothers' movies were sillier than a reunion of all of Gracie's relatives. The whole purpose of the plot was to give Groucho the chance to say things like "This is indeed a gala day. That's plenty. I don't think I could handle more than a gal a day," or, "One morning I shot an elephant in my pajamas. How he got in my pajamas I'll never know," and give Harpo the chance to leave a trail of silverware, blow his own horn, chase a blonde across the screen and play one serious number on his harp. "The rest of the plot," as Groucho really did say, "was irrelephant."

You're right, my Groucho is not as good as my Durante.

When Gracie and I made a movie, we studied our scripts and learned our lines, showed up at the studio on time and went through the door when the director said, "Go in." The Marx Brothers worked very differently. It took them months of rehearsals to make their movies look so spontaneous. Before they started filming their classic pictures like *A Day at the Races*, *A Night at the Opera*, and *Go West*, they would break down the rough script into five or six basic scenes, then take the entire cast on the road and test each scene in front of a live audience. When the Marx Brothers toured with scenes from *Go West*, they actually handed out ballots to the audience, letting them vote on the scenes they liked best and least. That worked out very well; the picture was a hit and Groucho just missed being elected Homecoming Queen.

When the Marx Brothers were together, onstage or offstage, they were always onstage. Individually they were calm, smart fellows; but when they got together they were as calm as Mary Benny in Tiffany's. The day they arrived on the MGM lot, for example, they started work by putting the studio president's nameplate on the door to the janitor's office. Then they barged into the janitor's office and tried to convince him to give them a big raise.

He couldn't even convince them he couldn't speak English. One day, when the famous producer Irving Thalberg kept them waiting in his office for two hours, he found them sitting naked in front of his fireplace, toasting marshmallows.

Most of the chairs on their movie sets were wired so they could give guests a mild shock. Anybody who smoked a cigarette had it shot out with a water pistol—Groucho gave cigars a special dispensation. Once, when Jackie Coogan's father visited the set, they grabbed him, pulled off his pants, locked him in a limousine and ordered the driver to drop him off miles outside Los Angeles.

The Marx Brothers set out to make funny movies, I don't think they ever realized they were making classic comedies. I think that even they were a little surprised that their pictures stayed so popular for so long. I remember I asked Harpo about it once, and he explained it very well, "   ," he said, "   . . . !"

Okay, I do a better Harpo than a Groucho.

In terms of success in the movie business, Durante probably nosed out everybody except the Marx Brothers. But they had four noses. All right, all right, no more big nose jokes. In fact, let's cut that one out too. In terms of success in the movie business, Durante probably edged out everybody except the Marx Brothers.

In the movies Jimmy had a problem that was almost impossible to overlook. Wrong. I told you, no more you-know-what jokes. The problem I'm talking about was his character. When you looked like Durante, when you sounded like Durante, when you used the English language like Durante, you were what is known as typecast. Bert Lahr, who played the cowardly lion in *The Wizard of Oz*, once explained typecasting to me. "It means," he said, "that they call me every time a role comes up for a cowardly lion. Otherwise, they don't call me."

Now, how many roles were really right for Durante? Besides Cyrano?

Durante was great playing Durante. Hey, he created the role. He made his first movie, *Roadhouse Nights*, in 1930 and after that he made about four pictures a year in which all he had to do was speak funny and carry a big schtick. Jimmy costarred in classic pictures like *Hell Below; Cuban Love Song; Music for Millions; The Wet Parade; Palooka*—in this version Joe Palooka gets knocked out and goes back to his mother's chicken farm, sort of a boxing *Jazz Singer*—*The Passionate Plumber;* even Columbia's first musical, *Start Cheering*. That last picture was typical of the kind of movies he made; he costarred with the Three Stooges, Professor Quiz and Chaz Chase, the famous match-and paper-eater.

I don't think the movie studios ever understood Durante. "MGM sent me ta school to learn howda speak English," he once complained, "and then whatta they do? Everytime I improves they puts me in a pitcher with Xavier Cugat, and he speaks Cuban. Then I improves a little more and dey puts me in a pitcher with José Iturbi, and he speaks Spanish. And then the coop de grass, I gets so good they throws me in a pitcher with Lauritz Melchior and who knows what he speaks. I'm telling ya, if my English gets any better they're gonna put me in the foreign pitchers."

Durante did have two big movie hits. In *The Man Who Came to Dinner*, he played the role of Banjo, a character that writers George Kaufman and Moss Hart had based on Harpo, but since Harpo didn't speak in movies he couldn't play himself. A few years later thought, Harpo played Banjo in summer stock, and that was the first time he'd spoken onstage since vaudeville.

Jimmy also played the role of the owner of a small-time circus in *Jumbo* on Broadway and in the movie, costarring with Sydney, who played the elephant. It was the best role Jimmy ever had. In one scene he was stealing the elephant from a rival circus, and was caught by the sheriff as he was trying to sneak out. "Just where'd you get that elephant?" the sheriff asked.

Jimmy looked at him with all the innocence of a man who could break your heart just by saying goodnight and asked, "What elephant?"

To convince the sheriff that the elephant was his own pet, Jimmy had to lie down and let the elephant put one of its huge hoofs on his chest, then lift him up in its trunk. Doing that night after night on the stage, then again in the movie, took a lot more courage than doing a buck and wing with Captain Betts' seal. One night the famous animal trainer Frank "Bring 'Em Back

Alive" Buck saw the show and afterward he told Jimmy that elephants were unpredictable, and that the stunt was so dangerous he wouldn't do it himself. Jimmy immediately told the producer, Billy Rose, that he didn't want to do the stunt anymore. "Jimmy," Rose said in a producerly way, "Jimmy, that elephant wouldn't hurt a fly."

"Yeah, maybe," Jimmy agreed, "but I ain't no fly."

"Just be nice to the elephant and the elephant'll be nice to you," Rose said. "You know they say an elephant never forgets."

"Big deal," Jimmy answered. "What the hell has he got to remember?"

Jack Benny was great in the movies. He bought the popcorn, he didn't talk and he liked to sit near the front like I did. But on the screen he had the same problem Durante did—his personality was so well known that he could only play characters who were versions of his own. If Jack was playing Billy the Kid and he walked into a saloon and bought drinks for the house, who was going to believe it? But if he had walked in and bought one drink, and asked for thirty-eight straws, everybody would have bought it.

Well, maybe "bought it" isn't the best phrase to use when discussing Jack Benny.

Jack made his first movie, *Hollywood Revue of 1929*, in about 1929. As soon as the picture was released, the entire country went into a deep depression. Maybe it was a coincidence. In that picture he played a master of ceremonies, and his big scene was a trick shot in which it looked like he was taking actress Bessie Love out of his pocket. It was obviously a trick shot, because everybody knew Jack never took anything out of his pocket. He made a few films after that, including a series of "Buck Benny" films for Paramount, based on a Western character he'd created on his radio show. Two of his films that I particularly loved were the classics, *Big Broadcast of 1937* and *College Holiday*. And, purely coincidentally, Gracie and I happened to be in both of them. Jack was great to work with. The only thing he took seriously on the set was the comedy. Everything else was fun. Working with Jack was like working with my best friend. Only easier. Jack's idea of acting was to act like he wasn't acting. Well, he wasn't, and that's how he did it so well.

In 1939 Jack played the title role in the movie version of the very popular Broadway show, *Charley's Aunt*. He was very nervous about being in a real movie, so naturally I did my best to help him relax. "Jack," I told him, putting my arm around his shoulders, "Jack, in a picture like this, all you have to remember is that the clothes make the woman." He really enjoyed making that picture; sometimes after spending all day on the set he'd stop at my house on his way home to have a drink. The hardest part about making that movie, he told me, was going to the bathroom. With all the petticoats and underwear and the girdle he had to wear, it took him half an hour to undress and another hour to decide whether to go to the men's room or the ladies' room.

Jack made one classic motion picture, Ernst Lubitsch's *To Be or Not to Be,* with Carole Lombard and Robert Stack. It was a wonderful fantasy—it had to be a fantasy because in the picture Jack was married to Carole Lombard—in which a troupe of Polish Shakespearean actors end up working with the Polish underground against the Nazis. Because Jack never believed he was an actor, he had to be talked into doing the film by Lubitsch, who told Jack he'd written the part specially for him. Jack was so nervous that after two days he'd run out of fingernails to bite. Just before one take he turned to Robert Stack and asked his advice on how to play a certain scene. "I'd like to help you, Mr. Benny," Stack told him, "but this is only my second movie."

So Jack played himself and the picture worked. He was so good in that film that when his father saw his son playing a Nazi officer, he got up and walked out of the theater. Jack ran after him and convinced him that his character wasn't really a Nazi. I think he told him that he was really an Austrian.

By the time they'd finished the picture Jack and Lubitsch had become good friends. In fact, at the wrap party for the film, which Lubitsch held at his house in Bel Air, Jack was standing in a small group that included Lubitsch, director Billy Wilder and one other famous director. This other famous director had a very big mouth and wouldn't let anyone else talk. Every time Lubitsch tried to say something this other director would interrupt. The third time he did it Jack very quietly left the room. Maybe twenty minutes after he'd returned a telegram arrived for this man. He was really pleased—getting a telegram delivered to him at a party was a lot more impressive than just getting a telephone call. Then the director opened it up. It read: WHY DONT YOU JUST SHUT UP AND LET LUBITSCH GET A WORD IN! Now, Jack never admitted sending that telegram. But he always had that contented smile on his face when he told the story, and everybody knew that Jack just loved to send telegrams.

To Be or Not to Be was successful when it opened, but the studio didn't promote it because Carole Lombard died in an airplane crash just before the picture was released. But today people consider it one of the greatest comedies ever made. That picture was so good, in fact, that a few years ago they remade it. That's something I don't really understand—if a picture is really good, does remaking it make it twice as good? To me that's like something Gracie would do—if she could make a great meal in fifteen minutes, she'd cook it for thirty minutes so it would be twice as great.

Look, I'm not against remakes. For example, I'm a little surprised that nobody has done a remake of Gracie's classic *Here Comes Cookie*. It would be easy to bring that story up to date, too, all they'd have to do is change the title to *Here Comes Chocolate Macadamia Cookie*. And I admit that some remakes are much better than the original. For example, Milton starred in a film called *New Faces of 1937*. Believe me, Milton's face was not new in 1937. The plot of the movie came from a *Saturday Evening Post* short story about a phony Broadway producer who found the worst script he could, then sold more than one hundred percent of the rights to investors, figuring that when the show flopped he could keep all the money. Mel Brooks turned that same idea into a great movie called *The Producers*. I mean, what else could he call it, Same Old Faces From 1937?

Anyway, besides *To Be or Not to Be* Jack made a couple of other pretty good films, *George Washington Slept Here* and *The Horn Blows at Midnight*. When Jack told me the name of that second picture I thought it was another story that Kaufman had written about Harpo. Actually, *The Horn Blows at Midnight* wasn't a bad picture, but one Sunday night on his radio show Jack started talking about it. "When I made *The Horn Blows at Midnight*," he said, "that horn blew taps for my movie career." That line got a nice laugh, so Jack told another joke about how bad the picture was. The more laughs he got, the worse the picture became. Jack was such a funny guy that it became one of the worst pictures ever made. The problem was that everybody believed him and didn't go to see the picture.

I guess it didn't really hurt him that much. Only twenty-five years later he got another offer to make a movie. Producer Ray Stark signed him to play a seventy-year-old former vaudevillian in the film version of Neil Simon's big hit play *The Sunshine Boys*. Sometimes it's hard to play a seventy-year-old, particularly when you're eighty years old, like Jack was. But Jack was a very young eighty-year-old, and he had to learn how to "play" old. He actually had to learn how to walk slower. His co-star, Walter Matthau, was also supposed to be playing a retired vaudevillian, but Matthau had a handicap, he was only fifty-two. He was worried about looking old enough. I'll tell you something, Jack was worried about the same thing. "Oh, don't worry about it," he told Walter. "These people are very talented. They'll be able to make *both* of us look old enough."

About a month before they were supposed to start filming, Dr. Rex Kennamer, who had been Gracie's doctor, discovered that Jack had stomach cancer. A few weeks later Jack died. I thought it was ridiculous. I'd heard about people dying to get a role, but Jack already had the part.

I don't know, maybe it's not nice to make jokes about the death of the man who was my best friend. I loved Jack, but there's no money to be made by crying, and knowing him as well as I did, he'd want me to make the money.

So when Jack couldn't do the picture, Irving Fein, the man who could only get two clients in forty years, suggested to Ray Stark that they audition me for the part. I think *Honolulu* had been my last picture, and I'd made that about thirty-five years earlier. For the part they needed somebody from New York, which I was. They needed somebody from vaudeville, which I was. They needed somebody old, which I am. How they found out I was Jewish, I'll never know.

So Irving and I started working on *The Sunshine Boys* script and I learned it cold. Not just my part, the whole script. At the first day of rehearsal we all sat down and Herb Ross told us what scene he wanted us to do. Everybody else picked up their scripts, I didn't even have a script with me. I knew what they were all thinking—these big movie stars are so temperamental. Then we made the movie and it was very nice.

The only problem we had while we were shooting the picture was that whenever I had a close-up, Walter Matthau would turn around and drop his trousers to try to get me to laugh. Listen to me, there's nothing funny about what you see when Walter Matthau drops his trousers.

The thing that surprised me most when I made that picture was how much the movie business had changed since *College Swing*. When Gracie and I made movies we went to the studio and we made the movie. It was just so much easier then. Cantor, for example, made fifteen pictures, and he couldn't act his way out of a bad dream. He acted like he was Eddie Cantor. But Eddie did a very smart thing; he always made sure the movie was the star of the movie. He made spectaculars, pictures that had such lavish scenery or great special effects or so many beautiful women that the audience didn't realize someone had forgotten to put in a story. These were pictures like *Whoopee*, which also was the first movie made by the great choreographer Busby Berkeley, *George White's Scandals*, *Kid Millions*, *The Kid From Spain* and *Roman Scandals*.

The gimmick in *The Kid From Spain* was a stunt with a bull. Eddie was supposed to be fighting a bull— the real bullfighting was done by a professional with Eddie doing the close-ups—and when the bull charged him, Eddie had to leap over a wooden fence and run down a corridor. The bull was also supposed to leap over the fence and chase him down the corridor. But the bull didn't want to leap over the fence. After take after take after take, producer Sam Goldwyn was really angry, and blamed it on the director, Leo McCarey. "Why doesn't the bull jump?" Goldwyn asked.

"I'm trying to get him to jump," McCarey said.

"Well, you're the director, aren't you?"

"Yeah," McCarey told him, "but the bull's not a member of the Screen Actors Guild."

Even Frank Fay made movies. Performers like Fay got signed by the studios because they were famous, but the studios really didn't know what to do with them. When Fay arrived in Hollywood after signing a contract, a studio executive asked him exactly what he did. "I'm a juggler," Fay told him.

"But how can we build a picture around a juggler?" the executive asked.

"No problem," Fay told him. "I'm a dramatic juggler."

Fay always claimed he wanted to do a monologue on film and call it "—Minutes with Frank Fay." The number in the title would be filled in after the film had been shot and edited. "It would be somewhere between '62 Minutes with Frank Fay' and 'A Lifetime with Frank Fay,'" he admitted. Look, if you knew him as well as I did, "62 Minutes with Frank Fay" was a lifetime.

Probably the thing that almost all of the films we made had in common was that the plot wasn't important. Important? Sometimes it didn't even exist. The whole purpose of these films was to give audiences a chance to see the vaudeville and radio stars they'd seen or heard playing the characters they were known for. For example, Jack Benny and Fred Allen made a picture called *Love Thy Neighbor,* which was about their feud. And Jack Pearl made two movies in which he played Baron Munchausen. And Fanny Brice could play any type of character, as long as that character was plain-looking, got to sing a few songs and do a few comic bits, and at the end lost the man— because Fanny was known for being plain, singing and clowning and being disappointed in love. And even with trick photography she couldn't have played Baby Snooks in the movies. In Milton's big hit, *Hieronymus Merkin,* George Jessel played Death. He had a great makeup job, he walked into a room and somebody said, "You know, you look like Death."

Jack Haley and Cary Grant were real movie stars; they could play any kind of character. Jack costarred with Shirley Temple in films like *Rebecca of Sunnybrook Farm* and *Poor Little Rich Girl,* but his greatest role was as the Tin Man without a heart in *The Wizard of Oz.* To me that proved what a great actor Jack was, because in real life he had one of the biggest hearts in the world. The only thing I remember about Jack making that film was that he almost went blind. A few flecks of the silver paint they used to make up his face got into his eyes. He became extremely sensitive to light and had to lie in an absolutely dark room for more than a week. Everybody was very worried that he might lose his sight, but gradually his vision came back. And as soon as he could see, he went right back to the studio to finish the picture.

Gracie and I went to the premiere with Jack and Flo. I know that none of us realized we were watching one of the greatest films ever made. All I remember thinking as we were sitting there was, "It's no *College Swing.*" Once again, I was absolutely right.

I don't think anybody was more thrilled than I was when Cary Grant became a famous movie star. I loved Cary and I was really worried about him. When I first met him his name had been Archie Leach and he was selling hand-painted ties and trying to make it in vaudeville as a stilt-walker. If he hadn't made it in the movies I don't know what he would have done, because the truth is that Cary Grant was a rotten stilt-walker. I mean, he always looked like he was about to keel over, and there just isn't too much work for a stilt-walker with a bad sense of balance.

Cary and I were friends for over fifty years, and I knew him very, very well. I'll tell you how much I cared about him. In 1982 the Friars Club honored him and asked me to say a few words. Now, at these dinners you're supposed to insult people to get laughs. How could I insult Cary Grant? Of course I couldn't. So instead, I just talked about our friendship. "I love Cary," I told them, "and I have a lot to say about him because I know him so well. I was introduced to him by Minta Arbuckle, who was married to Fatty Arbuckle. Now, Fatty Arbuckle was one of the great comedians in silent pictures. His first name was Roscoe, and they called him Fatty because he weighed about 300 pounds. He came to Hollywood as a stagehand and was discovered by Mack Sennett, who only weighed 145 pounds." It was always easy for me to talk about Cary.

"Now, Fatty was a good friend of Buster Keaton, who was also one of the greats. Keaton originally started in vaudeville with an act called 'The Three Keatons,' he worked with his mother and father. . . . Now Keaton was a very good friend of Charlie Chaplin, who was the king of silent pictures. Charlie Chaplin, at that time he was married to Lita Grey. This was before Paulette Goddard. And Lita Grey had her dresses made in a little shop on 45th Street, right next door to Wiennig's Restaurant. And Al Jolson used to eat at Wiennig's. And right above Wiennig's was the

Jack Mills Publishing Company. Gee, I could stand here and talk about Cary Grant all night. . . ."

I'll tell you something funny. A few of my friends got to be so famous that the studios wanted to make pictures about their careers. In some cases these pictures turned out to be more successful than the pictures my friends actually made during their careers. I was responsible for *Somebody Loves Me,* the story of Blossom Seeley and Benny Fields, for example. One day I was playing gin rummy in Adolph Zukor's office and he was complaining that Paramount had Betty Hutton under contract for a lot of money but didn't have a picture for her to do. I had a great thought. "Have her do Blossom Seeley's life," I said. Then I told him how Blossom had started on the Barbary Coast with the tiger's head between her legs, how she'd been very promiscuous, and what I didn't know I made up very truthfully. And what I didn't make up wasn't true. Zukor loved my story, and I let him win a few bucks, so he decided Betty Hutton had to make this picture. I told him I thought I could get the rights to the story from Blosson for $50,000, then talked him into paying her another $10,000 to teach all the old songs to Betty Hutton.

I was thrilled. Blossom and Benny hadn't been doing so well for a long time. They weren't broke, but they were struggling. I figured $60,000 would be a fortune to them. So I'll never forget Blossom's reaction when I gave her the good news. "Oh,

Natty," she said, "maybe you could have gotten a little more at MGM."

On this page, the role of Jack Benny has been played by Blossom Seeley.

When Blossom started telling her story to Paramount's screenwriter an amazing thing happened—she became a virgin. That was known as the Immaculate Deception. I've seen a lot of miracles take place during my career in show business, but Blossom turning into a virgin was the greatest one of all. She just refused to tell the real story I'd made up, and instead made up her own story and the picture didn't do very well at all. When I tried to explain to her how important it was for her to tell the whole story of her past, she told me, "Listen, Natty, maybe Benny and I can't do anything about our future, but I can guarantee you our past isn't going to be a failure."

I think the same thing happened when Warners made *The Eddie Cantor Story*. Eddie became a virgin with five daughters. Not only didn't he ever do anything wrong, he barely did anything. That was a miracle created by Warner Brothers—they made Eddie Cantor's life boring. Eddie was a lot of different things, some of them good, some of them not so good, but he was never boring. Making that movie without showing some of the bad times was like making a film about World War II without the fighting. The only good thing about that film was that Eddie got to record the soundtrack, which included all the songs he'd made famous, "Yes Sir, That's My Baby," "Bye Bye

Blackbird," "How You Gonna Keep 'Em Down on the Farm," and "Oh! You Beautiful Doll." Those songs were so great that they make you hum along with the title.

They made two wonderful pictures about Fanny Brice, *Funny Girl* and *Funny Lady*. To me, that was real movie making—they never let the truth get in the way of a great story. And everything in those pictures was based on fact: there really was a Fanny Brice and she was plain and she could sing and tell jokes and she was married to a slick gangster named Nicky Arnstein and he did take advantage of her, then she married producer Billy Rose and he left her and she was still plain.

But the best film biography ever made was *The Jolson Story*. In real life Jolson made quite a few pictures after *The Jazz Singer*, including his first all-talkie, *Sonny Boy*. But most of his other films were more like *Big Boy*, in which he played two roles in blackface. At the end of that picture Jolson appeared on the screen without the black and did a couple of songs—even in the movies he couldn't resist doing an encore. At least the movie didn't follow the audience home.

But after his first few movies, Jolson wasn't a big draw, and gradually his career seemed to be over. I'd see him sitting in a corner all by himself at the Hillcrest Country Club and I'd go over to talk to him. Jolie was always very nice to me. In those days there was a law against bringing sturgeon into California, because it was only caught off the East Coast and it was so expensive to keep it refrigerated while shipping it west that it was usually spoiled by the time it got there. But Jolson had it shipped into California and kept his own supply in the Hillcrest kitchen. Then he'd sit alone in his corner eating it. I'd go and sit with him and compliment him, and every time I did he'd offer me a piece of his sturgeon. Believe me, I liked sturgeon almost as much as I liked Jolson. The best booking he had during that time was World War II; he traveled from Alaska to Africa entertaining the troops. Jolson was a big hit in the war, and with the entire United States Army, Navy and Marines, he finally had a large enough audience to play for.

After the war, Sidney Skolsky, a syndicated Hollywood gossip columnist who was also working as an assistant producer at Warner Brothers, wanted to do a movie about Jolson's life. A young actor would play Jolson, but Jolie would record all his old songs and the actor would lip-sync them in the picture. When Jack Warner turned him down, telling him, "We did *The Jazz Singer* in 1927, and that was his story. Besides, nobody wants to see Jolson anymore," Skolsky convinced Harry Cohn at Columbia to do it.

Jolson wanted to play himself in the film and it took Skolsky a long time to talk him out of it. But Jolson did manage to convince Cohn to let him perform for one of the two long shots, when the camera was so far away the audience couldn't tell who was actually onstage. To play Jolson Skolsky hired an actor named Larry Parks, then he hired Matty King, one of the tap-dancing King Brothers, to teach Parks how to move like Jolson.

While Parks was rehearsing, Jolson recorded the soundtrack for the picture. Finally, a few weeks before they were supposed to start shooting, the time came for Jolson to meet Parks and approve his impersonation. Jolson, Parks, Matty King, and a photographer met in an office on the lot. "Okay, Larry," Matty said as he put Jolson's new recording of "Swanee" on the record player, "let's do it."

"Swa-nee, da da da da, da da da da, my da da Swa-nee. . . ." Parks was terrific, he got down on one knee, he raised his arms, he did all of Jolson's moves.

Maybe two-thirds of the way through the song Jolson just couldn't take it anymore. He just couldn't bear to see anybody be as good as he was, even if it was supposed to be him. "Hold it, hold it," he said, jumping up. "No, no, Larry, you're doing it all wrong. Here, lemme show ya. Put dat record on again." So they put the record on again . . . "Swa-nee, da da da da, da da da da, my da da Swa-nee. . . ." Jolson did a great Jolson, probably just as good as Parks. He got down on one knee, he raised his arms, he did all his own moves. And when he finished, he got up slowly and brushed some imaginary dirt off his pants. "Kid," he said to Parks, "that's how you do it." Then he walked out of the room.

Parks was tremendous as Jolson, and *The Jolson Story* became one of the biggest hits in movie his-

All My Best Friends

That's William Paley, Jessel, me, Benny, Fred Allen and Adlai Stevenson at a Friars Club Dinner. Fred spoke before Stevenson and was hilarious—so Stevenson told the audience he'd switched speeches with Fred, and that was his speech Fred had just delivered and he was going to give Fred Allen's speech. And he thanked everyone in advance for their reception.

Jack Benny, Georgie Jessel, me and Al Jolson are probably cooking up a scheme at a Friars Club roast.

"The Not So Pee Wee Quartet," consisting of Danny Kaye, Frank Sinatra, Groucho and me.

A lot of my best friends: Cantor, Sinatra, Jessel and Judy Garland. Judy's the one without the bow tie. (Photo courtesy Frank Worth)

Here I am with two of my best friends, Ann-Margret and Carol Channing. I love them both. People often ask me why I don't go out with women my own age, and I tell them the truth—there are no women my age. (Photo © Las Vegas News Bureau)

This is me and Gracie with Jack and Mary Benny, probably at a party. Knowing us, we were probably discussing world affairs. Or Jessel's. (Photo copyright © 1936 Paramount Productions, Inc.)

tory, grossing more than thirteen million dollars at a time when people still thought a billion was a typographical error. Jolie, who got 50 percent of the profits, made another fortune. But much more important to him, he was on top again. Parks' impersonation of Jolson was so good that Jolson actually stole the picture without even being in it. Everybody wanted to sign him to do something. This was the greatest comeback in show business history. So one day I walked into Hillcrest and saw him sitting in the corner with his package of sturgeon. I went over and said, "That's the best picture I ever saw," and waited for my sturgeon. Nothing. So I tried again, "That's the best soundtrack album I ever heard." Finally, Jolie looked at me and said, "Forget it, Natty. I'm hot again. Get your own sturgeon."

The sequel, *Jolson Sings Again,* was also a huge hit. When it was released Jolson went on tour with the film to the big cities. At the end of the movie he'd appear onstage and get a huge ovation for Parks' performance, then sing a few songs and tell a few stories. That was the only time that people who went to see Jolson in the movies really saw Jolson in the movies.

Because both the radio industry and the movie business settled in Southern California, Gracie and I were able to live and work in the same place for the first time in our careers. In vaudeville, we were always on tour. Our home was whatever hotel we were staying in, and we kept in touch with our friends by writing letters, calling long distance and leaving messages on our dressing room walls. That all changed when vaudeville died. During the 1930s most of our friends moved out to California and bought houses, except Fred Allen and Portland Hoffa, who stayed in their apartment in New York. I think Fred claimed he didn't have to move to Los Angeles to be miserable, he was unhappy enough in New York.

Living in California and owning houses forced us all to learn a whole new lifestyle. Strange words like "lawn" and "garage" began creeping into our conversations. It took a little time for us to adjust—until then most of the people I grew up with in New York thought that "lawn" was what went with "order."

It was a wild time to be living in Hollywood. There were lavish parties almost every night, held in the most beautiful homes in the world, and at these parties every room was filled with champagne in sterling silver ice buckets and half-dressed movie starlets willing to do anything for a break. That's true. I know that's true because it was in all the fan magazines and those magazines wouldn't make that stuff up. But Gracie and I figured it all had to be happening around the block, because we knew it wasn't happening on North Maple Drive.

Maybe there really was a Hollywood wild bunch, but our friends could have been called "the mild bunch." I think the two wildest things Jack Benny ever did were to appear at his own party wearing his Boxer shorts and one of Mary's hats

216

and playing the violin, and crashing one of Lucille Ball's dinner parties dressed as a gypsy musician, and play two numbers on his violin, then leave.

In the early 1950s a United States Senate sub-committee was actually considering licensing movie actors. They sent New York Judge Stephen Jackson to Hollywood to investigate the supposedly loose morals of the movie industry. This is the absolutely real truth, so help me Jolson. We were all very excited when the Judge arrived in town to search for sin, because we'd been looking for it for a long time and knew we could use professional help. Harpo said that he was going to conduct his own investigation—he was going to start by taking a walk along Hollywood Boulevard to see what he could pick up. I guess the Judge didn't find anything, because the committee disbanded without passing a law against illegal acting.

There were a lot of people who listened to us on the radio or saw our movies and believed that we really were like the characters we played. I mean, Jack Pearl told them that wasn't true, but who would believe him? Once, in fact, Jack almost drowned because everybody watching him struggle in the ocean thought he was just playing Baron Munchausen. When Jack Benny went out he always had to leave a big tip just to prove he wasn't really cheap. And Gracie couldn't shop in stores where she didn't know the salesgirls because people who didn't know her would never take her seriously—she'd ask to see a white blouse and they'd bring her a red skirt.

Carol Channing and I do a nice little bit when we're working together in which I start by saying, "You know, Carol, people think that you're exactly the same person onstage and offstage. Why, I've even heard that a burglar came into your bedroom one night and when he shined a flashlight in your face you sat up and sang two choruses of 'Diamonds Are a Girl's Best Friend.'"

"Oh, George, that's not true and you know it," Carol would say. "I sat up and sang two choruses of 'Hello, Dolly!'"

That's not true either. That's the show business truth. The real truth is that offstage performers are just like you and me. Well, maybe more like me. Except Milton, of course. Milton is never offstage. Once, supposedly, Milton was in a cab in New York and he had the driver in hysterics. "You think I'm funny today," Milton told him, "you should have caught me last Tuesday in a cab on Fifty-seventh Street."

And, no matter what the magazines wrote, offstage our social life in Hollywood was really pretty simple. Sometimes, at night, Gracie and I would go over to the Bennys' or to Bill and Edie Goetz's to watch a new movie in their projection room, or we'd go for a bicycle ride on the bridle path that used to run alongside Sunset Boulevard. If we really wanted to have a swinging time Gracie and I would put on our Western outfits and go downtown for some square dancing. Sometimes a group of men would play golf or go out to Gilmore Field, home of our minor league baseball team, the Hollywood Stars, to watch a ball game and, on Friday nights, we'd go over to Legion Hall for the boxing matches. In fact, maybe the most exciting thing we did was read the fan magazines to find out what exciting things we were doing.

There were a lot of parties, but they were nothing like the magazines wrote about, and that disappointed a lot of people. I remember when the Italian wife of a famous movie star came to one of our parties and decided, "I theenk these must be the intellectuals. Nobody stripped."

Maybe the wildest thing I ever saw took place at a stag party thrown by Louella Parsons' husband, Dockey Martin. Lolly and Dockey were close friends of ours. They'd come over for dinner a lot and they'd always bring a Catholic priest with them. That had nothing to do with Gracie's cooking, it's just that they were very religious. And I knew that every time they showed up with a priest, I was going to end up with a bruised shin—because sometime during the dinner I'd tell a risqué joke, the priest would love it and Gracie would kick me under the table. But this particular party was just for the men. When I got there I saw a beautiful girl standing against the bar holding a cigar and cigarette tray, just like in the nightclubs. She was dressed in a long, tight-fitting black dress. She just stood there against the bar for about an hour while we had cocktails. Then Dockey announced that it was time for dinner and told her she could leave. When she walked out we saw, for the first time, that the part of her dress covering her rear had been cut out. I'll tell you something, if Matthau had looked like that when he dropped his trousers, I would have laughed for him.

Groucho did a lot of entertaining. When he lived up in the Trousdale Estates he had a little get-together almost every Sunday night at which he'd serve a nice, cold buffet. Jack Carter told me that the first time he was invited to one of these little parties he was standing at the buffet table and the great screenwriter Nunnally Johnson told him, "See those green beans? They're great green beans. The only place around here you can get those green beans is at Groucho's house." Then he paused, and added very slowly, "And you get them every goddamn time you come here. Those same goddamn green beans, week after week after week, those same goddamn . . ."

Groucho and I had one thing in common. Both of us believed that a real friend is anyone willing to sing harmony. When Gracie and I gave a party at our house I never asked anyone to get up and do a number. I wanted my guests to be able to relax—and listen to me. I'd hire a piano player who played in my key and after dinner I'd get up and sing a few songs. And then a few more songs. One night, after I'd sung four or five of my hits, Jolson stood up and said, "Thanks, George, I'll take it from here."

"Okay, Jolie," I told him, "but you can only sing one song." Well, you couldn't tell Al Jolson he could only sing one song. He was furious. He was married to Ruby Keeler at that time and he grabbed her hand and pulled her out of the house. I followed them right out the door, still singing. "Okay, Jolie, okay," I told him, "we'll compromise. You can do two choruses."

At Groucho's parties he would play the guitar and sing. He'd sing popular songs, vaudeville songs, Gilbert and Sullivan songs; he'd sing for two or three hours. Now, Groucho was one of the greatest comedians who ever lived, he had a wonderful mind, but he couldn't hit a note with a sledgehammer from two feet away. But he sang, and he sang, and he wouldn't let anybody else sing. Going to Groucho's house to hear him sing was like going to Caruso's house to hear him tell jokes. I tried to explain that to him once. "Listen, Groucho," I said, "I want to ask you something. When you go to Al Capone's house, do you want to hear him sing? No, of course you don't. You want to see him shoot somebody, right?" But Groucho wanted to sing, so if you wanted to eat those goddamn green beans, you had to listen to him. I'm telling you the truth—it would have been better if Capone had sung and Groucho had shot somebody.

One of the last big parties I went to at his house was in honor of his eighty-fifth birthday. I remember Milton walking in and saying, "Hi, Julius"—Milton always called Groucho by his real name— "how you feeling?"

"Clever," Groucho said. And he was. Later in the evening he told several people, "I'm in perfect health. Except mentally." That meant he was in perfect health. It really was a wonderful party; I think that was one of the very few times I enjoyed hearing him sing. Of course, he only did one song.

Harpo and Susan Marx threw a lot of parties after they'd moved down to Palm Springs, and they always ended up with people staying over. After one of those parties Ruth Henning woke up just after sunrise and thought she heard heavenly music. She went into the living room and found Harpo gently strumming his harp. "Thank goodness it's you," she said. "When I heard the music I thought I was dead."

No matter whose party Jack Benny and I were attending, I always tried to do something to make him laugh. Believe me, if I thought for one minute that he was really embarrassed by the things I did to him, I certainly would have done a lot more of them. I remember one night we were at a party at writer Norman Krasna's house; there were probably seventy or eighty people there and the party was pretty quiet. I saw Jack walk over to the mantelpiece and pick up some matches to light his cigar. "Ladies and gentlemen, may I have your attention please," I said loudly. Everybody immediately quieted down, and Jack hesitated. "Well, we're really in luck tonight," I said. "Jack Benny is going to honor us by doing his famous match bit. Jack . . ." Everybody looked at him and waited. Jack didn't know what to do, so he lit his cigar. "Oh," I said, "a new finish!" And Jack started laughing so hard he had to get down on his knees and pound the floor.

Unlike his very best friend in the whole world, Jack rarely entertained at parties. Sometimes, though, at the big parties and at charity events, Jack and I would recruit a third person and do an act we called "Goldie, Fields and Glide." We'd use the same material I'd used in vaudeville when I was part of the original "Goldie, Fields and Glide" and, this is true, time had not improved that material. It was a simple song and dance act; we sang "Me and My Shadow" and did some basic soft-shoe steps. If I tell you that that was the worst act in show business I'd be lying—we weren't that good. Jack and I did it with people like John Wayne, Gregory Peck and Bing Crosby. The only person who wouldn't do it with us was Gene Kelly. When Gene saw how bad the act was, he wanted to improve it. That was impossible; you couldn't make anything that bad good; the act was a hit because it was so bad.

At some big charity party one night Jack and I needed a third person, so we asked Debbie Reynolds' husband, Harry Karl, who owned a big shoe manufacturing company, to do it with us. Harry didn't want to do it, telling us that he wasn't a professional entertainer. Perfect. "Harry," I told him, putting my arm around his shoulders, "Harry, it's really easy. All you have to remember when we run out onstage is, start with your right foot. That's all, just start on your right foot. We'll write down the lyrics and put them in your straw hat, so if you forget them just take off your hat."

Harry was still reluctant. "Gees, George, I don't want to embarrass myself."

"Harry, how long have you known me? Would I do anything to embarrass you? Believe me, this is easy. Just start on your right foot and remember the lyrics are in your hat."

Reluctantly, I'll admit, Harry agreed to do it. A few minutes later we were all standing backstage, waiting to be announced. And just as the band started playing our music, I leaned over and whispered to Jack, "Start on your left foot."

Jack and Mary threw a lot of parties at their house. Mary felt it was her duty as his wife to prove to people that Jack wasn't really cheap by spending as much of his money as fast as she could. That was Mary, willing to do anything for Jack. But the one party that I really remember was their daughter Joanie's wedding. It was one of the most lavish parties I ever attended. With more than 600 guests, it was the biggest party that had been thrown in Hollywood in years. Joanie Benny had decided to get married just a week after she'd met this fellow, and the wedding took place three months later. It was such a beautiful wedding that Cantor could have released it as a picture. Mary even flew a top Hollywood costume designer to Paris to supervise the sewing of Joanie's wedding gown. The wedding was held at the Beverly Hills Hotel, and they served thirty-five cases of champagne, 1,400 pounds of breast of squab, 300 pounds of lobster and a 200-pound five-tiered wedding cake. Everybody in the Hollywood television and movie business was there—Cantor, Wynn, Berle, the Marx Brothers, Danny Thomas, Sinatra, the Jimmy Stewarts, the Ronnie Reagans, Ethel Merman, Louis B. Mayer, Danny Kaye and Sylvia Fine, Danny and Rosemary Thomas, Tyrone Power and Linda Christian, Robert Taylor and Barbara Stanwyck, Clark Gable, Joan Crawford, Jack Warner and Lucy and Desi. It certainly was a little more elaborate than the little get-togethers we used to have in Jack's hotel room in New York. During the party I took Jack aside and told him, "You'd better keep this out of the papers. If anybody finds out about it, it'll ruin your reputation."

Bob Hope said he wouldn't have missed the wedding for a war, "Because Joanie is the first thing Jack Benny has given away in years." Later he gave a nice little toast, reminding everyone that "Jack figures he's not gaining a son, but losing a deduction."

The next morning both the L.A. newspapers ran big stories about the affair on their front page: The *Examiner* wrote, BENNY WEDDING COSTS $50,000. The *Times* headlined, BENNY WEDDING COSTS $60,000. As soon as Cantor saw the newspapers he called up Jack. "Just read the *Examiner*," he told him, "you'll save ten thousand dollars."

It was an absolutely beautiful wedding. I'll tell you something, being there and seeing all that food and all those beautiful flowers and Joanie's dress with its seventeen-yard-long train and listening to the big orchestras playing made me very thankful for my own wonderful daughter, Sandra; who'd eloped.

The one person who almost never showed up at the big Hollywood parties, at least until much later in his life, was Durante. Jimmy traveled with a party—his "Vice-Presidents" and whoever else happened to be around, and when he stopped at a traffic light a party broke out. After a show there were always more people in his dressing room than there had been in the audience. There were all his friends, whatever performers happened to be around, professional athletes, policemen, people he'd worked with in vaudeville, salesmen, people waiting for public transportation, a small funeral procession. . . . When he was staying at the Astor Hotel his suite was always filled with friends coming or going or, as far as anyone could figure out, living there. Once though, only once, his Vice-Presidents decided they were going to throw a real party in his honor. It was a surprise, and Jimmy really was surprised and touched. How touched was he? I'll tell you. In the middle of the bash Jimmy found the banquet manager and asked him how much the party cost. Then he made out a check for that amount. Jimmy paid for his own surprise party—and that's what I call really being touched.

I think Jimmy didn't like going to other people's parties because he couldn't relax around people he didn't know. If he had to go to dinner with people he didn't know, for example, he'd eat his dinner before going out for dinner because he knew he'd be expected to entertain. Alan Young told me a sweet story I'd never heard about Jimmy. When Alan was doing Durante's radio show they had a broadcast on Alan's birthday. After the show he invited Jimmy to go out to dinner with him and his wife. "Ah no, Youngey," Jimmy said, "I got aperntments." So Alan and his wife went by themselves for a quiet dinner. Their house was dark when they got home, but as soon as Alan opened the door he heard a piano start playing and a familiar voice singing "Happy Birthday to Youse." Alan was really shocked— he didn't even have a piano. But someone turned on the lights and there was Jimmy, sitting at a piano, surrounded by Clayton, Jackson and many of Alan's friends. Durante sat and played the piano for more than two hours. "All I kept thinking," Alan remembers, "was that this was a rented piano." Before Jimmy left, with the piano intact, he led all the guests in an unforgettable version of "Good night, Youngey."

He did not, however, offer to pay for the party. That was the difference between being touched and being touching.

But of all the parties my mind bunch went to, there is one that I'll never forget. For several years we would all go down to Palm Springs to celebrate New Year's Eve at Susan and Harpo's. Usually, at the end of a party or when we were leaving a restaurant, we'd be standing outside and Harpo would shake hands with somebody, and when he did, dozens of knives and forks and spoons would pour from his sleeve. It rained silverware. We'd all laugh and Harpo would leave and, as he did, the very last thing we would hear was the tink of one last spoon hitting the pavement.

One New Year's Eve we were leaving Harpo's house about three o'clock in the morning. We were all standing outside, waiting for our cars; the sky was filled with stars and the air was crisp and we were all together and everybody felt wonderful. Then suddenly, from the sky we heard a clarinet playing a slow, beautiful version of "Auld Lang Syne." It was Harpo, standing at an opened upstairs window, playing goodnight to his friends. Nobody said a word. This was a group that couldn't say good morning without doing five minutes, but nobody said a word. And I'll never forget it.

7

There's an old story I've just made up specially for this page. A very famous comedian who I'd known for years died, and when he opened his eyes he found himself in a very bright room, and he couldn't tell if he was in heaven or hell. A man dressed in flowing white robes was sitting directly in front of him, looking at a big ledger. Finally, the man closed the book and said, "I've examined the whole record of your life, and I think you deserve this."

Then he handed him six beautifully handwritten pages. As soon as this comedian began reading these pages, he realized he was holding in his hands The Golden Routine, seventeen minutes of the greatest material ever written, one line even more perfect than the last one. The comedian looked up at the man with tears in his eyes. "Then I made it," he said. "I'm in heaven."

"Not exactly," the man said.

"What do you mean? You've just given me the greatest routine any comedian ever had."

"That's right," the man said smiling, "but what are you going to do for an audience?"

Let me tell you something. When a banker goes home at the end of the day, he doesn't give away money. When a garbage collector finishes work, he doesn't collect garbage. A comedian is always a comedian, though—except Joe Penner, of course, who rested his brain in the summer. But just about every other comedian I've known sees life as a setup in search of a punch line. A comedian needs an audience like Jessel needed a pretty woman, or Jolson needed a mirror.

When we lived in New York City we could always find an audience at the Friars Club. The Friars Club was to entertainers what Chase Manhattan Bank is to doctors. The Friars Club was started to give vaudevillians a place to go to relax when they were in New York; but it became the place to go, day or night, to catch up on all the show business gossip, see friends, play a little cards and find an audience. When we moved out to Los Angeles there was no West Coast branch of the Friars, so a lot of us started meeting for lunch at the Hillcrest Golf and Country Club.

Starting about noon, every single day, whoever was in town would meet at the big round table for twelve in the Men's Grill. The regular group included me and Jack, Jolson, Cantor, Jessel and the Marx Brothers, the Ritz Brothers, Danny Kaye, Berle, Lou Holtz and Danny Thomas. A lot of people thought that the round table was our home away from home. That wasn't true at all. We spent so much time there that our houses were really our homes away from home.

That was some tough lunch to work. As Durante might have said about comedians, "It takes two to tangle." And there were always at least ten comedians there. There's a joke that describes what these lunches were like: How many comedians does it take to tell a joke? Ten. One to set up the straight line and nine to deliver nine different punch lines. Believe me, to that group, "Pass the salt, please," was a setup.

The group started off pretty informally, but then we decided to establish a few rules for membership: anyone who wanted to sit at the table had to be a paid-up member of Hillcrest, had to work professionally as a comedian, had to have at least a 20-handicap on the golf course and had to be approved by at least fifteen members in good standing of the Round Table. That last requirement was the toughest one to meet; at no time were there more than eleven members of the Round Table.

Sometimes though, we did allow a person who wasn't in show business to sit with us. "It's always good to have someone in the dress business," Groucho decided, "because it's just too hard to get another comedian to play straight man." For example, one man who joined us on occasion was an investment banker. But he also thought he could tell jokes. Believe me, he could not have made any money telling jokes. He couldn't even make Jack Benny laugh, and Jack laughed at the menu. So for years, every time this person started to tell a joke I'd stop him. "Wait a second," I'd say, "wait a second. I think that's a switch on the old pineapple story. We all know that one."

Everybody else at the table would nod their head and he would stop.

One day, after listening to me do this for two years, Danny Kaye took me aside and said, "Come on, George, tell me, what is the old pineapple story?"

I shrugged my shoulders. I admitted, "I just didn't want to hear his joke. There is no pineapple story."

The conversation at the Round Table was mostly about current events: whose show was doing well, what jobs were available, what the critics were saying—just the really important things. There was an unwritten rule that if another member had a show on the air everybody else had to listen to it or watch it. The only acceptable excuse for missing a show was death. And even then you had to bring a note from your undertaker. If you had done a show you'd find out as soon as you got to the table what everybody thought of it. If they mentioned it at all, even to tell you they didn't like it, they liked it. But if you sat down at the table and people started talking about Vice-President Alben Barkley's summer vacation, you knew the show hadn't been very good.

For one season Gracie and I were on TV directly opposite Groucho's "You Bet Your Life." That was tough on everybody. If they talked about one show, that meant they hadn't watched the other one. Vice-President Barkley took summer vacations most of that winter. But one Friday afternoon, Lou Holtz told Groucho his show had been terrific. A few other people said the same thing. I coughed. "Uh, any of you happen to see my show last night?" I asked.

Nobody said a word. Finally Chico snapped his fingers and said, "Wait, wait, I know somebody who saw your show last night and thought it was great."

"Who's that?" I asked.

"I'll go get her," Chico said, getting up from the table and going into the main dining room. A few minutes later he came back—with Gracie.

As far as I was concerned, Jessel was the funniest man at the table. I remember once, for example, Georgie had just come back after raising something like $25,000,000 in bonds for the new nation of Israel. "That's a lot of money, Georgie," I said. "How'd you raise so much?"

"It wasn't that difficult, Natty," he explained, "I just left no Cohen unturned."

Georgie was always getting himself into trouble with some woman or somebody he owed money to or the IRS, or some woman at the IRS he owed money to. At that time the Prinzmetal brothers were members of the club. One of them was a very famous doctor, the other one was a top lawyer. So one afternoon Georgie came in and as soon as he sat down he started complaining. "I'm really in trouble this time," he said, "this time it's really serious."

Naturally, everybody was concerned. "How bad is it?" Harry Ritz asked.

"Real bad," Georgie told him. "I need two Prinzmetals."

The only regular at the table who wasn't working in show business was Lou Holtz. After failing to make it in radio, Lou had become a stockbroker. He made a lot of money for himself in the market, and became the table's unofficial broker. He was always willing to tell us when he was buying a stock—unfortunately, sometimes he forgot to tell us when he was selling it. So, whenever any of us lost money in the stock market, Vice-President Barkley had to go on summer vacation again.

The smartest person at the table was Harpo. That wasn't just my opinion, that was the official opinion of Alexander Woollcott, the famous New York newspaper critic. Harpo was actually a member of two unofficial Round Tables, Hillcrest and the better known group that met at the Algonquin Hotel that included Woollcott, Robert Benchley, George S. Kaufman, Dorothy Parker, Franklin P. Adams and Marc Connolly. Harpo rarely opened his mouth at either table except to order lunch. Once, in fact, he told Woollcott that he felt a little silly, sitting at the famous Algonquin table without ever saying anything. "My dear Harpo," Woollcott told him, "you're a smarter fellow than I am. I am the best writer in America and I have nothing to say either. But I'm not smart enough to keep my mouth shut."

So, based on the fact that Harpo said the least at our Round Table, he would have been the smartest person there too. Everybody else finished tied for second.

The only person at the table I didn't get along with so well was Groucho. Look, he got that name for a reason. If he had had a different personality they would have called him Niceo or Good Guyo. But he was called Groucho and the truth is that sometimes he deserved it.

He really could be very tough on people. Once, in late November, he was walking down a street in Washington, D.C., when a woman carrying several packages passed him. "How nice," he said to her. "I see you're doing your Christmas stealing early this year."

On another occasion he went with Irving Brecher to the Greenbriar Hotel in West Virginia for a brief vacation. There was still a lot of anti-semitism in the South at that time and as they arrived at the hotel, Brecher suddenly began getting nervous. "I was in the middle of WASP country, a place where they still tarred-and-feathered people—and I was there with Groucho. So I said to him, 'Why don't you take care of the bags? I'll go check in.'

"And he said, 'Why don't you do that, youngster?' I knew I was in trouble. I started walking towards the door of the hotel and I heard footsteps behind me. I turned around and there he was, back bent over, doing his famous Groucho walk.

"'Groucho, *please*,' I said. He flicked his eyebrows at me. I knew I was in serious trouble. We went inside and I walked up to the front desk.

Standing behind that desk were three men identically dressed in shiny black suits. None of them were smiling. I took a deep breath and said, 'You have a reservation for—'

"I never finished. Groucho came up next to me and said, 'Is it true that you people run a chain of brothels?'

" 'You don't have a reservation,' one of the three men said.

" 'But I didn't even tell you my name.'

" 'You don't have a reservation,' he repeated. So I begged and I pleaded for almost two hours and finally they gave us the smallest room in the entire hotel, a converted broom closet with water pipes running through it.

"When we got into the room Groucho looked around and frowned. 'You know,' he said, 'I'm beginning to think I was undiplomatic.' ' "

At one time Groucho decided to drop out of Hillcrest. In the late 1930s he'd started playing tennis and joined the Beverly Hills Tennis Club, so he didn't come to Hillcrest that often. When the Hillcrest membership committee asked him to send them a letter of resignation so they could return his unused membership fee, he wrote his famous letter telling them that he was resigning because "I don't want to belong to any club that would have me as a member."

Well, there were times that a lot of people would have agreed with him about that. Of course, his resignation didn't stop him from coming to the club for lunch as the guest of one of his brothers.

And a few years later, when he had gotten over tennis, he decided to rejoin the Round Table. When Groucho had quit, his membership had been worth about $350, by the time he was ready to rejoin, the membership fee was up to $7,500. Sometimes Groucho could have been called Cheapo, too. "I'm not going to pay that kind of money just to have a place to eat," he said. "It's worth money to escape my wife's cooking, but not that much."

When we finally told Groucho that he couldn't sit with us until he'd paid his membership fee, he showed up at the club with Gummo, carrying one of those small, folding TV-tray tables, which he set up in the corner. "I don't need you fellows anymore," he announced. "I'm going into business for myself."

I always admired Groucho's talent. Both on-stage and offstage he was fearless. He tried to top every line. If somebody sneezed, Groucho would try to top it. Sometimes he would, too, and if he got a laugh, he'd use that line again. Of course, I'd never do anything like that. Anyway, Sophie Tucker used to sing a great song called "If You Can't See Mama Every Night, You Can't See Mama at All." One afternoon at the club I ordered sea bass. And when I did, Groucho said, "If you can't sea bass every night, you can't sea bass at all." That was sort of cute, and everybody chuckled. The problem was that I liked sea bass, and they made a nice sea bass at Hillcrest. And every time I'd order sea bass, Groucho would say, "If you can't sea bass every night, you can't sea bass at all." Every time, every goddamn time. It was the green beans of lines. After two years it wasn't funny. After five years it was even less funny. After eight years there was absolutely nothing funny about it at all. Nothing. But I still liked sea bass, I liked sea bass more than I liked Groucho.

One afternoon I opened up the menu and there it was—sea bass. I wanted that sea bass. But I knew I just couldn't bear to hear Groucho say "If you can't sea bass every night, you can't sea bass at all" one more time. I even have a hard time writing it again. I looked across the table. Groucho was watching me, just waiting for me to order sea bass. So I held up the menu in front of my face and I signaled the waiter to lean over, then I whispered very softly to him, "I'll have the sea bass."

And the waiter whispered back just as softly, "Mr. Burns, if you can't sea bass every night, you can't sea bass at all."

The problems in my friendship with Groucho started at lunch one day when he asked me who I thought was the greatest comedian who ever lived. What kind of question is that to ask a comedian? That's like asking two surgeons getting ready to operate who could finish first. When Groucho asked that question I told him the truth. "I think it was Charlie Chaplin."

There were times when Groucho should have been named Ego. "I don't think so," he said, "I think I am."

So I told him the real truth. "Well, if that's

what you think, then I must be the greatest comedian alive. Because I'm funnier than you are."
And as long as Gracie and Jack weren't there, I
meant it too.

There's really nothing funny about two comedians fighting—unless it was the Three Stooges.
Groucho and I eventually made up, but we were
never really close friends again. And it was a silly
argument—everybody knows Chaplin was the
best. For a long time Groucho wouldn't even talk
to me. And during that time I did the best thing
possible under the circumstances—I looked
Groucho right in the eyes and ordered sea bass
every time I wanted it. Sometimes even when I
didn't want it.

One afternoon at the club Jessel and Lou Holtz
were wandering around looking for something and
they walked through the big patio doors onto the
terrace. And there, in front of them, was the golf
course. Georgie looked at the beautiful green fairway, the men dressed in golfing outfits, the cad-
dies lugging golf bags, and the sticks with the
numbered flags on them. "My God," Georgie said
to Holtz in amazement, "how long has this golf
course been here?"

Most of us played golf. Or at least played at
golf. I knew golf was the right game for me the
first time I played when somebody asked me if I
had a good lie. I'd been waiting for that line for
about forty years. Of course I did—my score.
Most of us had started playing golf when we were
working in big-time vaudeville. Because we were

239

always on the road and, in the big-time, we worked only two shows at night, we were free all day so we took up the game. I don't think any of us were ever really very good at it, golf just isn't the natural sport of people who grew up in big towns. We were the kind of players who measured the distance of our drives in city blocks. "Oh, great hit, six or seven blocks easy."

I was miserable to play with, because when I was playing well I'd sing, and when I was playing badly I was just miserable.

The Hillcrest course was a tough one. I remember one day when we were all sitting at the Round Table when someone came over and told us that Conrad Veidt, a good actor who always played villains, had collapsed and died on the first tee. "Gees," I said softly, "this course is even tougher than I thought."

Cantor hated the course, mainly because he was one of the few left-handers in the club. There was a big tree near the sixteenth tee that hung over the right side of the fairway and Cantor kept driving balls into its branches. He complained to the greens committee that that tree was unfair to left-handed golfers and asked that it be trimmed back. They turned him down. Miraculously, one night the tree got itself chopped down. Not only chopped down, but cut up and piled into firewood. The greens committee figured Cantor was behind this miracle and called a special hearing. Cantor denied he had anything to do with it. "Eddie," a member of the committee said, "that tree didn't chop itself down."

Eddie would never have been mistaken for George Washington. "Maybe it was termites," he told them.

"That's not funny," the greens committee chairman said. Of course it was funny; it was a great line. "You're one of the few left-handed golfers in the club," the chairman continued, "and you wanted to have that tree trimmed. It looks like you had a good reason to chop down that tree."

Eddie wouldn't have even been mistaken for Baron Munchausen. "Maybe it was left-handed termites."

Jolson's problem on the golf course was his ego. I remember once we were playing golf in a foursome with the club pro and Jolson was gettng ready to tee off. The pro suggested he use a one-wood. Jolson told his caddy to give him a three-wood. "Listen, pally," he said to the pro, "don't forget it's Jolson on the tee." If he hit a really good shot, he'd stand back and admire it, then say confidently, "Jolson sure hit that one." But if he flubbed a shot, he'd shake his head and explain, "I have fifteen different stances and seventeen different backswings. You can't expect me to get used to all of them." Jolson even made the greatest excuses.

Like the rest of us, Jolson's moods varied depending on how he did on the golf course. I remember meeting him one day just as he was coming off the course. "How'd you do?" I asked.

He held up his hand. "I'm not sore, Natty," he said, "I'm really not sore." Then he thought about it for a few seconds and admitted, "But I am irked."

I played a lot of golf with Harpo and Jack. Harpo's real game wasn't golf, it was croquet. Alexander Woollcott taught him to play, and eventually Harpo was elected to the Croquet Hall of Fame. That's absolutely true. Maybe he was a great croquet player, but I had a tough time playing golf with him because I never knew what he was going to do next. Once, we were playing a pretty good round, we were probably a stroke apart, and I was about to tee off on the eighteenth hole. I got all ready, I started my backswing and, just as I did, a fork fell out of Harpo's sleeve onto the grass. A fork! After seventeen holes of golf. Another day we both hit our drives and followed them down the fairway. After I hit my second shot I looked for Harpo and I didn't see him. I finally found him in the rough—hanging upside down from a tree, peeing.

When he and Susan moved to Palm Springs they bought a house on the fifteenth hole of the Tamarisk Golf Club. The course was lined with beautiful homes, and every one of them had a swimming pool. So when we played that course Harpo would go from hole to hole, hopping over fences and diving into these pools to cool off. People who lived on the course knew that whenever they heard a splash in their pool, it was just Harpo playing golf.

We got into real trouble at Hillcrest once. We were out on the course on a very hot day and we decided to take off our shirts. You couldn't take off your shirt at Hillcrest, that was against the rules. We got an official letter from the club reminding us of the rule and asking us not to take off our shirts again. So the next time we played we took off our shirts again, and our memberships were suspended for two weeks. The day we were reinstated we were back out on the course. When we reached the third hole, we took off our pants. And when members complained, we pointed out that we were wearing our shirts, then reminded them that there was no rule against playing in our undershorts. There is now.

Groucho didn't have the right temperature for golf. He didn't like to do things he wasn't good at, and he wasn't good at golf. Finally, one day he was playing a course on the ocean, maybe Pebble Beach. And he got so angry that he stood up on top of a hill and threw every one of his golf balls into the ocean. Then he took his clubs and, one by one, threw them into the ocean. And when he'd thrown his clubs away, he picked up his golf bag and threw that into the ocean. And then he turned around and looked at his partners—but they backed away. Finally he smiled happily, rubbed his hands together and walked off the course.

Danny Kaye was good at almost everything he

did, but I don't think he was a great golfer. I will say this for him though, when he hit a bad shot, he threw his clubs much further than anybody else.

Jack played a lot of golf, but he wasn't much of a golfer. Actually, Jack wasn't much of an athlete of any kind. Let me put it this way—he was uncoordinated at cards. One time, I remember, we were all playing in a charity baseball game and Groucho was managing Jack's team. Jack playing baseball, there's an idea for a very funny show. As Jack got up to bat, Groucho told him, "Hit a home run." Jack struck out on three pitches. When he got back to the bench Groucho was upset. "If you're not going to do what I tell you," he said, what's the use of my being the manager?"

On a golf course, Jack had the hands of a violinist. That was fair, because as a violinist, Jack had the hands of a golfer. Actually, I think he probably could have hit a golf ball just as far with a violin as he did with a golf club. I'll tell you how bad a golfer Jack was. Here's the sound of Jack hitting a golf ball: "Go ahead, Jack, take another swing."

As Jack got older, the only reason he kept playing was because his doctor told him the exercise was good for him. But I know he really didn't like it very much. Sometimes when we were supposed to play he'd say things like "Oh, what a beautiful day for golf. Let's go out and play one hole."

When Jack did play he had one thing in common with every other golfer—if he played well, the world was wonderful. Riots, revolutions, World War II, he didn't care if he broke 100. But when he played poorly he got very depressed. One afternoon he was playing in a foursome with his brother-in-law, Hilly Marks, and writers Sam Perrin and John Tackaberry. He was having a bad day, slicing drives, topping grounders, he just couldn't do anything right. But after almost every shot, Hilly would say, "Sounded good, Jack." Fifty yards on the ground, "Sounded good, Jack." Sliced into the rough, "Sounded good, Jack." It could have been worse, he could have been saying, "If you can't sea bass every night, you can't sea bass at all." Finally Jack had had enough. When he dribbled another shot down the fairway and Hilly said, "Sounded good, Jack," he turned around and said angrily, "Who the hell cares what it sounded like? I'm playing golf, not giving a concert!"

We always played for a few bucks and making Jack laugh so hard that he had to get down on his knees and pound the grass was always worth a few strokes, because it took him a little while to regain his composure. So, as the stakes got higher, the players got funnier. One day Jack was playing with Irving Brecher. They were on the green about to putt when a woman in the foursome playing behind them hit a terrific drive, and her ball ended up about thirty-five feet from the cup. Jack was very impressed, maybe a little jealous too. "That was some shot that woman hit, wasn't it, Irving?" he said wistfully.

Irving put it in perspective for him. "Yeah," he said, "but she must have some dirty house." Three strokes.

I played golf with Jack pretty regularly. I wasn't any better at it than he was, but I didn't care as much. Sure, I didn't. But when I was with Jack and he started complaining about his golf game, I was always sympathetic. One day as we walked along the fairway, he started shaking his head in frustration. "I keep thinking that this is going to be the day I break par," he said, "But I never do, never. Why did God make me such a lousy golfer?"

"Oh, stop complaining," I said, "you're a rich guy, Jack. You've got one of the most popular shows on television, you're famous all over the world. Golf is the only thing you do lousy, so be a little grateful."

"Oh, I wouldn't care about any of that," Jack said, "if I could just be a great golfer."

I stopped. "Wait a second, Jack. You're trying to tell me that if God came to you right now and said, 'Okay, Jackson, you can have your choice, you can have a lousy television show and a great golf game, or a great television show and a lousy golf game, you'd take the lousy show and the great golf game?"

"That's right," he insisted.

"All right then," I said, "how great a golfer would you want to be?"

Jack thought about that. "I guess that depends," he admitted, "how lousy would God want my TV show to be?"

Jessel never played golf. I think Jessel's philosophy about golf was something like: If all you're going to do is chase the ball, why hit it in the first place? Georgie was really a big baseball fan, that was his sport. Not only had he been the New York Giants' batboy when he was a kid, he had also introduced the sport of baseball to Israel. He went over there in the early 1950s with bats and balls and uniforms and helped them organize a league. It didn't surprise me that Georgie Jessel was the father of Israeli baseball—knowing Georgie as well as I did, it wouldn't surprise me to find out he was the father of anything.

The only sport I know that Jessel actually tried was fishing. Personally, I have never been much of a fisherman. It just never made a lot of sense to me that people would spend hundreds of dollars on sophisticated equipment and then feel so good because they'd outsmarted a fish. I just don't think fish are that smart. For years people have been telling me that fish are supposed to be brain food. "Yeah?" I'd always tell them. "If that fish is so smart, what's he doing on my plate?"

I think Jessel felt pretty much the same way. He went deep-sea fishing once and hooked a seven-foot sailfish. As he reeled the fish close to the boat, somebody hit it over the head with a baseball bat and killed it. Georgie never forgot that. He told me once, "I can't even look at gefilte fish without feeling remorse." About a year after catching the sailfish, he was invited to go marlin fishing by members of Palm Beach's exclusive Sailfish Club. He turned them down. "When I was a young man growing up in the Bronx," he explained, "I never thought I would be invited by sportsmen to go marlin fishing. But I must humbly decline that gracious invitation, because in the last ten years I can't recall a single time that a marlin was accused of being antisemitic." Only Jessel could turn a simple invitation to go fishing into a religious experience.

Maybe the worst golfer of all was Ed Wynn. For Wynn, golf was a contact sport. In 1932, while he was playing in a charity golf tournament with Grantland Rice and Ring Lardner, he tripped walking off the first tee and broke his arm. Naturally, everybody thought he was kidding and they just let him lie there, unconscious, for a few minutes. Only when the next foursome asked if they could play over did people realize he was seriously hurt. Wynn was the only golfer I ever knew who had to be carried off the course on a stretcher.

Maybe I wasn't such a good golfer, but in all the years I played, and I played some pretty tough courses, I never broke anything. Including par. Look, I'm not going to lie to you, I . . . Let me rewrite that, I'm not going to lie to you in this paragraph, the truth is that sports just weren't that important to us. If we could get out in the sun for a few hours, hit a few balls well, tell a few stories and watch Danny Kaye throw his clubs into the lake, we were happy. Golf wasn't really our game, making people laugh was. Onstage and offstage. And we were all pretty good at that game.

Harpo, for instance. Harpo would do almost anything to make people laugh. Harpo was the kind of person who would be at a restaurant like "21" and, when someone asked him how he was feeling, he'd say "Fine," then take off his tie, his jacket, his shirt and his undershirt, pound his bare chest and say, "See?"

Harpo would do things like that all the time. Once he was standing in front of a hotel in Baltimore when a taxi pulled up and a very dignified woman got out. Harpo suddenly had an inspiration. He picked this woman up, carried her to the front desk and told the clerk, "Register us quickly."

He was just such a wonderful person. He never hurt anybody with his jokes, but like his brothers he loved to poke fun at people who took themselves too seriously. Once, for example, he went into a dimestore and bought their entire stock of fake diamonds and rubies and put them in a small bag. And then he went to Tiffany's.

Now isn't that just the best setup? If you can't figure out what happened next, you have to repeat, "If you can't sea bass every night, you can't sea bass at all." At Tiffany's Harpo asked to see a tray of diamonds. As he examined them, he took out his bag and dropped the fake jewels on the floor. Bells started ringing, buzzers went off, people started shouting, the doors were locked. And

Harpo just stood there smiling. Clerks raced over and started picking up the dimestore jewels as quickly as they could. Harpo just stood there. Then the manager examined one of the fakes and realized what had happened. Harpo was quickly searched and thrown out of the store—but as he left he tipped the doorman a ruby.

Harpo saw the humor in life. The great artist Salvador Dali once sent him a harp whose strings had been replaced by barbed wire. Harpo immediately sent Dali a picture showing him standing next to the harp with all his fingers wrapped in bandages.

Most of the things he did though, he thought up on the spot. I remember we were driving along Sunset Boulevard one day, and we stopped at a traffic light. A car with two little old ladies in it pulled up right next to us. Harpo honked his horn, rolled down his window and indicated that the woman should do the same thing. And when they did, he leaned out and pointed to the right and asked, "Pittsburgh?"

Once when he was vacationing on the French Riviera he went to a boxing match with the great actress Ruth Gordon. Harpo liked boxing, but this was a terrible fight. These guys looked like two Jack Benny's trying to hit each other. So Harpo decided to liven things up: he offered a bonus of 200 francs—to the loser.

Most of Groucho's humor offstage was verbal. In the late 1930s spiritualism was big in Hollywood, and Groucho went to a séance. When the medium asked if anyone had a question for the spirits, Groucho said, "I do. What's the capital of South Dakota?"

One of Groucho's wives wasn't Jewish and they had a lovely daughter named Melinda. One day Melinda went with her friends to a club that didn't allow Jews, and she wasn't allowed to go in the pool. When Groucho found out, he wrote a letter to the President of the club, asking, "Since my daughter is only half-Jewish, would it be all right if she went into the pool only up to her waist?"

There actually were some very personal things that Groucho enjoyed sharing with his friends; his insomnia, for instance. Sometimes he would call up people in the middle of the night and tell them, "This is Professor Waldemar Strumbelknauff. Tell me, aren't you ashamed of yourself for beating your children that way? If you were a man you'd come over here and knock my teeth out. If you were half a man, you'd come over here and knock half my teeth out. . . . This is Groucho. How are you? As if I really care." Then he would hang up the phone before that person could say a word.

Chico's humor was even more obvious. At dinner, for example, Chico would eat all his food, and when the check came he would put salt and pepper on it, then eat that too.

Cantor and Jessel were always trying to top each other. Once, they were both going to speak at the same dinner, so they got together to go over their material. Cantor told Jessel the two stories he was going to use, then Jessel told Cantor the two stories he intended to use. You've heard that there's honor among thieves, right? Notice that they don't say anything about comedians. I think this was one of those situations where it just depended on who spoke first. It was Cantor.

Eddie did the bit he had prepared, then said, "And before I introduce the next speaker, a man known for his ability to ad-lib, I'd like to tell you two wonderful stories I just heard." And then he told Jessel's stories.

Of course, Jessel eventually got even. Jessel always got even. In the 1940s Cantor produced a live show at the Capitol Theatre. Jessel wasn't doing too well at that time, so Cantor hired him for the show. It was during that booking that Jessel, who was forty-two years old, married a sweet sixteen-year-old girl named Lois Andrews. When Cantor got to the theater one night, he opened the door to his dressing room and saw Jessel and Lois Andrews on the floor, naked. "Georgie!" Eddie said, "what are you doing?"

Jessel looked up at him. "Listen, you cheapskate. With what you're paying me, who could afford a honeymoon?"

Jack was a quiet riot offstage. He was also uncoordinated at jokes. When he tried to do something funny, it just didn't work. A few times he took small pieces of toilet paper and stuck them under his eyelids, messed up his hair, put his sports jacket half on and half off and staggered around as if he was drunk. He thought he was

252

hysterical. This first time he did this he sort of reeled into lunch at Hillcrest, expecting us all to start laughing. Well, maybe the biggest joke at the Round Table was not laughing at Jack when he was trying to be funny. Not laughing at Jack was very funny. Even Jack thought so. He would do something . . . mildly amusing, nobody would laugh and Jack would break up. He wasn't just everybody else's best audience; he was also his own.

Jack was a great editor of other people's material, but he was also a pretty good writer himself. Offstage. He loved to write funny letters and send telegrams. Sometimes he would send a telegram reading LETTER TO FOLLOW, and then he wouldn't send the letter. We used to kid him about that. But once Goody Ace got a telegram from Jack promising THREE LETTERS TO FOLLOW. Sure enough, about an hour later three more telegrams were delivered—the first reading "A"; the second, "B"; and the third, "C."

I was always getting wires from him. When we were in vaudeville Gracie and I were working in Chicago and he was finishing a booking in Milwaukee. He sent me a telegram telling me he would be arriving at Union Station at nine A.M. and asking me to meet him. I sent him a wire right back, saying, I'LL BE GLAD TO MEET YOU. WHAT TIME ARE YOU COMING IN?

He wired back, I'LL BE IN AT 9 A.M.

And I wired him, SKIP IT IF YOU DON'T WANT TO TELL ME WHAT TIME YOU'RE COMING IN.

Then I started receiving wires signed by half the people we knew in vaudeville, people like Sophie Tucker, Nora Bayes, Belle Baker; I got about twenty telegrams, and they all said exactly the same thing: JACK BENNY WILL BE ARRIVING UNION STATION 9 O'CLOCK.

Well, of course I didn't meet him. Would you? Instead, I hung up each of those telegrams; I hung them on my makeup mirror, on the walls, on the ceiling, everywhere. At a little after ten o'clock Jack walked into my room and asked, "So why didn't you meet me?"

"I'll tell you the truth, Jack," I said, "I forgot what time you were coming in."

Everybody loved sending telegrams to Jack, too. Cantor worked with him in San Diego once, and as they were getting ready to leave, the hotel manager told them he had a small gift for each of them. It turned out to be a full-color publicity pamphlet for the hotel. Naturally, Jack was thrilled, but somehow, he left it behind. Fortunately Cantor stayed a day longer, because he found Jack's pamphlet and wired him, NOTICE YOU HAVE FORGOTTEN YOUR PAMPHLET. AM ARRANGING TO HAVE IT FORWARDED.

DON'T KNOW HOW THIS COULD HAVE HAPPENED, Jack replied by wire, FEEL TERRIBLE GOING HOME TO MARY WITHOUT IT. When Jack got hold of a joke, he didn't let it go. So from that day on, for months, wherever he went, he'd send Cantor publicity brochures from every hotel in the city.

One of the things Jack loved to do was read

Robert Ripley's famous column of incredible facts, "Believe It or Not," then send long letters to friends telling them the real story behind the items.

In one column Ripley claimed that crocodiles cry when they eat. Jack sent this item to TV director Freddie de Cordova and his wife, and wrote "This is probably the silliest Ripley's that I have ever seen. The reason it's silly is because we all know it's true. . . . Naturally crocodiles cry when they eat. So would you, Freddie, and so would Irving Lazar and Ronald Reagan if all you had to eat day after day was that crap they find in the water.

"Let me tell you something, Freddie, you give a crocodile a nice piece of smoked salmon and a steak, or a lamb chop and a nice green salad . . . then maybe a nice dessert of ice cream or pie, and I assure you, a crocodile won't cry. . . ."

"Have you ever seen a crocodile in Chasen's or the Bistro or Dominic's? You're goddamn right you haven't. That's my answer to Mr. Ripley! Love, Jack. P.S. No wonder they eat people."

I loved playing jokes on Jack, and Jack loved me playing jokes on him. So I tried to make us both happy as often as I could. I think most people have heard about the things I did for Jack. But just in case anybody has forgotten some of these things, I thought I'd give you the highlights:

So when he walked in the hotel room I was standing on the bed, naked, holding his telegram in my hands.

So he was standing on the bed, naked, with a lampshade over his head, expecting me to walk into his hotel room—instead, I sent in the maid.

So I told him, "Absolutely, Jack. Just take off your pants and put on one of Mary's big hats, then come downstairs playing the violin. Everybody will love it."

So as we waited in the royal receiving line, I said to him, "Now remember, Jack, whatever you do, when you meet the Queen, don't laugh."

But in the end, Jack finally topped me. Just when I had the best bit of all planned, he died. Some friend he turned out to be. Some great friend.

Danny Kaye loved making Jack laugh almost as much as I did. I'll tell you how far Danny would go for a good joke. Once, when Jack was playing the Palladium, Danny flew to London the day before Jack did and picked Jack up at the airport the next day disguised as his chauffeur. Danny Kaye was the worst chauffeur who ever lived. He got lost, he stopped at green lights, he sang off-key—which was tough for Danny to do—and he kept talking to Jack in an incomprehensible cockney accent. Jack was going crazy, but he was too polite to tell the driver to shut up. Finally Danny turned around and said something to Jack in his best Charlie Chaplin accent—and Jack fell on the floor of the car laughing. And then Danny flew home. That's a long way to go for a laugh.

Look, we were all very lucky people. Not one of us went into show business for the money. Our reward was the sound of laughter. Of course, then we discovered that they actually paid you for making people happy. Getting paid for making people laugh—that has to be the best profession there is that you can do standing up.

Once, during a break in rehearsals for his television show in the late 1940s, Ed Wynn was talking to comedy writer Seaman Jacobs. "I just don't understand it, Sy," he said. "They have the baseball Hall of Fame. They build big monuments to the Presidents. They put famous scientists on stamps. But there's no place that honors the great comedians."

"Oh, sure there is, Ed," Sy corrected him. "It's called The Bank of America."

Almost all of us started in show business with nothing and became rich men. Millionaires. We had big homes, nice cars, beautiful clothes, investments, savings accounts, cooks and butlers and all the lead tops of seltzer bottles we wanted. Even back in vaudeville some of my friends were making thousands of dollars a week. Jolson got $10,000 a week. Cantor got $10,000. Lou Holtz made $7,000 a week. Even Gracie and I were doing very well. In those days people were very surprised when they found out that Babe Ruth was making more money than Calvin Coolidge, the President of the United States. "I deserve it," the Babe said, "I had a better year than he did." Well, we were making more money than Babe Ruth. We were making almost twice as much as Coolidge. And we deserved it. We were much funnier than he was. At least most of the time.

But since none of us had ever had any money when we were growing up, we really didn't know what to do with it when we got it. Besides spending it. One of the things that a lot of people did in the 1920s was invest in the stock market. The market seemed like a great deal. In those days all you had to do was put up 5 percent of the money you invested. So as long as the stocks you invested in went up, you made a lot of money. On paper. On paper everybody was rich. They just didn't do so well in money. When the market crashed in 1929 almost everybody lost their fortune. Groucho lost $240,000, his entire life savings. Benny Fields had invested all of Blossom's money, about $250,000, and lost it all. Jessel lost $400,000. Jolson wouldn't let Jessel beat him in anything, so he lost $460,000. Lou Holtz was worth more than $1,000,000 before the crash— six months later he got a check for $732. Ed Wynn, who had been listed with Cantor, Jolson, Chaplin and George M. Cohan as the five richest people in show business, lost more than $2,000,000 in three days. But Cantor was the biggest loser of all. In twenty days he lost over $2,000,000. Even after selling his estate on Long Island he was in debt. "They told me to buy this wonderful stock for my old age," he said, "and it really worked very well. I bought it and within a week I was an old man." One of the things Cantor did to earn enough money to pay off his debts was to make his losses part of his act. "I thought I was in the market," he explained, "not under it." He wrote a bestselling book about the crash called *Caught Short*. He even added a stooge to his stage act, a man who stood on the side of the stage trying to squeeze the last drop of juice out of a lemon.

"Just who are you?" Cantor asked him.

And the man said, "I'm the margin clerk for Goldman, Sachs."

Cantor eventually sued Goldman, Sachs for $100,000,000, claiming they had mismanaged his investments, but Eddie's suit was thrown out of court.

Fortunately, Eddie wasn't wearing it at the time.

Just think of that as me doing Milton doing Groucho.

Gracie and I were among the very few people who didn't lose any money in the crash. It's not that I was so smart, it's just that I didn't know anything about money. At that time my money was so new to me that I hadn't even taken the price tag off it yet.

The truth is I didn't understand the stock market well enough to risk investing. I guess I agreed with Will Rogers, who told Cantor he just couldn't seem to figure out why a perfectly good company who didn't know him from a hare would let him become a partner in their business, then be nice enough to give him a share of their profits. I was only tempted to invest once. I'll tell you why I didn't. Gracie and I were playing in Akron, Ohio, and I went to see my brother, George, who was an executive with the big department store, the May Company. While I was there, George brought me in to meet the owner of the store, who gave me the best stock tip I've ever gotten. "Our stock is selling at eighteen," he said, "buy it right now, and when it reaches twenty-five, sell." I figured, gee, this is the guy who owns the whole place, he's sitting in a big office, he's wearing an expensive suit, he must know what he's talking about. So I decided to take his advice.

I'd never bought stock before though, and I didn't know how to do it. From Akron, Gracie and I went to Syracuse, New York. Jesse Block was on the bill with us at the Empire State Theatre in Syracuse and I knew he had invested in the market. "I want to buy some stock in the May Company," I told him, "you know how I do that?"

"Yeah, sure," Jesse said. Then he opened the newspaper and looked at the latest closing prices. "That's a good buy," he decided, "it's selling at sixteen."

Sixteen! I hadn't even bought it and already it had dropped two points. If a stock could drop two points between Akron and Syracuse, I thought, what would it do when we went on a really long trip? So I didn't invest in the market and I didn't lose any money when the market crashed, which is why that was the best stock tip I ever got.

Nobody really complained too much about the money they lost. This was a group of people with very strong egos, and I think they just had too much pride to let anybody know just how badly they'd been hurt. So they did what Cantor did—they made jokes about it. "I was checking into a hotel and I told the clerk I wanted a room on a high floor," Jessel said, "and he asked me, 'Will that be for sleeping or jumping, sir?'"

"I've finally figured out why they call the man who sold me my stocks a broker," Ed Wynn explained. "It's because right now he's the only person who's broker than I am."

Fortunately, just about everybody was working regularly, and they were able to slowly rebuild their finances. Cantor was still getting $8,000 a week on Broadway. Wynn was getting that much on radio. Lou Holtz was getting $2,500 a week. The Marx Brothers were the hottest team in the movies. Clayton, Jackson and Durante were the top nightclub act, and Jolson . . . Jolson was loaning money to the banks. Not everybody recovered; Blossom and Benny struggled for the rest of their lives. Before doing *Harvey*, Frank Fay was hauled into court owing $600—he took three one-dollar bills out of his wallet and said, "I'm broke." Jesse Block and Eva Sully didn't do well again until Jesse dropped out of show business in the 1950s —and became a stockbroker.

Nobody ever forgot the lesson they learned though. I think the motto a lot of people lived by after the crash was, a penny earned is . . . mine. I really don't think any of my friends were cheap—though in some cases "cheap" would be considered a compliment. Eddie Cantor, for example, was not cheap. Eddie was . . . frugal. He was definitely frugal. We were at Hillcrest one afternoon, for example, not too long after Eddie had bought a house in Beverly Hills. That house didn't have a swimming pool, and somebody suggested Eddie put one in. Cantor admitted that he didn't want to do it because it was too expensive. "Eddie," I said, "what are you going to do with all your money? You can't take it with you, you know."

"Don't tell him that, Natty," Jessel interrupted. "If Cantor ever finds out he can't take it with him, he'll send it on ahead."

People in show business used to tell this story about Cantor and Jolson. During the Depression an out-of-work vaudeville comedian named Mel Klee, he used to bill himself "The Prince of Wails," and did the same act in small-time that Al Herman did in big-time, went up to Eddie and told him he was really in a jam. He owed $600 back rent to the hotel and the manager was going to throw his wife and kids out into the street. "Oh, that's a shame," Eddie told him, and he meant it too, "A talented guy like you to be in such a sad situation. I just loved your act, and I'd love to help you out, but I just put all my cash in the bank. I do wish you the very best though, and if I can ever help you again, please let me know."

An hour later Klee walked into Lindy's and saw Jolson, and told him exactly the same story. "Well, for crying out loud," Jolson said, "what am I supposed to do about that? You never should have been in show business in the first place. You had a terrible act. Why don't you just go out and get a real job?" Then Jolson took out his wallet and handed Klee $600. "Here," he told him, "take this, but don't ever ask me again."

A little while after that Klee ran into a friend of his. "I just saw Cantor and Jolson," he said, "and I told both of them I was in a bad jam."

"So who helped you out?"

"Never mind that," Klee said. "Cantor told me I had a great act."

Jolie was tough to figure out when money was involved. Sometimes he could be so generous— when he visited the St. Mary's Home in Baltimore where he'd spent some time growing up, he handed the priest $1,000 cash, but other times he could be so . . . frugal. "I got a little money," he liked to say, "but I'm a nice fella." One season he had a hit radio show that was being written for him by Charlie Issacs and Manny Mannheim. It was traditional at Christmas for the star of the show to give gifts to each member of the staff. Because Jolie's show was a big success, Charlie and Manny sort of assumed they were going to get pretty nice gifts. Maybe a car, Charlie figured, that's what he had given Martha Raye. A house, Manny said, he can afford it. So, two days before Christmas, one of Jolie's assistants came into their office and told them, "Boys, when you get out into the parking lot, there's a gift waiting for you."

A car, Charlie thought, I knew it. The two of them casually raced outside. And right in the middle of the lot was a big station wagon—with the entire crew lined up behind it, each of them being given a smoked turkey for Christmas.

Groucho was also tough to understand sometimes. When he drove his car to a restaurant he'd park on the street several blocks away so he wouldn't have to pay for parking, and he would never check his hat or coat. Some people believed that the only reason he starting wearing a beret was because he could fold it up and keep it in his pocket. "I just resent having to buy back my hat or my car from a restaurant," he once explained, "after I've paid those fancy prices for eating there." I don't know, maybe he regretted that after his car was stolen—with his topcoat in it.

On the other hand, Groucho would often pick up checks, and paid his ex-wives a lot more than he had to.

Fred Allen was just as hard to figure out as Jolie and Groucho. Once Fred met a friend on the street and invited him up to his hotel room for a drink —then served him a glass of water. Technically, I guess, Fred was correct. A glass of water does qualify as a drink. But when was the last time you heard somebody walk up to a bar and order "water and water," or "water on the rocks"? And Fred would never spend money on a taxi. Even if it was raining, he'd just put on his rubber boots, open his umbrella and walk. Who knows, maybe he was just collecting water for his drink.

One year, just after he'd finished doing his radio shows for the season, a producer offered him

$10,000 a week, four weeks guaranteed, to do a stage show. Fred turned him down. The producer raised the offer. Fred turned him down again. Finally somebody asked him how he could turn down a sweet deal like that. "I can't do it," Fred explained. "I've already given a deposit on a summer house in Maine and it's not refundable."

But Fred could also be very generous. Not only would he overpay for newspapers, he was the only person I ever knew who paid panhandlers in advance. That's true. Nobody gave the panhandlers who waited outside the Broadway theaters and studios more of his own money than Fred Allen. Fred not only gave them money, he became friends with them. Once, I remember, he came out after his show and one of the regulars was missing. Fred was concerned and asked about him. Another one of the regulars explained it was his birthday, and he'd taken the night off. So Fred reached into his pocket and took out a big bill. "Give this to him, would you? Tell him I'm going on vacation tomorrow so I won't be seeing him for a few weeks."

Maybe the cheap . . . the most frugal . . . nah, cheap is right, the cheapest person I've ever known was Maurice Chevalier. He wouldn't even give you the time of day. He wouldn't give you his best regards. One summer, Gracie and me, and Jesse Block and Eva Sully sailed with him to Europe on the *Ile de France*. We'd meet in the bar every night, and either Jesse or I always picked up the check. Not once during the week did Chevalier offer to pay. When we got to France, though, he invited us to his house. It was a nice place. Filled with real French furniture. And on every table he had an inexpensive ceramic ashtray that looked like the trademark straw hat he always wore on the stage. These ashtrays were cute, and Eva asked him if she could have one as a souvenir. Not only did Chevalier say no, he also had the *gall* to tell her where she could buy one for a quarter.

That's actually a pretty smart pun for me. I must be doing my Fred Allen.

Jack Benny made a fortune by being cheap. He was so cheap, for example, that when Mary asked for diamonds for her birthday he bought her two of them—the eight and the Queen. He was so cheap that when he worked in a nightclub he'd insist Mary stand up and take a bow, explaining, "Now I can deduct the dress. If you'd wave your hand I could deduct the ring too." And he was so cheap that he once gave Gracie a coupon for a year's subscription to a magazine as a gift—and all she had to do was fill it out and send it in with a check.

That Jack Benny was one of the greatest characters ever created. And it proved what a good actor he was, because one thing he wasn't in real life was cheap. Mary made sure of that. What's the word for the opposite of cheap? Don't tell me. Oh, I know, Jessel.

The truth is that Mary provided Jack with an awful lot; a lot of bills for clothes, a lot of bills for furs, a lot of bills for jewelry. . . . The real

truth is that Jack did buy Mary a lot of jewelry
—he knew he bought it for her because when she
showed it to him she always said, "Look what you
bought me today." Maybe the most expensive
piece of jewelry she had was a large diamond ring
that she wore all the time. My son Ronnie used
to warn her about that. "Aunt Mary," he told her,
"you shouldn't wear that ring in public, because
somebody's going to hit you over the head and
take it." And Ronnie knew what he was talking
about because one day Mary was held up in her
suite in the Pierre Hotel and her jewels were
stolen. Jack was on an airplane when it happened,
but as soon as he heard about it he tried to get
Mary on the phone. She wasn't in the suite, so he
kept calling and calling. Finally she answered.
"I've been worried about you," he said, "where've
you been?"

She told him that she had been at Harry Winston's jewelry store looking at diamond rings.

Jack couldn't believe it. "You were robbed four
hours ago and you're already looking at another
diamond?"

"I have to, doll," she said. "It's like when you
fall off a horse, if you don't get right back on, you
might never do it again."

Mary really didn't have any concept of money.
Once, for example, she decided she was going to
have a garage sale. She put all her old dresses on
racks and invited the secretaries at CBS, the
women who worked in Dr. Kennamer's office and
some of the girls from Flo Haley's beauty salon,

then marked her dresses down as low as $2,000 apiece!

Of course, Jack didn't have any concept of money either. I think that as far as he was concerned, the most important thing his money did for him was keep Mary happy. I remember when he showed up at the club after signing a $2,000,000 deal with CBS. He was as excited as I've ever seen him. "Congratulations, Jack," I said, "you really look excited."

"I am, Natty," he said. "You know what I just found out? Did you know that if you drive up Wilshire Boulevard at exactly twenty-eight miles an hour you miss every red light?"

"What's the matter with you, Jack?" I asked him. "I'm talking about the contract with CBS. Aren't you excited about that?"

"Of course I am," he said. "If it wasn't for that I never would have driven up Wilshire Boulevard."

Jack was really a very generous man. He was the kind of person who would buy tickets to a charity appearance he was making and give them away. One night, I remember, he had dinner at Cantor's house and Eddie started telling him about Israeli Bonds. Jack made out a check right there for $25,000. The next day though, he came into the club and immediately started warning people not to accept an invitation for dinner at Cantor's house because, "He serves the most expensive meal in town."

Because of the character Jack created, he was

forced to overtip. He'd give a cabdriver five dollars for a one dollar ride. We were leaving Earl Carroll's nightclub one evening and Jack tipped the hatcheck girl a buck, a big tip in those days—she handed it right back to him, telling him, "Please, Mr. Benny, let me keep my illusions."

As generous as Jack could be though, for some reason he hated to pay cash for anything. If he could pay for a meal or a gift with a credit card or personal check, he'd always pick up the bill; but if he had to pay cash he wouldn't do it. I never knew why. But for years he carried a $100 bill in his money clip, and if the check totalled something like $14.75, he'd take out his $100 bill and ask, "Does anybody have change for this?" Nobody ever did, of course, then somebody else would pick up the check. That $100 bill appeared more regularly than Old Faithful. I think it might have been the most valuable $100 bill they ever made —I know it saved Jack a small fortune. One night, just before going onstage, he handed his money clip with the $100 bill on top to Irving Fein to hold. Irving and Hilly Marks had been seeing that same $100 bill for too many years. So before Irving gave it back to Jack they wrote an appropriate message on it: "Thanks for entertaining the troops. Sincerely, Abraham Lincoln."

Now, Jessel was really a generous man. In fact, we all used to say that as long as any one of us had a dollar in his pocket, Jessel would be a generous man. For a man who later in his life became so closely associated with conservative causes, when it came to money I think Georgie must have had a little touch of communism in his heart—because he certainly believed in the redistribution of other people's wealth.

Georgie was someone who always believed in helping the little man. And the little woman. And the big woman. The Broadway panhandlers knew he was an easy mark. When he was doing a show with Fanny Brice on West 44th Street, for example, they'd wait outside the stage door every night and he'd give each of them a buck. One night, after handing out the money, he told the regulars, "The show's moving to Forty-ninth Street tomorrow, so come there after the show." That was Georgie, making appointments with panhandlers to give his money away. Well, to give somebody's money away.

And Durante? Durante was the only man I ever knew who really threw money away. Durante would always share whatever he had with whoever was around. In the 1950s he opened The Durante Music Publishing Company just to make sure his friends had a steady income. This was the kind of company that had Vice-Presidents only Fred Allen could make up titles for. Vice-President in Charge of Thinking Up Good Song Titles. Vice-President in Charge of Going For Coffee. I think the only note any of these Vice-Presidents ever wrote was an I.O.U. But Jimmy didn't care, this was his way of making sure his pals were working in show business.

Years earlier though, when Jimmy's Club Durant was the most popular speakeasy in New York, Jimmy and his partner, Lou Clayton, decided to check the cash register one morning. The receipts from the night before came to something like $7,000, but there was just over $6,000 in the till. When Lou asked the bartender where the rest of the money was, the bartender told him, "This is an old cash register and it jumps a lot."

Club Durant was one flight up. "Open the window, Lou," Durante said. Then he picked up the old cash register and carried it over to the window.

"Hold it, Jimmy," Clayton said, grabbing as much money out of the register as he could.

Jimmy looked out the window to make sure nobody was there, then heaved the register onto the sidewalk. "I'll tell you something, Lou," he said, with a satisfied look on his face, "that damned register ain't never gonna jump no more."

8

What did we know about money? Look, when you grow up with nothing, like I did, and Jolson did, and Jessel did, and Cantor did, and the Marx Brothers and Berle and so many other people, you learn what the important things in life really are. You learn how important love is, and your family, and your friends, and a good wool blanket. And you learn very early in life that there are some things all the money in the world can't buy—like poverty.

We were comedians, not businessmen. And most of the time, when we got involved in business, we proved it. As far as dealing with money, most of us were like Ed Wynn, who admitted after settling a tax lien with the government for more than $500,000, "When it comes to money my stage billing reads: I'M THE PERFECT FOOL."

I think the W.C. Fields Investment Plan was probably pretty typical of the way we dealt with money. Fields had lost a lot of money when the banks closed, so to make sure that never happened to him again, he carefully deposited small amounts of money in banks all over the country under an assumed name. That way, he figured, nobody could ever find it. And he was absolutely right, after he died, nobody did.

The two people who made really smart investments were Bob Hope and Jack Haley. Both of them could look at an empty lot and see the future. I looked at the same lot and saw piles of dirt and old tires. So both of them bought land and became very rich men, and I didn't. I admit it, I just didn't understand real estate; I figured, even if I bought land, where was I going to keep it?

I had some opportunities. In the late 1930s, for example, somebody offered me and Jack and Harpo the chance to buy land for $350 an acre. We got pretty excited about it. So we called the man who managed our business affairs and told him about it. I think he told us we shouldn't buy the land because it had too much water on it. He made it sound like a Florida swamp. Today that land is called Lakewood, California. Look, it wasn't our business manager's fault, we were dumb enough to listen to him.

Jack and I did invest in a few things together. We bought a ranch once. I guess that's jus' the ole country-western boy in me comin' out. At that time everybody was investing in ranches, so Jack and I bought a piece of property with Leonard Firestone, of the tire and rubber company. I figured if anybody knew about land, it had to be him, because every time I saw an empty lot, some of his tires were on it.

Our spread was way out yonder by the town of Indio. Indio weren't much more'n a watering hole.

273

My pardner, Buck Benny, and I rode out a fur piece one day to lay eyes on the place. When we got there, why ole Buck, he jus' looked to his right and said, "I don't see anything but sand."

"Well, pardner," I said, "look on the other side of the road."

He did. There wasn't anything there except sand either. That was my big joke. Other people had cattle ranches and sheep ranches, a few people had horse farms; Jack, Leonard and I had a grapefruit ranch. 'Course, there were a lot of advantages to a grapefruit ranch. Grapefruits don't have to be milked every day. They don't have to be branded. They never have to be sheared. They don't eat anything at all, and, maybe best of all, we never had to worry about grapefruit rustlers. On the other hand, we never did have the satisfaction of riding out to the north forty and seeing our herd of prize grapefruits grazing in the setting sun. Actually, that ranch turned out to be a pretty good deal—we made a little money and got all the grapefruits we could eat. People who owned horse farms could never make that claim.

The best investment I ever made was joining Hillcrest. My original membership cost $300, then they discovered oil on the property. I think Hillcrest was the only country club in the world that members got paid for belonging to. Of course, with my luck, if I had intentionally invested in an oil business, they probably would have discovered a pinochle table.

Jack did invest in the oil business and he lost a

lot of money. He put more than $300,000 in the Home-Stake Production Company, along with people like the Chairman of the First National City Bank, the best financial writer in the country, the head of PepsiCo, Andy Williams and Alan Alda. The whole thing turned out to be a fraud. That had to be some smart operator to cheat Jack Benny out of money. People invested more than $130,000,000 in the company, and when Home-Stake declared bankruptcy and its president was asked how much oil they had actually discovered, he said, "That's relative."

Comedians may not make good businessmen, but sometimes businessmen can be pretty funny. I don't think Jack laughed at that line.

Jack actually did make some pretty good business decisions. He had a lot of stock in MCA, he invested in cattle, he even owned a shopping center. Most of us formed our own television production companies that owned and produced our shows and several others. Jack's company was called Amusement Enterprises. I formed Mc-Cadden Productions for a very important reason —my business manager told me to do it. What did I know about owning a business? If the company stole seltzer bottles and melted down their lead tops, then I could have really contributed. But balancing books? That's the only time I regretted not keeping in touch with Captain Betts' seal.

In 1948 Jack sold his company to CBS for $2,400,000. As soon as I heard about the sale I wanted to change the name of my company. I wanted to call it something like "Jack Benny's Other Company." Of course, CBS wasn't really interested in his company, they were buying his radio and television programs. I remember that Jack and the IRS had a big fight over his profits. They both wanted them. I mean, that was really an unfair fight, the entire government of the United States of America against Jack—the government had no chance. Eventually the courts ruled in Jack's favor, and that turned out to be a landmark case for people in show business who wanted to profit from their own companies.

Ed Wynn wasn't satisfied with his own company, he tried to form his own radio network. In 1933, he spent more than $250,000 to start the Amalgamated Broadcasting System, which was a chain of thirty-three independent stations. The biggest station in the chain was New York's WNEW, which took its call letters from Ed Wynn's name. So, for a little while at least, the three biggest broadcasting networks in America were NBC, CBS and Ed Wynn's—and that's the way it stayed for the entire three weeks Ed's network was in business.

Harpo had some decent investments, some stock, a ranch, a J.C. Penney store and some land in Palm Springs. But Zeppo was the best businessman of all the Marx Brothers. He quit the act after making five pictures and started several very successful companies. He made millions of dollars from a defense plant he owned, he invented several pretty good products—including a wristwatch that sounded an alarm to warn about an irregular pulse beat—and he teamed with Gummo to open a talent agency. He represented his brothers, Barbara Stanwyck, Fred MacMurray, he really had a first-class list. At one time he was trying to convince Norman Krasna, a great writer-producer-director, to leave the William Morris Agency and sign with him. They'd had lunch at the Brown Derby and, as they left, some autograph-seeker outside started bothering Krasna. I don't know exactly what happened, but this guy wouldn't leave Krasna alone. Finally, Zeppo had had enough, he knocked the guy down with one punch. Then he turned to Krasna and asked, "Tell me, Norman, would the Morris office give you that kind of service?"

People say that you can't buy happiness. Well, we had to be convinced. Even if we didn't know how to invest money, we learned how to spend it. When it came to spending, we were very talented people. And maybe we learned that money really couldn't buy happiness—but we found out that it could make a substantial down payment.

We spent our money on the things we never had, which was everything except the lead tops of seltzer bottles. Houses and cars and clothes and jewelry and even vacations. Vacations. Most of us had never had a real vacation in our life. In vaudeville, for example, a vacation was what we called it when we couldn't get a booking. "How you doing?" "I'm on vacation." "Sorry." Besides, even if we had had a little time and the money, where could we have gone that we hadn't been? We played every city in the country. Once you've worked the Grand Canyon Palace and the La Brea Tar Pits Orpheum there just aren't many places that you haven't seen. But after we'd made it in radio we had our summers off and a lot of money. For the first time we could just sit by the pool and relax; but the travel bug is like one of Gracie's relatives—they're both impossible to get rid of. So when we finally had the luxury of staying home, we traveled.

If I have any regrets at all about those days it's that the airlines didn't have frequent-flyer programs. Of course, in the days I'm talking about, the airlines barely had airplanes. But if they had given travel bonuses Gracie and I would have done very well, because we always seemed to be going somewhere.

Believe me, if you gave me a map and asked me to find something, I couldn't find the map. I don't know geography, I know theaters. But we always seemed to be going somewhere over the water, and I knew we weren't going to Lakeland. We went to Europe, Hawaii, New York, but maybe our most memorable trip was the summer vacation Gracie and I took with Winnie Pearl in 1934.

I'd like to show you some slides from our summer vacation, but unfortunately they hadn't invented the slide camera yet. So instead of slides I'd like to read highlights from Gracie's diary of that trip. Naturally, Gracie was very tough to please. We sailed to Italy on the SS *Rex*, "The most beautiful boat," she wrote in her diary. In Naples we stayed at the Excelsior Hotel, "A beautiful hotel overlooking the Bay of Naples. . . . We could also see Vesuvius foaming and fuming." Pompeii, she wrote, was "another dream come true. We saw . . . a laundry shop that the inscription said was donated by a Princess. . . ." Then we went to the Amalfi coast, "The Amalfi Drive is the most beautiful drive in the world." We stayed at the Victoria Hotel in Sorrento, "One of the prettiest hotels I've ever seen." The Excelsior Hotel in Rome, "Looked and felt like heaven. Then we went to St. Peters, the most beautiful church in the world." Outside of Rome we went to a roadhouse named "Grotto of the Pigeons," that meant real pigeons, by the way, not American tourists, and it had "The most beautiful lighting effects." One night we went dancing at "Chez-Vos," "The most beautiful spot in the world." From Italy we went to Budapest, Hungary, which was "The loveliest city. Directly opposite our hotel is the gorgeous Franz Joseph Palace, one of the most beautiful palaces in Europe. . . ."

See, that was the problem with Gracie, she was just never satisfied.

We went to all the museums and the palaces, we had an audience with the Pope, but you know what fascinated Gracie the most? "The Church of the Cappucini Monks is most interesting due to the fact the monks once they go in can never leave so they must be buried there. When their graves

279

became overcrowded their bodies had to be dug up and room made for later monks' bodies. Not knowing what to do with the bones they decorated the walls and ceilings and made the most unique designs with skulls, arms, legs, etc. . . ."

Fortunately, Harold Grieve decorated our house. I could tell you it cost me an arm and a leg, but even I wouldn't use a bad joke like that.

The only place we went on this trip that we didn't like was Moscow, Russia. We spent two weeks there in three days. It was such a depressing place. The first thing the guide supplied by the government told us was that we weren't allowed to tip, because "The capitalistic practice of tipping is degrading." So we didn't tip, and we got exactly the kind of service we paid for. As it turned out, the problem was that we were there at the wrong time of year. Anytime. There was nothing to do there except look at other tourists looking for something to do there. So we went home early.

Harpo also went to Russia during this period. President Roosevelt had just recognized Communist Russia—I mean, what'd he think it was, Switzerland?—and Alexander Woollcott decided that it was appropriate that a Marx be the first American to perform there. I guess the Lennon Sisters were booked. So a trip was arranged for him.

He almost didn't get there. He brought his old vaudeville trunk with him, and when he got to the Russian border the guards searched the trunk. His clothes were on top, but when they looked under his clothes they found his props—hundreds of knives, two revolvers, bottles marked "poison," a can marked "gasoline," one automobile horn, and all his disguises—wigs, mustaches, beards and makeup. It was just exactly the sort of equipment you need to either put on a show or stage a revolution. The border guards didn't believe Harpo when he told them he was a comedian—maybe they'd heard about performers killing an audience, but they knew it didn't mean one person at a time. So Harpo was detained.

The thought of these Russian border guards trying to interrogate Harpo sounds like a scene from a Marx Brothers film, *A Night at the Torture Chamber*. Can you just imagine Harpo sitting in a wooden chair, smiling, while a Russian soldier sneered at him, "Oh, so you won't talk, huh?"

Eventually Harpo was permitted to go into Russia. As long as he didn't tip. Then he had a lot of trouble getting official permission to put on his pantomime show in Moscow. At that time the most popular show in town was *The 14th Division Goes to Heaven*, a light comedy about dead soldiers from the 14th Division debating the Holy Trinity, so it's not hard to figure out why they had trouble appreciating Harpo's act. They wanted to know the political meaning of dropping dozens of knives out of his sleeve. Harpo explained it to them, "If something gets a laugh," he said, "you do it again. That's all the meaning you need."

Cantor also had problems with soldiers, but his took place in Rome. While vacationing in Italy in the mid-1930s, Cantor was supposed to meet Premier Mussolini at his palace, but he left his letter of appointment in his hotel room. So when he got to the palace Mussolini's guards poked him with their bayonets and wouldn't let him pass. To prove who he was, Cantor did his act for the soldiers. "I got right down on the floor," he told me, "and I rolled my eyes at them, and I went through all my tricks, but they still wouldn't believe I was a comedian."

I want you to know what a loyal friend I am. That is probably the single greatest setup I've ever heard. Cantor's been dead for more than twenty-five years, and I'm still not going to touch it. I'm not going to tell you what to do, though.

Eddie finally did get to meet Mussolini. During their meeting, he said, they talked about the really important things in the world. "He's a great man," Eddie explained. "He's seen all my pictures."

Jimmy Durante also went to Italy on his vacation. He said that one of the most thrilling moments of his life was visiting his relatives' homeland in Sorrento. I knew just how he felt the first time I'd played the Essex Street Theatre. Jimmy said he received the greatest reception he'd ever gotten when he arrived in Sorrento. "Dey had my name all over the houses. This one 'Durante,' that one 'Durante.' It was only later that I found out that in Italian, Durante means 'For Rent.' Ain't that somethin. All these years I been for rent, you'd think somebody woulda made me an offer."

Coming home from Italy, Jimmy sailed on the same boat as the Queen of Spain. "So we gets innerduced and I takes off my hat, and I bows low to show I got manners and I say, 'It's a pleasure to meet ya, Queen.' And she don't say a thing, she just busted out laughing in my face, which naturally I don't mind, seein' as that's what I get paid for." I'll say one thing for Jimmy, at least he never complained that people in Europe spoke funny.

Jack Benny might have traveled more than anybody except Bob Hope. Now, even though Jack spent a lot of time in Europe, the only language he could speak or understand was English. The main problem with that was that he could never order his favorite breakfast, cornflakes with milk. Once, though, he was visiting Norman Krasna, who was living in Switzerland. Norman's staff spoke only Swiss, so Jack complained that he still wouldn't be able to order cornflakes with milk. "Don't worry about that," Norman told him. "Tomorrow morning when you wake up, just pick up the telephone and say, 'Bonjour.' The girl will bring you your cornflakes with milk."

So the next morning when Jack woke up, he picked up the phone and said, "Bonjour," and a few minutes later a girl showed up carrying cornflakes with milk. Well, Jack thought that was just terrific. "Don't you see what that means," he told Norman. "From now on, wherever I am in

Europe, I know how to order cornflakes with milk. All I have to do is pick up the phone and say, 'Bonjour.' "

Mary was no better at languages than Jack was. During one of the few trips they took together, they were in Paris on the Champs-Elysées when they saw a Frenchwoman scolding her small dog. "Isn't that amazing," Mary told Jack, "that little dog actually understands French."

Jack loved to tell that story, and whenever he did, he'd add, "And she even said it without any writers around."

Jack's favorite country, outside of the United States, was England. He played the London Palladium many times. "One of the things that surprises me about your country," he told a London audience in 1952, when England was still suffering from postwar shortages, "is that everywhere I go I see people standing in lines. Or queues, as you call them. Well, this morning I was standing on a corner waiting for the light to change and I noticed there was a man standing behind me. Naturally, that made me a little nervous, so I moved to the next corner. And this fellow came right along and stood behind me again. So I moved one more time—and he followed me again. Finally, I turned around and said to him, 'What's the idea?' 'Oh,' he said to me, 'I don't know what you're queuing up for, but whatever it is, being second ain't bad.' "

One of the greatest shows Jack and I ever did together was a command performance at the Palladium in the early 1960s. Quite a few times, after Gracie had retired, Jack would put on a wig and a dress . . . and stockings . . . and high heels . . . and he shaved his legs . . . hmmm, maybe he liked being Charley's Aunt more than I figured. Anyway, he'd dress up as a woman and play Gracie's part and we'd do a typical Burns and Allen routine. Jack was just great as Gracie, although his voice was a little higher than hers. I'll tell you something interesting—one of the first times we did that bit was at a charity dinner. The president of Columbia Pictures, Harry Cohn, had the studio costume department dress up Jack. They gave him the sleek, black-sequined suit that Rita Hayworth had worn in the movie *Gilda*. It all worked out great. The act was wonderful and, as long as Jack lived, that was his favorite outfit.

I think people loved Jack because he seemed to be such a sweet, unaffected man. And that's true, that's exactly what he was. I'll tell you what Jack's idea of a great vacation was: even though he was invited to go all over the world by royalty and presidents and prime ministers and lawyers, the thing he liked to do most on vacation was get into his car with a friend and go for a long drive. He just wanted to get as far away from telephones and show business as he possibly could. So almost every summer he'd get into his Rolls-Royce with a friend and drive across the country, stopping in little towns, eating in greasy spoons, maybe playing a round of golf at the local golf course. He had a great time, he'd just casually stroll into some diner in a small town in Mississippi or Texas and sit down at the counter. People would notice him, but nobody could believe he was really Jack Benny. When they finally got up the nerve to approach him, they'd get very nervous and say things like, "Jack Benny, you're my favorite fan," or "Didn't you use to be Jack Benny?" Finally the counterman would ask him what he wanted, and with real pleasure Jack would look at him and say, "Just give me the usual."

The person who took the most trips with Jack was his good friend Frank Remley. One summer, for example, they planned to take Route 66 through the south to New York, then go north through Canada for the return trip. But when Jack picked up Frank, Frank suggested they switch it around and take the northern route to New York, then return on Route 66. Jack thought about it for a minute then asked, "Which way is the car facing, Frank?"

"North," Remley told him.

"That settles it then. Let's go through Canada, because it would be a waste of time to turn the car around."

Maybe the greatest story I ever heard about Jack's trips took place at the beginning of a drive from Los Angeles to New York he was making with Jesse Block and the great songwriter Johnny Green. Jack was going to drive, so Jesse turned to Johnny and asked him where he was staying in New York. "At the Astor," Green told him.

"Okay," Jesse told him, "that's on Forty-fourth

Street. I stay at the Essex House on Fifty-ninth Street. So you'd better sit in the middle because I get out first."

More than anywhere else though, the one place that Jack loved to go for a short vacation was into the hospital. Other people had snapshots of their vacation, Jack had X rays. He'd just lie in bed and watch television. While he was there he'd have a complete physical and they'd take all kinds of tests, but for him the real purpose of his stay there was just to relax completely. I don't remember ever going to visit him there; I mean, how could I, you never bother somebody while he's on vacation.

People have asked me how Jack and I were able to remain such close friends for more than fifty years without ever having a real argument. It wasn't that hard. We both loved show business and the people who were in it, neither one of us had terrible tempers and, most importantly, we never played cards together.

Almost all of us loved to gamble. Cards, the racetrack, professional sports; it didn't matter. It wasn't so much the winning and losing, it was just the winning. I think that maybe when you start with nothing, you feel like you have nothing to lose. I know psychologists can explain why most of us liked to gamble so much. I used to know the exact reason—I knew it because I used to play cards with a psychologist at the club and everytime he'd lose he'd tell me why I liked winning so much. And when he finished explaining it to me, I explained it to him, "I just like the money."

The biggest gambler of all was Chico. Chico was once asked how much money he'd lost gambling. "Ask Harpo," he said. "As much money as he has, that's how much money I've lost."

I tried to talk to him about it once. "Cheek," I said, "it isn't good the way you gamble on everything. It's gonna break you eventually."

I think he understood; in fact, he wanted to bet me $1,000 he could stop gambling anytime he wanted to.

Chico gambled on everything. "The first crap game I ever played in I lost forty-seven thousand dollars in one night," he said one day, "but I learned as I went along. In time I was able to lose much more than that."

Once he was playing a hotel in Las Vegas for $25,000 a week. The first night he was there he lost $27,000 in the hotel casino. The owner of the place had him barred from the casino for his own good—so the next night he went across the street and lost $13,000 at a competing place. "See," he told the owner of the first hotel, "I got even with you."

Groucho and Harpo were worried about him, so they talked him into letting them hold part of his income. They put it in the bank, and when the bank account reached $100,000 Chico decided he wanted it back. When Groucho and Harpo refused, he sued them to get it. They finally had to give it to him, and as soon as he got it he lost it gambling. "If he made ten thousand dollars a day, he'd spend ten thousand dollars a day," Groucho used to complain. "I don't mind that. What I do mind is that he still sleeps better than I do."

Chico would bet on almost anything, but his real love was cards. He was such an expert card-player that Charles Goren even wrote about him in his classic book on bridge. But winning didn't matter to Chico as much as the excitement of a good game. So sometimes, to make the game more interesting, he'd do things that nobody could explain. If he was playing against somebody he knew he could beat, he'd play with two of his cards exposed to even up the game. Or when he was playing poker and was dealt three of a kind, he'd throw one of them away and try to make a more difficult hand. But that was Chico. I was at the club one day and he was just desperate for a gin game. "Give me a game," he asked, "we'll play for two cents a point." I told him I didn't want to play cards. "All right, one cent," he said. I told him I really didn't want to play cards. He shook his head, "Okay, you can start with fifty points on each hand and you can blitz me but I can't blitz you."

"Chico," I said, "I don't want to play cards."

He threw up his hands in frustration. "Have it your way. We'll play for nothing."

Chico made a lot of money in his lifetime, but he was almost always broke. He didn't care, though, he was a happy man. "I came into the world even," he used to say. "All I want to do is go out even. If they'll just put a good two-iron, a golf bag, a pack of gin cards and a beautiful blonde in my coffin, they can send it anywhere they want."

Maybe the only person I've known who gambled as much as Chico was Matthau. He just loved the action. When we were making *Sunshine Boys*, for example, he came over to me and said, "George, I can't get hold of my bookmaker, who do you like in the basketball game? Syracuse or St. John's?"

Basketball game? What do I know about basketball? I remember telling Dr. James Naismith, when he was inventing the game, that he should put the peach baskets higher, but he wouldn't listen to me. Other than that though, I didn't know anything about the game. So that's what I told Walter.

"C'mon, George, make a bet, please. You like Syracuse or St. John's?" He just couldn't enjoy the game unless he had a bet down.

I'd worked in Syracuse dozens of times. "All right, I'll bet on Syracuse."

Walter frowned. "Okay, I'll take the bet. You got Syracuse for five bucks, even money." Then he went off to watch the game. Walter doesn't watch a basketball game like other people. He turns off the sound and listens to classical music. He told me that Mozart's early symphonies go particularly well with basketball because they have a lot of allegro and practically no adagios. I agreed with him.

After we'd made the bet Walter would come over every half hour to tell me, "Your team is winning" or losing, or whatever. Finally he handed me a five-dollar bill. "Here," he said, "so you beat me. I'll get you next time."

"Walter," I told him, "I don't want your money."

"No, go ahead and take it. We made a legitimate bet. You beat me, that's all."

"Well, all right, if you insist," I said, and then, as long as I was taking it, I asked, "Are you sure we only bet five dollars?"

Walter knows he has a problem with gambling though. He told me about the night he was at dinner with Jack Nicholson and Johnny Carson and Angie Dickinson and Henry Kissinger and several other people and for more than an hour they talked about making certain drugs legal. Walter was very surprised when Kissinger agreed that it was a good idea, so he asked him, "Then how about legalizing gambling, Henry? How do you feel about that?"

"Oh," Kissinger said, "I think gambling should be legalized too. I don't think gambling hurts anyone physically."

"Henry," Walter said, shaking his head, "you really think it doesn't?"

Kissinger opened his eyes in surprise. "It does?"

Actually, Walter has used his gambling for at

least one good purpose. His mother was a very independent woman and she didn't want to take any money from him, so when he went to visit her in Florida he'd take her to the dog track. He'd bet on five or six dogs in every race, putting one ticket in each of his pockets and memorizing which ticket was in which pocket. When the race was over, he'd reach into the right pocket, take out the winning ticket and hand it to his mother. "Here," he'd say, "you won again." She'd go cash the ticket and keep the money. His scheme worked out very well, it only cost him maybe $125,000 to give her $75,000. And then one day she took him aside and said, "You know, Walter, you're pretty good at picking dogs. If the acting thing doesn't work out, you maybe could make a living at it."

Most of us did our betting at the horse track. When Del Mar was being built we all bought shares in the track and had box seats there. Gracie loved to go to the races and would do anything to get to cash a winning ticket. Sometimes she'd bet like Walter, risking $2 on every horse in the race. Jessel spent so much time at Del Mar that he became known as the Honorary Mayor of the track. Jolson was at the track almost every day when he wasn't working, and he was a big bettor. He'd bet thousands of dollars on a race. Jolson knew horses too, and at one time he even owned several horses. Fanny Brice loved the horses. She loved to bet so much, in fact, that when they showed films on television of races that had already been run, she'd bet on them with her friends. The day after Fanny had a serious heart attack, Cantor walked into her hospital room and found her lying in an oxygen tent—reading the racing form.

Jack Benny actually owned a thoroughbred racehorse, although Jack wasn't much of a horse-player. The horse's name was, what else, Buck, and he had great bloodlines. His father was Upset, the only horse to beat Man o' War, and his mother was a good stakes horse named Helen T. But Buck never won a race. He was terrible. And Jack just couldn't understand it. "How can he not win with those parents?"

"Well," I suggested, "maybe he was adopted."

One afternoon Jack and Cantor took Jack's father, Meyer Kubelsky, to the track with them. Cantor always said that that was the day he found out where Jack's character had come from. Jack and Eddie would bet a few dollars on every race, but Jack's father would study the racing form, then make big bets—in his mind. He wouldn't put up any money. And before every race, Jack would ask his father which horse he was betting on, and his father would tell him, then explain why he was making that bet. Finally, just before the final race on the card, Jack asked his father, "Who are you betting on?"

Meyer shook his head. "I'm betting nothing is what I'm betting. I'm out too much already."

Apparently Jack's character had great blood-lines too.

But the real horseplayer was Durante. Jimmy used to say, "Everything I knows about in the world I learnt in the racing form." When Durante was young he'd spend hours every day handicapping races at tracks all across the country. Some days he'd bet as many as twenty different races at eight different tracks. Now, he had no problem picking the horses, but he played so many different parlays that sometimes he had trouble figuring out if he'd won or lost for the day. And if he hadn't had a winner in a few races, he'd use the Gracie System, betting several horses in the same race. Once he was at Del Mar with his wife, Margie, and two horses had led the race from the start. But on the last turn several horses started gaining ground and Jimmy jumped up and started cheering. "Which one are we rooting for, Jimmy?" Margie asked.

"It don't matter," he said, "I got that whole bunch back there."

I think it was Cantor who once asked Jimmy why he would bet on four horses in the same race. "Well, I look at all the figures," Jimmy explained, "and the way it looks to me, the race is gonna come out a tie. So I know that one a them horses is gonna make me a happy man."

But one beautiful afternoon at Del Mar Jimmy finally had the kind of luck every horseplayer dreams about. He was there with Cantor and they'd lost the first two races. Then Eddie ran into a horse owner he knew from Louisville, Kentucky, who gave them a good tip. Cantor, feeling very confident, decided to risk ten dollars. "Nah, Eddie," Jimmy told him. "On this kind of an FBI inside, I'll bet fifty bucks." The horse won, paying more than twenty dollars. That was just the beginning. Jimmy and Eddie didn't lose another race. It didn't matter which horse they bet, the favorite, a long shot, the horse won. On that afternoon, they were touched by magic. It's a good thing Jessel wasn't there, or they would have been touched by him too. Suddenly though, after they'd cashed five straight winning tickets, Jimmy stopped, looked at Eddie and said very seriously, "Eddie, you gotta promise me one thing. No matter what happens in the last two races, we go back to show business."

When Jimmy was sixty-eight years old he and Margie adopted a little girl that they named Ce Ce. And Ce Ce grew up loving horses just like her father, except that she loved riding them in horse shows. Less than a year after Jimmy died in 1980, Ce Ce competed in a big show at Madison Square Garden in New York. "My only regret," she said, "is that my father wasn't able to see me ride. He would have loved the horses."

"Yeah," Margie agreed, "and he probably would have bet on all of them too."

Jimmy was also a substantial investor in the Las Vegas casinos, but he did it the hard way—one bet at a time. Durante actually opened Las Vegas, he was the first act to play Bugsy Siegel's Flamingo Hotel when gambling was legalized there. He loved Vegas or, as he always referred to it, "The place where the money comes from." Jimmy's game there was craps, and he'd spend hours at the dice tables. Like Chico, a casino once tried to keep him away from the tables—not because he lost too much, but because as soon as people heard his familiar voice pleading with the dice, they'd stand around watching him play instead of losing their own money. So that made Durante one of the few people who could cost the casino money by losing.

Lou Clayton was an even bigger gambler at the tables than Jimmy. There was a story that he once wired Jimmy asking him for $5000 pocket money, and Jimmy sent a wire right back telling him, "NOBODY'S GOT POCKETS THAT BIG."

Jack Benny used to say, "The only way I'll ever get hurt in a casino is if there's an earthquake and a slot machine falls on my foot." He wasn't kidding either. Jack was one of the highest-paid performers in Vegas, making as much as $50,000 a week in the 1950s, but he wasn't a gambler. He liked to shoot craps and play the 25¢ and 50¢ slot machines, and set a $100-a-day limit for himself. As soon as he lost $100 he'd quit—even if it only took him ten or twelve hours to lose it.

Mary made up for Jack. Jack always used to say that Mary was a good gambler. Maybe that's true; who knows, except for the Indians maybe Custer was a good general too. Mary and Jack were really a team; as much money as he could make, she could spend. She played blackjack mostly and she wasn't very good at it. The object of that game is to get cards whose face value is 21 points or lower, but to end up closer to 21 than the dealer. I think Mary's personality may have created some problems here—I think she just wanted to have more cards than anybody else.

I've played Vegas quite a few times; I've worked there with Carol Channing, the DeCarlo Sisters, Ann-Margaret, Bobby Darin, and I loved them all. Bobby was just a twenty-two-year-old kid when I hired him to be my opening act. I think that was the first time he'd ever been to Vegas, and naturally he was overwhelmed. Sure, he was about as intimidated as Milton is shy. Bobby was the most confident kid I've ever known. One night I went into the casino after the show and I saw him standing there with Elvis Presley; they were probably the two hottest young talents in show business, and both of them were beautiful, polite, talented kids. I thought I'd make them laugh. So I went over to them and I whispered, "I see you fellows are alone. If you need any help meeting some girls, don't be embarrassed to ask me."

Presley thought I was serious. "Thank you, Mr. Burns," he said. Toughest audience I ever worked to.

Okay, so they didn't ask.

Bobby and I got very close. He was some kid. The day of Gracie's funeral he was worried about me staying alone in the house. So he stayed with me that night. Nobody asked him to, he just did it. That was very important to me.

The only game I played in Vegas was "21"— because you do it sitting down. I also played the

297

horses a little, but I would have enjoyed the horses a lot more if, instead of just running around in a circle, they would have sat down and played some cards. Card games have always been my favorite kind of gambling. Cards don't really require that much skill; if you can yell at your partner and reach your wallet, you can play cards. And if you're not very good at it, and you can reach your wallet, you can play cards with me. I still go to Hillcrest to play bridge almost every day when I'm not working. I have a little lunch and I look around and I see that big round table where we all used to sit with all those empty chairs around it. It's not so bad, now I'm definitely the funniest man at the table.

The business of making people laugh was profitable, but every one of us made a lot more money for people who really needed it than we ever made for ourselves. I kid around a lot, kidding around is my job, but I'm very serious now. We all donated a lot of money to charity, and we all appeared at countless dinners and testimonials and fund-raising events. I really don't think there is another group of friends who did as much for other people as we did. I'm proud of that.

Cantor, for example, raised more than $300,000,000 cash for charity during his career, maybe more than anyone else who ever lived. Jessel used to tell a story about a group of men living in a small village who decided one day to find the strongest man in the world. They took an orange and they had men squeeze it and squeeze it until there wasn't even a single drop of juice left. They knew that only the strongest man in the world could get another drop of juice out of that orange. People from all over the world came to this village and squeezed the orange, but no one could get a single drop of juice out of it—until Eddie Cantor arrived. Cantor picked up the orange and not only did he get two quarts of juice out of it, he also got fifty dollars cash and a pledge to buy two hundred dollars in bonds.

Cantor raised money for Jewish charities and Catholic charities and Protestant charities. He would make more than 150 appearances for charity every year. Cantor named "The March of Dimes," which raised millions of dollars to fight polio. He loved making up catchy slogans—for the Red Cross he created "From all quarters of the nation all quarters" and "Give—keep the Red Cross out of the red." Eddie was also one of the very early leaders in the fight against drunk drivers—he took W. C. Fields' car keys away.

After eighty-six years, it's tough to resist a straight line like that one.

Nah, he didn't take Fields' keys away, he wrote slogans like "If you drive drunk, you'll have a cop as a chaser" and "Have you noticed that the people who were slowest going through school drive by them the fastest" and "Drive carefully—children should be seen and not hurt." They could still use that last one.

Cantor's favorite charity was his summer camp for poor kids up at Surprise Lake, in Cold Spring,

New York. Every year Eddie raised enough money to provide a few weeks in the country for 2,000 city kids. Eddie practically singlehandedly brought poison ivy to New York City. We were talking about the camp one day and he told me how important it was to him. "I have to do it, Natty," he said. "I'd just hate to see these kids have to go through the same terrible things I went through when I was growing up."

"You mean living in the basement and never having enough to eat?"

"No, I mean rooming with Jessel."

Jessel spoke at more charity dinners than anyone who ever lived. There were times when he worked 90 charity dinners in 100 nights; I mean, the man would do anything for a free meal. Jessel claimed he raised more than $100,000,000 for causes ranging from the State of Israel to the City of Hope Hospital. "I played God across the board," he said. But not for Warner Brothers, that was my job.

Jessel did pretty good for a man with an eight-month public-school education. He was very well read, he wrote beautifully and he made the most wonderful speeches. Jessel was one of the greatest dinner speakers who ever lived. Of course, as far as I was concerned, anybody who didn't say, "If you can't sea bass every night, you can't sea bass at all," was a great dinner speaker. He was so good that one night he walked into the wrong reception and gave a long speech praising a man that nobody in that room had ever heard of, and still got a standing ovation.

Let me give you an example of how good he was as a speaker. He was a guest at a dinner honoring Amelia Earhart. The person who was supposed to introduce her didn't show up, so they asked Jessel to do it. Now Jessel didn't know anything about Amelia Earhart except that she was a woman who flew airplanes. So he just stood up and said, "Ladies and gentlemen, as I stand here before you tonight I am reminded of a little colored mammy living in a small town in Mississippi. This lovely old woman, her back bent over with age, had barely enough food to survive. One day, as she shuffled along the side of the road, she came upon a mangy old dog. This little dog was useless to everyone, and was just barely holding on to life. But this old woman picked him up in her frail little arms, and somehow managed to carry him back to her ramshackle hut. And there she nursed him back to health, sharing her meager provisions. And that woman took care of that dog until the day she died. And when she died, she went directly to heaven, where St. Peter himself was waiting to greet her. And he said unto her, 'Because of your sacrifice for a helpless creature, you have earned your heavenly wings.' The great St. Peter pinned the heavenly wings on this little colored mammy. She stretched them out and saw that they were beautiful, more beautiful than anything she had ever seen. Then she tested them, and as the wind itself, she was lifted off the ground. And then she flew, and she flew from cloud to cloud experiencing a joy and a freedom unlike anything she had ever felt during her mortal life. And oh, it was a truly beautiful moment. Watching this was Our Lord Himself, who was sitting on a cloud with his Only Begotten Son. And as he watched this little old black mammy flying on the wings of heaven, he turned to his son and said, 'Jesus, can that woman fly!' Ladies and gentlemen, Amelia Earhart.''

People used to say that Jessel would appear at the opening of a TV dinner carton. Jolson was just the opposite, he really didn't like performing at charity functions and avoided it whenever he could. Instead, he made out a check to the charity for the money they would have gotten if he had appeared. Naturally, it was always a big check—Jolson figured if he was there, the place would have sold out. Jolson donated a lot of money to charity. When he got tired of his fourteen-room mansion on top of Mulholland Drive, for example, instead of selling it he just gave it to Cedars of Lebanon Hospital. But he didn't like having to show up in person. I mean, there were exceptions. I remember once we were having a twenty-fifth anniversary fund-raiser at Hillcrest and he agreed to perform. His only condition was, as usual, that he go on last. Eight great acts went on before him, Danny Kaye worked, so did Jack Benny and me and Gracie, and it was very late when they reached his spot on the bill. But instead of coming right out, Jolson made everybody wait. Eight violinists, that he had hired himself, came onstage and started tuning up, as if the show was just beginning. Time passed. People started getting edgy. Then Jolson finally came onstage. He sang for two hours. And he sang for free. In fact, with paying the musicians, it cost him money to perform. But he didn't care; money never mattered to Jolie, "I got so much money that fourteen guys couldn't spend it," he once told me. "But I'd rather die than quit show business." Fourteen guys, huh? It's a very good thing that he and Jessel didn't get along.

Milton estimates he's done more than 10,000 benefits, working as many as seven different dinners—in one night. Knowing Milton, I can understand that. He always said that there was no such thing as an old joke as long as there was a new audience—and he's never stopped searching for that audience. Among the many charitable things Milton has done are setting up the Berle Foundation for Crippled Children, serving as Mayor of Mending Heart, Florida, the site of the National Children's Cardiac Home, and acting as the host of many telethons. Once, for example, he spent twenty-two straight hours on television raising hundreds of thousands of dollars for the Damon Runyon Cancer Fund. Look, if there was an audience, Milton would host a fund-raiser to prevent chapped lips.

Durante, Harpo and Jack used to perform at fund-raising concerts, in addition to donating hundreds of thousands of dollars to charity.

Jimmy did his piano-wrecking act and Harpo appeared with symphony orchestras, doing things like playing pick-up sticks with the conductor's baton, playing traditional harp favorites like "Chopsticks" and "Swanee," and forcing the bass player to turn his instrument upside down to play it. Sometimes, when Harpo was conducting Haydn's C Major Symphony, "The Toy Symphony," he'd replace members of the orchestra with their children, who played the music on toy drums, a triangle, a water-filled whistle known as a nightingale, and a ratchet.

Jack was always doing something for charity. He would go to fund-raising auctions and raise the bidding on an item one cent at a time. He would appear at lottery drawings—once he gave away a million dollars in New Jersey, then fainted. And if he couldn't show up himself, he'd donate items. During World War II, for example, his famous Maxwell was auctioned off and, in 1943, he made the ultimate sacrifice for the war effort —he donated the seventy-five-dollar violin he had learned to play on to a war bonds auction. The auction was held in Gimbel's basement and was conducted by Danny Kaye. Besides Jack's violin, they were auctioning off Thomas Jefferson's Bible and a letter from George Washington. But the violin was the thing that most people were interested in; I guess Jefferson just wasn't that funny. It sold for $1,000,000 in war bonds, making it the most valuable violin in the world. That's a lot of money. I mean, I always knew people would pay a lot to keep Jack from playing the fiddle, but a million dollars? The buyer was the owner of the Garcia Grande Cigar Company. When he was asked if he could play the violin, he said, "If I was a violinist, I wouldn't be able to buy a million dollars' worth of war bonds."

Jack pretty much gave up playing the violin, except as a prop in his act, when he became a big radio star. Sometimes, when he was appearing in a theater, he'd tell the audience that someone had requested he play a song for them. Then he'd look into the wings and ask for his violin. After a few seconds, someone in the wings would throw it out onstage. Jack would just stare at it—and then they'd throw the bow onstage. When the audience finally stopped laughing, Jack would say, "Obviously, that's not the person who requested it."

But in 1956 he did an episode on his television show in which he dreamed he had become a concert violinist, and in order to look like he knew what he was doing on the show, he started taking lessons again. And he discovered that he loved playing the fiddle. Sixty-one years old and taking violin lessons. Of course, Mary made him go into a bathroom in the back of the house and close the door when he practiced, but he didn't mind. "It sounds better there," he said, "just like singing in the bathtub."

And with the lessons and the practice, by the time they filmed the show Jack was actually pretty go . . . I mean, Jack was . . . Look, I'll tell you how good Jack was on the violin. At a testimonial dinner, Dick Cavett said, "Jack Benny's violin playing is every bit as good as George Burns's singing."

After the show was broadcast, former President Harry Truman asked Jack to appear with him at a fund-raising concert for the Truman Library and the Kansas City Symphony Orchestra. Truman had appeared on Jack's show several times, so Jack couldn't turn him down. At about the same time people in New York were planning to tear down the beautiful Carnegie Hall concert auditorium, and The Committee to Save Carnegie Hall asked Jack to play at a fund-raising benefit for the theater with the New York Philharmonic. Jack Benny at Carnegie Hall. What some people wouldn't do for money. As his close friend, the great violinist Isaac Stern said, "When Jack Benny walks onto the stage in tails, in front of ninety great musicians, he looks like the world's greatest violinist. It's a shame he has to play."

Both concerts were very successful, and Jack enjoyed doing them so much that he began performing all over the world to help raise money to support symphony orchestras. Jack really did play the best he could in these appearances. He used to say he considered his performance a success if he finished playing at the same time as the rest of the orchestra. He got the kind of reviews I had gotten with the seal: "Last night Jack Benny played Mendelssohn . . . Mendelssohn lost." "He came, he sawed, he conquered." I think his good friend, the great conductor Zubin Mehta, probably summed it up best. "There was one particular moment during that concert that I shall recall as long as I live," he said. "It's when the entire audience jumped to its feet and shouted, 'More! More!' That was right after Jack had announced there would be a five-minute intermission."

Seats for these concerts were priced from $5 to $100, but Jack claimed that the more expensive seats were those furthest away from the stage. "In fact," he said, "for two hundred fifty dollars, you don't have to come at all."

Over a fifteen-year period Jack raised almost $6,000,000 for the benefit of classical music. Of course, a lot of people felt that that was his way of paying for the damage he'd caused it.

I've done some things for different charities, but if I tell you about them people would say I was blowing my own horn, and that's Harpo's act. But there was one memorable evening I would like to tell you about. Not too long ago I donated the first, then the last, million dollars to Cedars Sinai Hospital for their $100,000,000 building fund. And to thank me for my contribution, they had a big dinner. At that dinner they said all sorts of nice things about me, which I appreciated, and then they said words as sweet as any I have ever heard. "Okay, George, you can sing one song now."

9

I think everybody loved being married. In fact, some of my best friends loved it so much that they got married three or four times. Let me tell you something, in the battle of the sexes, this group was the infantry. Standing up, the most important thing in any of our lives was making people laugh; lying down, it was women. Believe me, lying down, nobody wants to make people laugh.

On one of our radio shows Bill Goodwin said to me, "George, I'd like to ask you two questions. How long have you been married to Gracie?"

"Seventeen years, " I told him. "Why?"

"That's the second question."

Well, that was probably the easiest question I've ever had to answer. Gracie made being married to her easy. I've said this before; she was my wife, my lover, my partner in our act and, most important, my best friend. I think that after a while we saw the world through each other's eyes. There were no surprises, I knew what Gracie looked like with her makeup off, and she knew what I looked like without my toupee. And she still loved me. We had a great life together. And we weren't the only ones: Jack and Winnie Pearl were a wonderful couple, and Jack and Flo Haley, Louella

Parsons and Dockey Martin, Walter and Carol Matthau, Milton and Ruth Berle, Danny and Rosemary Thomas, Charlie McCarthy and Marilyn Monroe, Danny and Sylvia Fine Kaye, Harpo and Susan Marx, Jimmy and Margie Durante, Bob and Dolores Hope, Eddie and Ida, even Jack and Mary. I make a lot of jokes about Mary, but Mary knew how to make Jack happy and so she did those things—he was happiest when she was happy, so she did everything possible to make herself happy. But she did it all for Jack.

Not everybody was so lucky. Jolson was married four times. Jessel was married three times. Groucho was married three times. Wynn was married three times. Cary Grant was married five times. Even Fanny Brice was married three times—although legally she was only married twice. I think she was only sixteen years old when she married the local barber because, she always said, "He smelled so nice." Her parents had that marriage annulled after one night because she was underage, so legally, it didn't count.

Of course, legally Jessel was married five times. He married his first wife, Florence Courtney— one of the Courtney Sisters, a good harmony act —three different times. Georgie was a man who couldn't take yes for an answer. He married her for the first time in 1919, then divorced her in 1921, married her again in 1922, then divorced her again in 1923, then married her again in 1924 and divorced her again in 1930. That's not just a simple "I do"; that's "I do," "I did" and "I've already done it." I think that after the third marriage Georgie tried to claim his divorce attorney as a dependent.

I remember that when Georgie was trying to win her back for the second time or the third time he sent a wire to Cantor, saying, SEND ME $1500 IMMEDIATELY. DESPERATE. LOVE, GEORGIE. So Cantor took the cash out of the theater box office and sent it to him. That was the last time Cantor heard from Jessel until he got back to New York six weeks later. Eddie was so upset he went right to Georgie's hotel room to make sure he was okay. He was fine. "I used the money to pick up a beautiful bracelet for Florence at a bargain," he told him.

"A bracelet?" Eddie was really angry. "But you wired DESPERATE."

"Sure," Georgie said. "Would you have sent me the money if I'd wired BRACELET?"

Georgie's problem was that he thought love and marriage were like the sun and the moon—they never appeared at the same time. As he once said while toasting somebody else's marriage, "May they have as much happiness as I have had on several different occasions." Cantor loved to tell the story about the time he was working with Jessel in Gus Edwards' "Kid Cabaret." "Jessel celebrated his thirteenth birthday while we were in the show, and he was going to be bar mitzvahed. The morning of the bar mitzvah he called me on the phone and said, 'Eddie, I want you to wear a high hat, a frock coat and striped trousers.' I told him that that wasn't what I usually wore to a bar mitzvah, and he said, 'Oh, I'm also getting married.'"

The truth is that the only woman Georgie ever really loved was the great silent movie star Norma Talmadge. He used to say, "Even her sneeze made Debussy sound like a bum." Now, I never knew what Florence Courtney had, but I know what she got: $100,000. That's what it cost Norma Talmadge to keep Florence from filing an alienation of affections lawsuit, claiming that Norma had stolen Georgie away from her. Imagine that, a woman claiming that another woman had had to steal Georgie's affections. Believe me, nobody ever had to steal Georgie's affections—he gave them away at the drop of a skirt.

Maybe the best part of Georgie's marriage to Norma was his memory of it, because while they were together they were always fighting. "We were married ten years," he used to say, "and I never unpacked."

Their marriage ended when Norma kicked him out of their house. He was desperate to get back together with her, so he bought her a beautiful bouquet and a $14,000 diamond necklace. Then he went to the house on the servants' day off and rang the doorbell. "These are for you," he said when she answered.

Norma looked at the flowers and smiled. Then she looked at the necklace and smiled. Then she looked at Georgie. Well, at least he got two out of three. She threw the flowers and necklace at him and slammed the door in his face.

Georgie leaned on the doorbell until she opened the door again. Then he said, "I guess this means I can't use the swimming pool?"

"You know what the problem with you is, Georgie?" she said angrily. "You have an inquisitive mind." Only she didn't say mind. Her thoughts went much lower than that.

Georgie got so depressed about splitting up with Norma that he bought a gun in a hockshop and decided to commit suicide. This is absolutely true. He even wrote a suicide note. But he didn't like the way the note sounded so he called up his friend George M. Cohan to help him fix it up. Cohan made some suggestions, Georgie added a few things, Cohan made a little more, and the note got so good that instead of committing suicide, Jessel sold it to a music publisher for $500.

Cantor couldn't believe it. "Who else could try to commit suicide and make a profit?"

Their divorce wasn't any friendlier than their marriage. One day Georgie called her up to discuss their settlement, and when she answered he said, "This is Georgie. You remember me, honey."

And Norma said coldly, "Sure I do. You're the fellow who used to be in vaudeville with Eddie Cantor."

Sometimes in my stage act I tell the story of the rich young man who was only eighty years old when he married a beautiful twenty-year-old girl. After the ceremony one of this young man's

312

friends said, "Tell me the truth. Why would a pretty young girl like that marry somebody your age?"

Seems like a silly question to me, but he did ask it.

So this man smiled and told him the truth. "I lied about my age. I told her I was ninety."

I used to call that "The Jessel joke." The year after Georgie and Norma finally got divorced he met a beautiful young girl named Lois Andrews. I mean, a young girl. When they met, Georgie was forty-two and Lois was fifteen. But I'll be honest, even though she was only fifteen, she had been living on her own for a while and was easily as mature as a seventeen-year-old.

Anyway, when they met it was love at first sight. Well, at least it was lust at first sight. After their first week together Georgie announced that they were going to get married in Detroit, Michigan. Georgie picked Detroit because of its great natural beauty, because he was booked there, and because it was the only state where a sixteen-year-old could get married legally without her parents' permission. Okay, so it really wasn't because of Detroit's great natural beauty.

It wasn't really surprising that Georgie would want to marry a girl twenty-six years younger than he was—his father had married a woman thirty-three years younger than he was. Lois's mother, who was only nine years younger than her future son-in-law, gave the marriage her blessing after meeting Georgie, calling him "A fine young man."

Actually, Lois was a pretty smart little girl. "The matter of our ages isn't important," she said. "Some girls start going out with guys when they're sixteen. I'm old enough to marry the man I love, and I love Georgie more than any man I've ever loved before."

She also said that they were going to wait a little while before having children. "We won't have our first child for a year, not until we really get to know each other really well. We're in love, deeply in love, but we do need to get acquainted." And she was right, they had a beautiful baby a year after they got married.

I don't remember if I tried to talk Georgie out of this particular marriage. Georgie got engaged the way other people got haircuts; it was just something he did every few months whether he needed to or not. Who knew he was serious this time? Besides, he never would have listened to me. Georgie spent his whole life looking for somebody to love, and believe me, Lois had some body.

Georgie was just like a little kid after the marriage. Two months after the wedding he had to cancel some bookings because, he said, "I was playing ball with Lois in our backyard and ran to catch a fly ball. I burst a blood vessel in my temple, which caused a temporary paralysis on the left side of my face. But I'll come back as good as ever."

Georgie Jessel playing catch in his backyard with a sixteen-year-old girl? Playing with a sixteen-year-old girl, sure. But catch? Outdoors? The

314

only thing Georgie ever tried to catch outdoors was a sixteen-year-old girl.

Gracie and I went to their house a few times. The thing I remember about the house was that it was filled with kewpie dolls. Lois collected kewpie dolls. That was fair, Georgie collected real dolls. Their marriage lasted two years, but Georgie always said that it taught him a good lesson. "I figured out the best way to buy a new house," he said. "Find a guy who built a house for his beautiful young bride. She divorces him and he decides he's got to get rid of the house at any price. That's the time to buy it."

Somebody asked him if that was the way he'd bought his house.

"No," he admitted, "that's the way I sold it." It took Georgie several hours to get over that marriage. Georgie was the kind of man who always liked to drown his sorrows in a tall blonde. So as soon as one relationship ended he'd start another one. One thing you can say about Georgie, he was never afraid of commitment. In fact, he used to tell me that several of his former girlfriends should have been committed.

Poor Georgie, he was always in trouble with some girl. I remember when he was engaged to a beautiful young girl named Tommy Adams. Beautiful, but very tough. One night Georgie was with her and Lou Holtz and a good friend named George Pallay at the Mocambo nightclub. Maybe they had a little too much to drink, but Georgie and Tommy got into an argument and she threw

315

a glass of whiskey in his face. Jessel walked out of the nightclub. Lou Holtz told Tommy, "We'll take you home."

"I want a cab," she said.

"No, we'll take you home." They all piled into the front seat of Pallay's car and headed toward Tommy's apartment. Lou was sitting between Pallay and Tommy. "Tommy," he said, "you should be ashamed of yourself. A nice girl like you, embarrassing everybody like that. You know that Georgie means well, but it doesn't look good for the two of you to be fighting—" Tommy suddenly turned around and slugged Lou in the mouth. She cut his lip wide open, and blood spurted all over George Pallay. "Stop the car," Lou said, and he got out, leaving Pallay alone with Tommy.

When they got to her apartment she told him to come upstairs and wash off the blood. But she was still furious, and as Pallay was standing over the sink in the bathroom, she took off the diamond engagement ring Jessel had given her and threw it in the toilet. Before she could flush, Pallay reached into the toilet and grabbed it. He wiped it off and slipped it on his finger so it wouldn't get lost. So Pallay was standing in the bathroom, covered with blood, and engaged to Georgie Jessel.

Tommy told him, "Call Georgie and tell him I'm sorry."

Pallay did, but Jessel was pretty angry too. He told Pallay, "Tell her to get lost."

When Pallay told Tommy, she said, "Tell Georgie that if he doesn't come over here right now I'm going to kill myself."

Pallay called Jessel again and told him what Tommy had threatened. Well, at least Georgie didn't offer to write a song. Instead he said, "Tell her if she does, I'll put on my striped pants and be over there in the morning to say a few words."

Everything finally quieted down—then Tommy swallowed a handful of sleeping pills. Pallay called the emergency room at the hospital and they told him to keep her walking around the room until the paramedics got there. Now Pallay was covered with Lou Holtz's blood, engaged to Georgie Jessel and walking around the room with a woman who was trying to commit suicide. Let me tell you, Pallay had some tough night.

A few days later I was with Jessel. "I don't understand it, Georgie," I said, "she throws whiskey in your face, she yells at you, she goes out with other men. What do you need somebody like that for?"

Jessel smiled and said to me very softly, "Natty, it fits."

Georgie got engaged more than any man I've ever known. It seemed like every few months Gracie was going out to buy sterling silver candlesticks for Georgie and his new fiancée. He was briefly engaged to Rita Hayworth, for example. That ended while they were driving to Las Vegas to get married—Rita woke up from a nap, snuggled up against his shoulder and said sweetly, "I love you,

Phil." He was also engaged to an actress who announced that they were going to be married as soon as she got out of the sanitarium where she was recovering from a nervous breakdown. When Georgie was sixty-three-years old he got engaged to a twenty-nine-year-old actress who had brought charges against him in a paternity suit. Five years later he got engaged to a twenty-four-year-old model who stood him up at the altar. It took me a long time, but I think I've finally figured out why he got engaged so often; it turns out it had nothing to do with women—Georgie was in the used sterling silver candlestick business.

Okay, so maybe he didn't get engaged to every single woman he went out with. I know he was about to get engaged to the Mexican movie star Lupe Velez, but called it off when she stuck a steak knife through his hand and into the table. Seems to me she just could have said no. And he didn't get engaged to actress Joan Tyler, who also sued him for paternity. Georgie was sixty-five years old at the time and didn't deny the charge. "At my time of life," he said, "this is a compliment." And he certainly didn't get engaged to the actress he was dating, who he found alone with the great actress Eva Le Gallienne, who was a well-known lesbian. Instead of getting engaged, he looked at this girl and shook his head sadly. "I don't know what you're doing with her," he said. "I can do anything with you that she can do with you, and besides that, I'm a great Jew comic."

Jessel never changed, he spent his whole life

chasing women. I remember one day when he was in his late seventies, we were at the club and some girl called him there. He started romancing her right on the telephone. We listened to this for a few minutes, then I finally turned to Jack and said, "Can you believe this? After all these years, Georgie is reduced to giving phone jobs."

Jessel may have been engaged the most, but Durante was engaged the longest. Jimmy and Margie Little went out for sixteen years, and were engaged for ten of them, before they finally got married. I don't want to say Jimmy was nervous about it, but Eskimo surfers in December don't have such cold feet. Of course, Jimmy did have a good excuse—he was booked that decade.

The women loved Jimmy—and when he was single Jimmy loved them right back. As often as possible. Maybe the girls liked him so much because he was always a perfect gentleman. He always tipped his hat and opened doors for them. "They's all perspective mothers," he used to say. Unlike some men, Jimmy never cared what a woman looked like, "To somebody," he explained, "she's beautiful."

Once, when Jimmy was working in radio with Alan Young, they were on tour and staying at different hotels. Alan was in conference with the writers when Jimmy called him. "Youngey," he asked, "you be using your room right now?" Alan said he was going to be working with the writers all afternoon. "Well, you mind if I borrows it for a little bit?" Jimmy said. "I've got a date with a girl who works in my hotel. And lemme tell you, a gentleman never takes a lady to the hotel in which she woiks."

Jimmy had been married to his first wife for twenty-two years before she died. A few years later he met Margie at the Copa and they started going out. And they went out, and they went out, and they went out. Finally, Margie gave him an ultimatum, "I told him I would get a divorce from him if he didn't marry me."

"She's a very voracious girl," Jimmy said when he announced that they were getting married. "I mean, what's the word? Vivacious. Anyway, we're very congenital."

Jimmy claimed to be a "nervous wretch" when they got married in front of 700 of their closest friends. And after the wedding just Jimmy and Margie, and thirteen friends, went on their honeymoon.

Jimmy was not the kind of man who let marriage change a good relationship. For a long time after they were married he lived in his house and Margie lived in the house he'd bought for her. "I'm the only guy in Hollywood who keeps him-and-her houses," he said. "I even got two swimmin' pools, one for swimmin' and one for rinsin'."

Houses never mattered to him anyway. Material things never mattered to him. Once, for example, he met with his writers in the den of the new house he and Margie built, which had beautiful oak-paneled walls. A few weeks later Jimmy held another meeting in the same room, but one of the writers said that something about the room was different. "Yeah, that's right, you got it," Jimmy explained. "See, last time youse guys was here the room wasn't finished. They hadn't painted the walls."

Jimmy was sixty-seven when he finally married Margie. On his wedding day, when reporters asked him if he had any advice to give, he said, "Yeah. Marry young."

Jessel had done that. Of course, Jessel also married middle and married old. But Georgie certainly wasn't the only person to marry someone much younger. Jolson was at least fifty-six years old when he married twenty-one-year-old Erle Galbraithe. Groucho was sixty-three when he married a twenty-four-year-old model. Lou Holtz married a girl thirty-seven years younger than he was— and they had two children. Zeppo was only fifty-eight when he married a twenty-eight-year-old showgirl. Ed Wynn was fifty-two when he married his twenty-seven-year-old showgirl. Even Fanny Brice was ten years older than Billy Rose when she married him. And you know why they did it? Because they could.

Most of these marriages didn't work, though. Ed Wynn's marriage to a girl twenty-five-years younger than he was pretty typical. Ed did everything he could to make the marriage work. As soon as they got married he bought her a good dictionary and tried to teach her good manners. And more importantly, when they started fighting a week after they were married, he tried to make up with her by giving her a limousine, jewels and other gifts. But it didn't matter. She announced their divorce to the press while she was busy recovering from her nervous breakdown. And sitting next to her when she made that announcement was a man she introduced as "My gigolo. He costs me twenty dollars a night," she said, "but he's lots of fun."

Believe me, Jessel would have worked cheaper. Maybe not as often, but cheaper.

Of all the marriages between older men and younger women, I think Jolie's was the most successful. That was pretty surprising, because the only person Jolie always got along well with was himself. Jolie even paid his brother Harry not to use the name Jolson professionally. Of course, when Al didn't pay Harry all the money he owed him, Harry sued to recover use of his own name.

I can't even imagine what it would have been like to be married to Jolson. First of all, you would have to have separate mirrors. His first marriage broke up just after he hit it big at the Winter Garden. As soon as he became a big star he told his wife to go back to her home in Oakland, California. When she went, happily, he told her to come right back. Jolie couldn't bear the thought that somebody would be happy to leave him. After a while though, he sent her back to California. Finally, his lawyer went to see her to find out what kind of divorce settlement she would demand. "I don't want any money," she said, "I just want to be free." Well, that was much more than Jolson was willing to pay. He just couldn't believe that a woman wouldn't want to be with him, particularly when he didn't want to be with her. So he wanted her to prove how much she loved him by demanding a large settlement. It was a matter of pride with him. He finally took the train to Oakland to convince her to fight him over the divorce. When he got there, she met him at the station with her new boyfriend. He got right back on the train and came back to New York. Maybe that was one reason that Jolson never really trusted women.

I think Jolson's biggest problem with women was that they came between him and himself. I know that when he got back to New York after honeymooning in Europe with his second wife, Jessel asked him how he was feeling and he said he didn't know. "How can you say that?" Georgie asked. "You've just come back from your honeymoon. Aren't you in love?"

"Love," Jolson shrugged, "what's love? Who wants to go to Europe alone?"

Sometimes it seemed to me that Jolson didn't even want to be with a woman, he just wanted them to want to be with him. He had an unusual way of courting them. For example, when he met a young woman named Ruby Stevens—she later changed her name to Barbara Stanwyck—while judging a Charleston contest, he told her, "It's a funny thing about your name being Stevens. That's the same name as the president of one of the banks I got six million dollars in. . . ."

His third marriage, to nineteen-year-old Ruby Keeler, whom he met when she was dancing at Texas Guinan's speakeasy, lasted eleven years. At first they seemed to be pretty happy together. In fact, Jolie even started one of the most publicized fights of the 1930s defending Ruby's honor. Men did things like defending women's honor in those days. What happened was that Walter Winchell, one of the most important gossip columnists in the world, had written a screenplay titled *Broadway Through a Keyhole* that was supposedly about Jolie and Ruby. In Winchell's script, the showgirl had been involved with gangsters before meeting the famous singer. Ruby was really upset by that story. So when Winchell showed up for the boxing matches at the Hollywood Legion Stadium, Jolson stood up and decked him with one punch.

Winchell did the honorable thing—he sued Jolson for $500,000. Just about every paper in the country made it front-page news. Jolson wasn't too upset. "You can sing Mammy songs for a hundred years," he said, "and you can wear out your poor old kneecaps on splintery stages, but you have to sock a columnist before you really become famous."

Winchell eventually dropped the lawsuit, but he still managed to keep everything in perspective. "I'll shake hands with Jolson," he said, "after I've had more publicity. And not until then."

But eventually Jolie and Ruby split up. "He very often ridiculed me," Ruby told the court during their divorce hearing. "He called me stupid every time I expressed an opinion. . . . It gave me a slight inferiority complex." A slight inferiority complex? Ruby must have been pretty tough, then, because Jolson's ego was so big he could give the Lord himself an inferiority complex. Even Jolie admitted the divorce from Ruby bothered him. "My mind's completely at ease," he said. "I get up late, have breakfast in bed and then receive all the producers who want me to star in their shows. I have a fine lunch, go to the track, then receive the radio officials who offer me programs. I go to dinner, to a show, then to some nightclubs and finally go home to my elegant hotel suite and get into my soft, downy bed—and then I take three sleeping pills and go right to sleep."

And I thought I was too sentimental.

He met Erle, who was an X-ray technician in a military hospital in Hot Springs, Arkansas, while visiting wounded soldiers for the USO. Six months later she moved out to Los Angeles to be with him, and he got her bit parts in a few movies. Her real job, though, was taking care of Jolson, and that was a full-time job. She must have done it well, because the last few years of his life Jolson was as happy as I had ever seen him. Al Rylander, a good friend of Jolson's, told me that he was with him in Washington, D.C., just after *The Jolson Story* had made him a big star again, and remembers Jolie telling him, "It's amazing. Here I am, seventy years old, I've got more money than I can spend, everybody wants me to work for them, and I have a beautiful young wife who I really love."

Then he frowned, and said, "If only she didn't want sex, I'd be the happiest man in the world."

Maybe the toughest person of all to be married to was Groucho. You notice that he wasn't called Romeo either. I just don't think Groucho ever took marriage seriously. I think he thought marriage was like a country club—he just couldn't respect anybody who would marry him. While he was getting married the first time he started insulting the minister performing the ceremony, telling him, "Why are you going so fast? This is a five-buck ceremony, aren't we at least entitled to five minutes of your time?" He wasn't much nicer to his wife. When they got divorced after twenty-one years he shook her hand and told her, "It's been nice knowing you. If you're ever in the neighborhood again, drop in." He did sign one of the most unusual alimony deals I've ever heard of—he had to keep paying his first wife alimony until he divorced his second wife.

Groucho spent the last six years of his life living with a nice girl named Erin Fleming, whom he called his companion-secretary. I don't know if they lived in sin, but I hope so. Three years before he died, the court appointed Erin his legal guardian. I thought she was great for him. Until she came along he was acting like he was in rehearsal for being dead. He just stayed in his house, he didn't go anywhere, he didn't do anything. Maybe I didn't like his singing—let's be honest, he was no Durante—but I still wanted him to sing. One song. Besides, without Groucho around, I didn't have anybody to be mad at. I have to love some-body before I can spend the time being mad at them; and I loved being mad at Groucho. So as long as he didn't say those two words, "sea" and "bass," I wanted to see him active again.

Erin forced him to go out of the house, to give concerts, answer letters from his fans, she threw lots of parties at their house. He did a one-man show at Carnegie Hall, he did some television in-terviews, he even did a series of photographs for a magazine showing him lying in bed with other famous people. Like Burt Reynolds. In fact, when Burt and Groucho were lying on his bed, waiting for the photographer to get ready, Groucho told Burt, "Not tonight, I have a headache."

Groucho left Erin two houses, money and other gifts when he died. The Bank of America sued to get them back, claiming that she had forced him to give her those things. There was a big trial and the bank had a psychiatrist who testified that in the last few years of his life Groucho had "an infantile personality, poor self-control, and was given to temper tantrums."

Sounds like the same old Groucho I always knew.

He never changed at all. Before Erin had come to live with him he had twenty-four-hour nursing care, but she had fired the nurses. The bank's attorney's claimed that was proof she was trying to control him. Erin said that wasn't the reason she fired them. "It's my opinion that he found out he could have the nurses for free," she said.

"He was covered by three insurance companies. The girls were all gorgeous. He wanted tall blond ones with large . . ." She paused to look for the right word. ". . . personalities." Wrong word. But it still sounds like the same old Groucho.

I testified at the trial. I told them that I didn't think that Erin was entitled to half of Groucho's money. "If she was with him six years," I said, "she deserves it all." It had taken me a long time, but I'd finally got even with him for his abuse of a sea-bass joke.

Erin's attorney asked me about a party I'd gone to at Groucho's. "He never stopped singing," I said. "He sang all the time. He wouldn't even let me sing." Everybody in the courtroom laughed when I said that, I don't know why. I didn't think not letting me sing was so funny. The attorney then asked me if I'd seen love and affection between them. That was a silly question. "There were one hundred fifty people there," I pointed out.

Then one of the attorneys for the bank started to question me. "Excuse me," he began, "but I've never questioned God before."

I'd sworn to tell the truth, so I did. "I'm only God when I get paid," I told him. Later I was asked if I thought an eighty-year-old man could really find happiness with a thirty-year-old woman. "No," I admitted, "not too often. Only once or twice a night."

I was a big hit in court. In fact, I was such a

big hit that they offered to extend my appearance for three weeks guaranteed, two trials a day.

I thought Groucho had been very lucky to find someone like Erin; some of my friends never really managed to find happiness with another person. Fanny Brice, for instance. Fanny had more friends than I've got great vaudeville songs, and she had kids, but I think she was still a lonely woman. Sometimes she'd call Cantor in the middle of the night and wake him up to ask him what he was doing, and he'd get dressed and go over to her house and sit and play cards with her. She just needed somebody to keep her company. Most people don't have to read about their love life in the newspaper headlines, usually they can just hear about it from their neighbors. But Fanny's loves and marriages and divorces were so public that they became part of her stage character. Fanny became the woman who loved deeply and lost; she was the scorned woman. And for someone who used to admit she was homely, her romances made more headlines than any of the great beauties. Now that's talent.

After her one-night marriage to the barber she married a smooth con artist named Nicky Arnstein. She used to tell people, "Nicky stood for manners, education, good breeding and an extraordinary gift for dreaming." Like I told you, he was a smooth con artist. Nicky even had made a record—only his was with the police. The real police, not the singing group. Fraud, I think. They were married in 1919 and Fannie supported them. A year later he was accused of master-minding a theft of $5,000,000 in Wall Street bonds. Even though he was convicted on a lesser charge, and long after they'd split up, Fanny never believed that that he was guilty. "Listen," she'd tell people, "Nicky Arnstein couldn't mastermind a bulb into a socket."

She spent a fortune fighting to keep him out of prison, but he was finally sent to Leavenworth for two years. The story got national headlines, and Flo Ziegfeld would never let a headline go to waste. One night, just before Fanny went onstage, he put a little soot under her eyes to make it look like her mascara had been smudged from crying, and told her to cry when she sang the ballad "My Man." Well, it's a nice song, and she started crying when she sang it, and the audience knew she was crying for her man who was in jail, so they started crying too. The only person who was happy was Ziegfeld, but the song got so big that Fanny demanded he triple her salary—then he started crying. "My Man" became the most popular song in the country. You just can't imagine how happy people were to feel bad for Fanny. That song made her one of the biggest stars in show business.

Nicky was released from prison a year early for good behavior. It turned out that the only place Nicky could behave himself was in jail. Because as soon as he got out, he started with the new deals and new women. Two years later Fanny found him with another woman and filed for divorce.

Maybe she wasn't so happy about it, but it was a great career move. A man betraying the woman who had given everything she had for his love? That's the kind of story they invented movies to tell. The more people cried for Fanny, the bigger star she became.

"I married Nicky for better or worse," she said, "and it's come to worse." A reporter asked her if she would ever marry again. "No," she said sadly. "If you can fall in love another time you weren't so much in love the first time. Love is like a card trick—once you learn how it's done, you can't be fooled any longer." Love is like a card trick? I wonder who was writing her divorces?

So Fanny never married again as long as she lived, or one year later, whichever came first. Her next husband was Billy Rose, who eventually became one of the great Broadway showmen. Rose was a very smart guy. Years earlier, for example, the day before he was to compete in the finals of the world speed-shorthand contest, he broke his finger and couldn't hold a pencil. So he stuck a pencil through a potato and held on to the potato to win the title. That's a true story. Even I couldn't make up something like that. I mean, I could, but why would I? Fanny and Billy were married by Mayor Jimmy Walker. The fee for the wedding was normally two dollars, but Rose gave him a dollar and said, "I'll give you the other one if it's successful." So everything worked out fine—Rose saved a buck. Fanny's marriage to Billy Rose broke up when he produced the Aquacade, a water

331

ballet, and met a swimmer named Eleanor Holm. Fanny found out Rose was leaving her to marry Holm when a reporter called her up to find out how she felt about it. "Listen," she said, "I can do everything better than Holm—except swim!"

Offstage, Fanny never liked to talk about her private life. It was her private life, and if we were interested, we could read about it in the newspapers. I don't know, maybe she talked about it with Cantor, but never with me and Gracie. There was a real difference between the material she did in public and the things she would talk about when she was with friends. In public she would talk about her loves, in private she talked about the things that were important to her—show business and interior decorating. She decorated a lot of homes in Hollywood, sometimes with things she'd found in old barns and attics. She really did a beautiful job for her friends, but if you walked into a house, and it looked like it had been decorated with the type of things you put up in your attic or store in a barn, you knew Fanny had decorated it.

I've always said that marriage was like a cafeteria: A man grabs what he wants and pays for it later.

Congratulations! You've just read history being made. After all these years, I've stole a joke from Berle! Of course, in the case of this particular joke, you've just read ancient history being made.

But the thought's a good one, even if Berle's joke isn't. Divorce has always been pretty common in Hollywood. Success and fame and money cause people to change; at least that's what I've heard. But people do change, that's why studios have costume departments and motels have hourly rates. Look, show business marriages are like any other type of marriage, some of them are good, some of them are bad, and some of them are like the Sophie Tucker-Al Lackey marriage. When they were splitting up, Al said nostalgically, "I'll say this for Sophie. She never gave me a bad check." I don't know for sure that show business people have more divorces than other people, but I do know that their divorces get more publicity. Show business divorces make headlines. Women all over America cried for Fanny when first Nicky Arnstein, then Billy Rose left her. And men all over America cried for Ed Wynn when the judge told him how much alimony he would have to pay.

Ed Wynn's divorce was a big hit. Every newspaper made it a front-page story when he left his wife of twenty-one years for a Follies girl who was a former Miss America. As Ed probably would have said, when it came to getting married, his stage billing held—he was The Perfect Fool. During the divorce trial Ed told the judge that his wife was a dipsomaniac. That was what we used to call an alcoholic. That, and "Hey, W.C." When she sued Ed for divorce the details of their unhappy marriage became public. "I found out that a pint a day wasn't enough to keep the doctor away," he said, "I spent two hundred fifty thousand dollars in doctors' bills alone." Once, he claimed, she ordered thirty-one drinks during dinner. When they had guests in their home she would sit there for hours without saying a word, then the next day she'd call each guest and tell them that Ed didn't allow her to talk. Sometimes, late at night, she'd wake up and have their chauffeur drive her to a nightclub where she'd get drunk.

Hey, maybe I'm old-fashioned, but I just don't think people should talk about those kind of personal problems—I think they should write about them in books, where they belong.

Ed did try to help her. He hired private nurses for her. He had religious people pray for her. When a doctor told him the house they were living in was too big, he bought some land and had fifty-one men working twenty-four hours a day to build a smaller house in three days. Nothing worked though. Now, the only reason I'm telling you all these things is to make a point—see how important it is to be able to sing! Fanny turned her tragedy into a great career because she could sing. Ed had all this tragedy in his life, if he could have even hummed a sad song or two, he would have been a huge success. Believe me, if Flo Ziegfeld had been in charge, Ed's divorce could've run on Broadway for years.

Of course I'm kidding. It was a terrible thing for Ed to have gone through, and I know he would never have wanted to commercialize it. Besides, I don't really think it would've run for more than a year anyway.

Now, Frank Fay's divorce from Barbara Stanwyck was sensational. Ed Wynn once said that the second-nicest thing Fay ever did was marry Barbara Stanwyck—and the nicest thing was divorce Barbara Stanwyck. His nickname for her was "Smack." And as she revealed during their divorce, there was a good reason for that—according to her testimony, that wasn't just what he called her, but what he did to her. Before meeting Barbara Stanwyck, Fay had been married twice. One of his wives was Frances White, of "White and Rock," a good singing act. But Fay was so religious that he had both of his previous marriages annulled so that he and Barbara could be married in the Church.

Berle also used to say, "Marriage is like a bathtub full of hot water. After a while it ain't so hot."

Blame Milton for that, not me. I just write here.

Fay and Stanwyck started out hot. "I love you as much as it is possible for a woman to love a man," she wrote to him, ". . . Please, Frank, whatever you do, love me. And wherever you go, take me. For there I shall be content." And he designed and built an estate for her that had four different houses, including one with thirty rooms and a huge rose garden, and was surrounded by a running track.

Some men I've known say that love goes out the window when her husband comes home. Fay and Stanwyck's marriage lasted almost eight years. But when it cooled . . . it got colder than Durante's feet. At their divorce trial she demanded that he take psychiatric tests, claiming that he was a drunk, that he had knocked her into the swimming pool with one punch, that when he was driving he'd take both hands off the steering wheel to light a cigarette then scream, "God help us, Amen," and that he loved his new false teeth more than he loved her. I knew Barbara Stanwyck, those must have been some great false teeth.

Fay was great in the courtroom. When he testified they put him under oath and asked him to state his profession. "I'm the greatest comedian in the world," he said. When his lawyer criticized him later for boasting, Frank shrugged and said, "What could I do? I was under oath."

That might have been the funniest thing he ever said.

Now, some wives throw surprise parties for their husband, Berle's first wife gave him a surprise divorce. Milton was in a hotel room with his wife, a starlet named Joyce Matthews, when he answered the telephone. "I'm a lawyer and I represent your wife," the caller said. "You'd better have your attorney see me before I file suit for her divorce."

Milton turned to Joyce and told her, "There's a crazy man on the phone. He says you're getting a divorce."

Surprise!

"Well," Milton could have said, "don't tell the judge that I complained about the way you make coffee, because those are weak grounds." Fortunately, he didn't.

Actually, it turned out to be a bad divorce. In fact, it was so bad that it didn't work and they got married again. Only this time, when they took their wedding vows, they left the word "obey" out of the ceremony. Knowing Milton, that was probably one of the most honest things he's ever done. When they got divorced for the second time they were much more experienced, and that time they got it right, because they were divorced happily ever after.

It took a very strong woman to handle Milton. Trying to follow his mother was about as easy as following Jolson at the Winter Garden. When Milton was growing up, Sarah Berle had tried to keep him away from the women, but when that became impossible she began fixing up dates for him. She must have been pretty persuasive, because Milton's reputation with the girls was very big. He went out with everybody from silent movie star Pola Negri to evangelist Aimee Semple McPherson to Marilyn Monroe. You'll notice I use the phrase "went out," but that's not exactly what I mean. I can't tell you exactly what I mean, because I do a clean act. I don't even drop cigar ashes on the page. But if you want to know what Milton did with these women, think of a train going into a tunnel. And based on Milton's reputation, this train was so popular with the passengers that he couldn't keep it in the station.

Okay, so I lied about the cigar ashes.

As Milton got a little older he was able to make his own dates. Bert Granet, who wrote for Milton, remembers being with him in a San Francisco bar one night. Two very pretty girls were sitting together at a table, and Milton kept trying to get their attention. It wasn't going too well. Let me put it this way: it didn't look like the train was going to run. The bar was dark and Milton probably figured the girls didn't recognize him. So he did the best thing possible in that situation, he went to the pay phone and dialed a number. Then after waiting a few seconds, he said loudly enough for the girls to hear, "Hello, Mother, this is your son, Milton Berle."

Ruth Cosgrove was strong enough to handle Milton. I'll tell you how strong she was—during World War II she was Walter Matthau's commanding officer. She was a captain in the WACs, and Walter served under her.

That's an old joke of Berle's. When you're writing about Milton, you can use any joke and say that it's an old joke of his. Even if it isn't, it will be.

Everybody loved Ruth Berle. She was a smart, feisty, warm woman with a great sense of humor. Besides marrying Milton, I mean. In fact, when Milton finally got around to asking her to marry him, she looked at him lovingly and said, "Please, Milton, don't put me on the spot."

Milton likes to tell people about the time they were having dinner at Chasen's and a new busboy put much too much pepper on Ruth's salad. Finally, Ruth tasted it. Putting down her fork, she said, "Needs salad."

Ruth could always handle Milton. When anybody mentioned his well-known sexual escapades, she'd say, "With practice, he'll get better." She just wasn't a jealous woman. "She once found powder on my arm," Milton remembered, "and she accused me of going bowling."

They had a great marriage until the day Ruthie died. She was so important to his success. Once, years ago, writer/producer Hal Kanter was working on Milton's TV show. Hal made a terrible mistake, he tried to tell Milton what to do. Milton got angry and walked off the show. "I stood there thinking, now what have I done?" Hal told me. "I've just fired my star. Well, I thought, they're going to come and tell me to turn in my parking space and leave. But an hour or so later the phone rang and it was Ruth. Very calmly she asked, 'Now what did you do to my little boy?' I told her the whole story. 'Well,' she said, 'if I let the cobra out of the basket, will you be kind to him? Will you be nice to him and apologize?'

"I couldn't say no to her. 'Okay,' I said, 'send your cobra over.' Then Milton and I apologized to each other and went back to work."

Milton once said that the greatest love affair since Romeo and Juliet was between him and show business. I know exactly what he meant. Show business is some wonderful lover. Once you feel that embrace . . . well, I never got over it. And I'll tell you something else, it's a relationship in which there's never been a divorce; oh, there've been a lot of forced separations, but once you fall in love with show business that love never ends. That can make it pretty tough on the person you're married to. Particularly if they're jealous. Of course, the good news is that show business doesn't leave lipstick stains on your collar.

The best show business marriages have always been the ones in which the husband, the wife and show business are all very happy together. Like Ida and Eddie and Eddie's career. Ida knew every word of every song Eddie sang, she knew every move in his act, every cue. Eddie's career was their business. They never argued over the bills or their girls or decorating the house; they argued whether a joke was funny or whether he missed an entrance.

Eddie and Ida were together their whole lives. They were married for forty-eight years, it really was until death did them part. They had the kind of marriage that makes divorce lawyers cry. The funny thing was that Ida's father had been against the marriage. He was in the men's clothing business and he didn't like actors, he didn't think there was any security in show business. The only thing he liked about actors was that they wore men's clothes. For years he tried to talk Eddie into going into the men's clothing business. Finally, when Eddie became a big star, he took his father-in-law to Broadway and pointed to a big sign in front of the Paramount reading, EDDIE CANTOR IN PERSON! Then he took him around the corner to a movie theater and showed him another sign, EDDIE CANTOR IN ROMAN SCANDALS. His father-in-law didn't say too much, instead he took Eddie over to 44th Street to the well-known men's clothing store, NAT LEWIS'S HABERDASHERY. "There," he finally told Eddie. "That sign will always be there."

Eddie had Ida, I had Gracie, and Walter Matthau has Carol—who he claims is a lot like Gracie. For example, Carol Matthau does crossword puzzles the way Gracie's character would have done them. That's not easy to do. Here, you try. Give me Carol's answer for a three-letter word for a beverage. A three-letter word for a beverage, the way Gracie would have answered it. Dum, dum, dum dum dum dum, dum, dummmm. Time's up. Carol's answer is: 7-Up. Now that you see how it works, give me the four-letter name found in the Bible for the son of Ham. Son of Ham, four letters. I'll give you a clue, the right answer is Shem. And Carol Matthau's answer? The son of Ham? What else, Spam.

The truth is that Carol Matthau is really a very smart lady. Walter gives her a lot of credit for helping him in his career. When Walter was doing Neil Simon's play *The Odd Couple* on Broadway, for example, he played a wisecracking, sometimes very nasty character. A wisecracking, sometimes very nasty character? Who does that remind you of? (Seven) letters. Not found in the Bible. When he was creating the role, Walter said, he based a lot of the character on his close friend, Groucho. Sometimes, in fact, during rehearsals, he'd catch himself doing an imitation of Groucho, something he didn't want to do. On opening night, as he and Carol were driving to the theater, he was very nervous. Carol gave him just one suggestion, "Remember," she said, "not too much Groucho."

A few months after that, Walter was with Groucho and he told him the story. Groucho nodded understandingly. "I know just what she meant," he said, "sometimes I have the same problem."

Most men in show business marry women in show business because those are the girls they meet. People usually marry people they meet at the office, even if that office is the stage of the Palace Theatre. Winnie Pearl was in show business when she met Jack. Flo Haley was a chorus girl when she met Jack. And Sadie Marks was a salesgirl at the May Company when she met Jack. I guess all of these women decided they'd settle for Jacks or better. Personally, I don't think there were any better than these Jacks.

The difference between these three women was that Winnie and Flo got out of show business when they were married, except for an occasional appearance with their husbands, while Sadie became Mary Livingstone and had a long career.

I don't think people ever gave Mary enough credit—because I know she used to spend right up to the limit they gave her. But it was Mary who kept Jack working. I mean, somebody had to pay her bills. All right, I am just kidding. Mary and Jack had a show business marriage. Who knows what it is that makes a person happy in a relationship. Could I have been happy with Mary? No, of course not. First of all, Gracie would have had a fit. But it didn't make any difference what I thought about Mary, Jack loved her and I loved Jack. So I loved Mary too, once removed.

Listen, Jack was a handsome guy, and before he married Mary he did a big job with the women. The funny thing was, though, he never wanted me to know about it. I don't know why, but he didn't talk about the girls with me. I remember once we were sharing a room at the Forrest Hotel and I was getting dressed to go over to the Friars Club to play cards. Meanwhile Jack had showered and put on a white silk robe and a white silk scarf. It was obvious he was going to be entertaining a woman. "So Jack," I asked him, "what are you doing tonight?"

"I don't know," he said. "I think I'm just gonna stay here and practice the fiddle." In silk pajamas? "And Natty," he continued, "do me a favor, would you? Call me before you come back tonight, so I can put my instrument away."

"Sure, Jack," I said, "but you do something for me. When you're playing with your fiddle, make sure you use resin. If you don't you might get Cupid's eczema."

I think Jack married Mary because Gracie and I had gotten married and he was afraid he'd have nobody to play with. They really didn't even know each other that well when they got married. "I wasn't very much in love with him when I married him," Mary admitted. "My love for him came after." She never did say after what. They got married in Waukegan, Illinois, in front of six or seven friends. Everybody at the ceremony was really surprised when, as soon as the rabbi pronounced them man and wife, Mary fainted. The reason they were surprised was because they expected Jack to faint.

The truth is that Mary made a nice home for Jack; in fact, Mary made several nice homes for Jack, and that was what Jack wanted. Jack needed somebody like Mary to take care of everything in the house because he couldn't do anything at all. I mean, Jack couldn't turn off the lights. Seriously, Freddie DeCordova, who directed Jack's TV show for years, used to say that when a light goes out in Jack's bedroom, he wants to move to a new house. Before Jack and Mary started sleeping in separate bedrooms, every night before Mary got into bed she'd pull down the shades and turn out the lights. One night she risked asking Jack to do it. It was actually a trick question—the lights were already out. But Jack got out of bed, pulled down the shades, turned on the lights and got back into bed. Mary waited a few seconds, then asked, "Don't you notice anything about the lights, Jack?"

Jack opened his eyes. "What's wrong with them?" he asked.

George S. Kaufman used to say that Jack didn't understand the hammer. He was right. Jack and Mary lived in the same house on Roxbury Drive for twenty-five years and for most of that time he thought someone had to go into the basement and stoke the furnace to bring up heat. He was working with his writers in his den one day and one of them asked him to turn up the heat. "I can't," Jack apologized, "the butler's off today." The writer then taught him how to use the thermostat. Well! Who knew? Jack just loved the whole idea of the thermostat. He thought the thermostat was the greatest thing he'd discovered since he'd found out that he could make all the lights on Wilshire Boulevard by driving exactly twenty-eight miles an hour. He called me immediately to find out if I knew all about the thermostat. When I told him I did, I think he was just a little disappointed. Then he asked me, "Did you know you could also *lower* the temperature?"

I kid a lot about Mary Benny. The truth is that Mary was my friend and Gracie's friend for fifty years, and we both loved her, but sometimes she was hard to figure out. I don't think Mary was ever a really happy person. As she got older, she became sort of a recluse, staying in her bedroom all day, playing solitaire. Eventually she didn't even go out of the house to have her hair done, she had a one-chair salon built onto her bedroom, and had the hairdresser come to the house. That was sad. But Jack never stopped loving her. There's an old expression, politics makes strange bedfellows. Well, sometimes so does marriage.

Even I can't tell you with a straight sentence that nobody had girlfriends. Look, some people cheated on their wives. Some of them even cheated on their girlfriends. But I think what people did in their private lives was their own business. Everybody had their own relationships and worked out an arrangement that was best for them. The only possible reason for me to write about these affairs would be to sell more books, and get a big sale to one of the weekly supermarket papers, and make a lot of money and I'm not . . . I mean, I can't . . . well . . . so, would it really hurt to mention that what's-his-name kept an apartment for you-know-who—who was married at the time? Or that the famous singer once found guess-who, wearing his only shirt, hiding in so-and-so's closet? And ---t-- and ---i-- --o--? And one of my best friends did have that girl in England when we. . . . But I'll tell you who was always faithful to the great love of his life. Jolson. Jolie never cheated on himself.

But please, don't quote me on any of this.

10

So, some of us were happily married, some of us were happily single, and some of us didn't know the difference. Then one day they invented television and we all went into it.

All right, maybe that's not such a great transition. But that's a hard transition to make. And if it's tough to make the transition to television in this book, imagine how tough it was to do it in real life.

I think I loved being in television more than any other part of my career. Television meant show business, and I wanted to be in show business. Television was that place where performers who could act like they knew what they were doing, could act. Maybe my friends didn't invent television, but we were right there at the beginning. As far as most people believe, television began with a closed-circuit demonstration at the 1939 World's Fair. But it started a long time before that. Berle made his television debut in 1929, for example. He was working at the Palace in Chicago when an inventor named V. A. Sanabria asked him to do a comedy bit over a closed-circuit network of about 200 sets. Milton remembers that he had to wear a lot of makeup for the test. Doing the test was actually a pretty daring thing for him to do—I mean, he was the first comedian on TV, who was he going to steal from? It worked out pretty well, though, Milton was the biggest star on the Sanabria, with a rating of almost 200 sets.

Jessel also claimed to be the Father of Television. No comment. In 1930 Georgie and Benny Rubin and newspaper columnist Bugs Baer and writer Harry Hershfield were asked by an inventor named Allen B. DuMont to be on his television. That's how things have changed—in those days you weren't on someone's television show, you were on their television. The entire DuMont Network consisted of one set in William Paley's suite at the Ambassador Hotel and the other set in General Sarnoff's suite at the Waldorf. The best thing about it was that there was no competition; no competition, there wasn't even another channel.

The show was broadcast from a studio in New Jersey to New York, and for the telecast their faces had to be painted green with brown lips. I know there's a New Jersey joke there somewhere but I'm not going to do it. Hey, I like New Jersey; if it wasn't for New Jersey being there, think of all the people who would fall off the end of the George Washington Bridge! Anyway, this was probably the first time any of them had ever performed in greenface. Who knows why they had to wear green makeup, maybe it was St. Patrick's Day. All I know is that Jessel made a phone call to his mother: "It's Georgie, Mama, Georgie from the money," and came out in black and white.

Ed Wynn did a telecast from the Radio City Music Hall in 1935 that went all the way to the top of the Empire State Building, almost twenty blocks away. Matthau once thought that he was in the first production of Shakespeare on TV. He told Laurence Olivier that he'd made history by playing Iago in a performance of *Othello* on the Philco Playhouse in 1952. Olivier just shook his head, pointed to himself and said "Macbeth, 1938."

"There was no television in 1938," Walter said. Olivier told him that there was. "Okay," Walter said, "how many people saw it?" Olivier put up one hand—but he raised all five fingers.

Just like radio, the first star of television was the television. People were so thrilled that a picture with sound was coming into their living rooms that they didn't even care what was on. The truth is that nobody could figure out exactly what television was. They didn't know if it was the rebirth of vaudeville, or legitimate theater, or an advertising gimmick or just a novelty. A lot of people, including some very smart movie studio executives, thought it was just a fad that was going to be forgotten in a few years, because they knew it was impossible for anyone to do a real show every week like they were doing on radio. One syndicated radio columnist even decided, "The more televiewers see telecasters groping to make television commercial as an advertising medium by displaying guns to kill insects, cereal boxes, cakes of soap, test tubes of gasoline, etc., the more it is

349

realized they are not on the right track. The eye doesn't like it. It becomes apparent that the movies have trained the eye not to tolerate such exhibits mixed with entertainment."

Within a year after that was written, Milton's show was the biggest thing on TV. And compared to guns that killed insects, Milton was brilliant.

Most people who were still successful on radio didn't go into television right away. Gracie and I didn't, Jack didn't, Bob Hope didn't. Of course none of us knew it then, but having a successful radio show was about to become as important as being nominated to run for vice-president on a ticket with Tom Dewey. But the people who weren't doing so well on radio had nothing to lose. Nobody knew what kind of material would work on television. As Ed Wynn said during his first telecast, "I know as much about television as anybody. I've already been on it for fifteen minutes."

It didn't take people long to realize that television was different from anything anybody had ever done—even without the greenface. It wasn't like vaudeville—in vaudeville if you made a mistake only a few hundred people saw you and you could correct it during the next show; in television millions of people were watching and you only got one chance. It wasn't like radio—the audience could see you; so Fanny couldn't play a six-year-old and Amos 'n' Andy had to be black. And it wasn't like the movies—everything had to be done live. There were no second takes. Let me put it this way, TV did something that vaudeville, radio and the movies hadn't been able to do—television made a big star out of Ed Sullivan.

A lot of great comedians had real trouble making the adjustment to television. Ed Wynn, for example, was one of the first comedians to have a regular weekly network show. His variety program went on the air in 1949 from Hollywood, the first national TV program to be done in Los Angeles. In those days everything anybody did was a first—an actor tripped, people said it was the best trip they'd ever seen on TV. Because the coaxial cable that connected New York and Los Angeles hadn't been laid yet, Wynn had to make a kinescope of his show and sent it to New York to be telecast on the East Coast.

Ed had some problems getting used to performing in front of a TV camera. He wanted to be free to move around the stage, just like he had in vaudeville, but the director insisted that all his moves had to be planned. Ed just couldn't understand why he had to change for the camera. Once, when the director asked him during a rehearsal if he intended to make the same moves during the actual telecast, Wynn asked, "Why do you have to know that? When you telecast a baseball game, do you ask the ball where it's going next?"

Ed had a tough time getting used to hitting his mark, the spot where he was supposed to be standing. Finally, when the director stopped a rehearsal to tell him that he'd missed his mark, Ed lost his temper. "I'm off my spot? I'm off my spot? Get Pat Weaver down here right now."

Pat Weaver was then the head of NBC. He came right down to the studio and asked, "What's the matter, Ed?"

"What's the matter? What's the matter? I've been in show business for fifty-eight years, and this young man wants me to stand over there, when I feel the humor right here. I just don't understand it. Why would I want to stand over there when all of the humor is right here?"

The biggest problem Ed had, and a lot of other people too, in making the adjustment to television was remembering his lines. He was sixty-three years old when he went into TV; gee, that's hard to believe, he didn't look that young, but it must be true, because I just wrote it. It had been years since Ed had had to memorize more than a few lines of dialogue, and it was hard for him. So somebody came up with a good idea: they wrote the first line of every paragraph on a piece of shirt cardboard and held it next to the camera Wynn was supposed to be looking at. That one line reminded him of the story he had to tell. But after six or seven shows practically the whole script had to be written out for him. And that's how cue cards were invented. Everything worked out fine; Wynn won the first Peabody Award given to a TV performer and two Emmys, and the usher who held the cards went into the cue card business and became the top cardman in television.

Smith and Dale, the greatest comedy team in

vaudeville, had a different problem adjusting to television when they made their debut on Berle's show. In vaudeville, time limits were flexible. As long as the audience was laughing, you could stay onstage until you were finished. But in television, everything had to be timed to the second. They only gave you ninety-five seconds to cook a three-minute egg. In rehearsal, Smith and Dale's famous Dr. Kronkhite sketch was running too long, and Milton asked them to cut a few lines. Neil Simon used a similar bit in *The Sunshine Boys*, and even when I wasn't really Smith or Dale I didn't want to cut the sketch. So I can imagine how Joe Smith and Charlie Dale felt when Berle asked them to cut their greatest sketch. Joe Smith took Milton aside and told him, "Listen, I could do it easy, it's not me, it's Charlie. We've been doing this sketch exactly the same way for forty-eight years, and it's a little hard for Charlie to change all of a sudden. So I was thinking, don't you think there's something else you maybe could fasten up a little?"

I think the most frightening thing about working in television in those days was that everything had to be done live. If you didn't get it right the first time, you didn't get it right forever. Live television really scared a lot of people. Groucho, for instance, wouldn't do it. He only agreed to host "You Bet Your Life" when the producer decided to film it in front of an audience and telecast it much later. It was really strange, nobody was nervous about working in front of an audience they could see, it was the people they couldn't see that they were worried about. Old "Lonesome George" Gobel had a very common way of dealing with camera fright—before going on the air he'd throw down two quick shots of scotch in his dressing room. One night Pat Buttram was the guest star on the show and, just before George and Pat had to go onstage, George offered him a shot. Pat turned it down, which surprised George. "You mean to tell me," he said, "that you're going out there . . . *alone?*"

Maybe Durante was the only performer who wasn't terrified about working live. I mean, with Jimmy, what could happen? If he said something wrong, how would anybody know? Jimmy's malaprops were an important part of his act and his writers would always give him two or three in every script, but they'd also put in enough hard words to ensure that he'd mess up a few more. They knew, for example, that Jimmy could always be counted on to ask his orchestra to "reprieve da music." And when the audience laughed, he'd say proudly, "Dey writes 'em, I says 'em!"

But maybe the real reason that Jimmy wasn't afraid to do live television was that he worked as hard as anybody in show business, and when his show went on the air he was ready to do it. Carol Channing once appeared on his show as his guest star. They had one big scene together and they rehearsed it until both of them knew it perfectly. Then they rehearsed it a few more times. In the middle of the final rehearsal Margie Little interrupted them and said something like, "What are you still rehearsing for? Both of you know the scene. I think maybe you're just a little nervous."

Jimmy looked at Carol and smiled. "Ah," he said, shaking his head, "the confidence a the amateur."

Look, I could understand why people didn't want to be on live TV. Things did happen. On the "Philco Playhouse," for example, in the middle of the big dramatic finish, a "dead" person in the background suddenly got up and walked off the set. When Ezio Pinza was on Berle's show he was ready to lip-sync one song, but some technician put on the wrong song. Wynn forgot a line one day and couldn't see his cue card. "I must have something to say," he ad-libbed, "otherwise I wouldn't be standing here." Sometimes the props didn't work. During a commercial for Maxwell House coffee on Red Buttons' variety show, the announcer poured steaming-hot coffee into a cup—and the cup split in half. Red immediately said, "And no other coffee can make that claim." Let me give you an example of the kind of things that happened. John Wayne was Durante's guest star one week. In their big skit, Durante was supposed to rescue Wayne from some bad guys holding him prisoner in a log cabin by punching the bad guy so hard that he flew through the wall of the cabin. Now I'll tell you a behind-the-scenes, inside-show-business secret: this had to be done with special effects. Durante really couldn't hit anybody that hard. So what they did was attach a wire to a harness worn by the stunt man, and when Durante threw his punch they yanked the wire and the stunt man flew away. At least that was what was supposed to happen. But a propman had forgotten to cut a hole in the balsawood cabin wall, and when they yanked on the wire the stunt man was lifted two feet into the air, and instead of going through the wall, he knocked it over. The wire then got snagged on the wall, and the stunt man just hung there in midair. I mean, he just hung there. Every few seconds he'd suddenly be jerked up another few inches as they worked backstage to get him free. Durante just stood there, looking at his miracle fist. That was one of the few times in show business history that a performer really was left hanging.

Durante didn't say a word, which was a great ad-lib. What could he say, "I've met people with bad hangups, but this is ridiculous," "Every wall wants to get into the act, "Why are you still hanging around?"

Live TV did give performers the chance to ad-lib, and some of them could take advantage of that. Berle knew a joke for every situation, although Jack used to say that Milton couldn't ad-lib a blister if he touched a hot stove. Wynn was a terrific ad-libber. I'll tell you a cute story. One week he had the beautiful actress Ann Sheridan on his show. After they'd done a scene together he thanked her and told her that he was going to do a big Western scene with his next guest star, Gary Cooper. Cooper was playing the desperado and Wynn was playing the sheriff. But just as Ann was about to go offstage a stagehand gave Ed an urgent message—Cooper hadn't shown up. So Ed asked Ann to play Gary's part in the skit. It was a nice setup.

After a commercial, Wynn came out in a cowboy outfit, wearing a badge that had "Sher" written on it—and Ed told the audience, "There are no ifs about it." Look, folks, but those were the jokes. When Ed spotted Ann he said, "Oh, there you are, the most dangerous man in the West."

"No, Sher," Ann told him, "you've got the wrong man."

Then Ed unrolled a poster with Cooper's face on it, reading, "WANTED $5000." He held it up next to Ann. "That's you," he said, "you can't deny it." It got a big laugh and he started to roll up the poster. But all of a sudden he stopped, and he looked at it, and he pointed to Cooper's picture and told the audience, "Incidentally, that's why Gary Cooper isn't here tonight. He wanted five thousand dollars."

Probably the best ad-lib I ever saw, maybe one of the best in the history of TV, took place on one of Jack's specials. His guests were the Marquis Chimps, a good chimp act done by three monkeys. All they were supposed to do was sit on their stools and make faces while Jack played a violin solo. But a minute or so after Jack started playing, and without being signaled by their trainer, two of the three chimps jumped off their stools and ran offstage. The third chimp just sat there, looking so sad. Looking a little like Jack, actually. But finally even he couldn't take it anymore. He looked over at Jack, who was still scratching on his fiddle, jumped off his stool, picked it up and carried it offstage. Without saying a word, the chimp had stolen the show. He'd also stolen Jack's act.

The two most popular types of shows on early television were professional wrestling and variety shows. I'll tell you something, the wrestling matches usually were better written than the variety shows. For the most part the variety shows were just televised vaudeville. In fact, NBC announced Milton Berle's show, "The Texaco Star Theatre," as "Old-time vaudeville . . . patterned after the shows of New York's Palace Theatre, for many years vaudeville's national headquarters, the show will feature jugglers, song and dance teams, tightwire artists, impersonators, magicians, ventriloquists, and the multitude of other acts that packed them in at the Palace." The only thing NBC didn't say, of course, was that Milton intended to play all the parts himself.

It was really something. It turned out that vaudeville hadn't died after all—it had just been in a coma. A lot of the old acts started rehearsing again. In fact, I got a very nice note from the seal asking me if I wanted to dump the girl and team up again.

The three biggest stars of early television were Berle, Wynn and Gorgeous George. Nobody was bigger than Berle. Milton would be the first person to tell you that. Also the second, and the third. It's true, though. In fact, it was only because of Milton's success that a lot of other comedians finally decided to go into TV. In fact, I can remember Bob Hope telling me that he just had to get into television before Berle used up all of his material.

. . . and the fourth . . .

When Berle moved to New York to do his show, someone asked Hope if he'd stolen anything while he had been out in Hollywood. "Well," Bob said, "I won't say he stole anything, but they now call the studio where he worked Warner Brother."

Those first few years on television were the greatest of Milton's career. He'd never really been a major vaudeville or radio star, but he dominated the early days of TV the way Morse had dominated the telegraph. Until television, Milton's biggest success had come in nightclubs, but nightclubs were really too small for him. On television he could perform for the whole country. Who knew that the whole country was also too small for him?

I guess the best way to describe "The Texaco Star Theatre" is to say that Milton went for broad comedy—in fact, he'd usually open the show by coming out dressed as a broad. "One thing I'm convinced of," he said, "custard pies, seltzer bottles, tripping on banana peels, a bag of flour in the kisser, falling into an open manhole, will always be funny." I think I can explain the show like this: probably the most intelligent joke on the program consisted of Milton shouting "Makeup" as loud as he could, then getting hit in the face with a powder puff full of flour.

But it was the most successful show in television history. I mean that right up until you're reading this sentence no show has ever been more successful. Three out of every four television sets in America were watching Milton. Movie theaters, which had helped close vaudeville, had to close on Tuesday nights when he was on, and put up signs like, WERE HOME WATCHING MILTON TOO, or WE GIVE UP MILTON TUESDAY NIGHTS ARE YOURS. People said Berle was responsible for selling more television sets than anyone else in history— "I know that's true," Joe E. Lewis said, "I sold mine. My brother sold his." But when Berle, when Berle . . . I have to stop stuttering when I type . . . Berle was the King, and the Queen, of vision between 1948 and 1952, more than 17,000,000 sets were sold. The competing stations tried 111 different shows against him, but he just killed everybody else in the ratings. It got so bad that CBS finally went for the Big One—they put God on opposite him. That's what's known as serious counterprogramming. Bishop Sheen's show didn't do so well either, but they kept it on the air anyway. Nobody is going to cancel God's show.

You never know.

Milton was the whole show. He was the star, the director, he planned the lighting, the scenery, the costumes, the choreography, he approved the script, he was the musical director, he even wrote lyrics for some of the songs he sang. He even invented a device called "The Berlite," a light on top of the camera that blinked until the audience had stopped laughing, so the actors would know when to say their next line, and he invented the isolated camera, which made editing much easier. About the only thing he didn't do was operate the cameras—but he did plan the camera shots.

During rehearsals he'd walk around with a towel and a police whistle around his neck, and he'd constantly be blowing that whistle to get everybody's attention. I think I would be exaggerating if I said Milton was the best-liked person on the set.

Hal Kanter was one of Milton's writers on that show, and he was telling me about the day the great comedy writer Larry Gelbart and his wife came to watch the rehearsal. Gelbart and his wife were close friends of Milton and Ruth. "For some reason," Hal remembered, "Milton was on his worst behavior that day. He was yelling at everybody and correcting everything. It was just a bad day. When we finally finished I was saying goodnight to Larry and his wife and he said, 'Let me ask you a question. After watching what went on here all day, there's something I just don't understand. How can a man with your track record put up with all the crap he gives you?'

"And I told him, 'I do it because he's paying me five thousand dollars a week. Now let me ask you a question. Why are you his friend for free?'

"I worked with Milton for a long time. And we

had our fights, but when he starts talking about staging and music and lights and jokes, you have to listen to him because he knows what he's talking about. He's a very astute showman and I have tremendous admiration for him. But I have to tell you, while we were working together there were several times when I considered homicide. Never suicide, always homicide."

Milton could be very difficult. Every night he'd tell his manager to call him the next day at a specific time. Once, for example, he told him to call at exactly 10:42. When the telephone rang at 10:44, Milton answered the phone and said, "Hello, stranger." Onstage, he was even tougher. Somebody once wrote that the man who said that nothing was impossible had never tried to get between Milton and a camera. Milton just couldn't let anybody else do their act on his show without interrupting them. He had to be part of every bit on the show. In fact, they used to say that Milton did everything to remain the center of attention except shoot a guest star. Sometimes, when he thought a guest was getting too much attention, he'd grab him by the lapel of his jacket and turn him away from the camera. When Jackie Gleason was his guest star, Gleason put straight pins under his lapels to stop Milton from doing that. It didn't bother Milton at all. He just screamed and turned Gleason around.

Look, I'm not going to criticize Milton, he knew what he was doing. And the audience loved him. But there was one thing that he did that I objected to, and that took place when Marilyn Monroe guest-starred on his show. During the show Marilyn, who just happened to be in and out of her most revealing gown, bent over to take a bow, and Milton stuck a program in front of her. I always thought there was a law against something like that. If there isn't, there certainly should be.

Actually, Milton was a very generous performer. He only interrupted those guests whose acts he thought he could improve. It was just a coincidence that that turned out to be everybody. A lot of performers wouldn't do the show because Milton wouldn't leave them alone, and some of those who did do the show regretted it. Singer Gloria DeHaven walked off the show because Milton wouldn't stay out of her act. Ethel Merman only agreed to do the show when Milton guaranteed he wouldn't bother her. And Mahalia Jackson . . . Mahalia Jackson was a wonderful gospel singer, she sang about trouble and hardship and having faith in the Lord. But until she worked with Milton, she didn't know what trouble really was.

During rehearsals he made her change her costume several times, and he cut the three songs she was supposed to do down to one. They just didn't get along. Somehow, they made it through the show. But after the show Hal Kanter stopped by her dressing room to thank her. "Mr. Kanter," Mahalia said, "that Uncle Miltie sure is a genius, isn't he?"

Kanter thought about that for a few seconds,

then said, "Well, yes, I suppose you might say that in his particular field, you could consider him a genius."

"Yeah, well, that's what I heard," she said. "Well, let me tell you something. If I ever come on this show again, which I really doubt, you best tell him not to genius all over me."

Just like in vaudeville, the most important thing on these variety shows was the bill. Ratings really depended on the popularity of the guest stars. In a lot of cases, this was the first time that people were able to see stars they'd been reading about their whole lives performing live, and right in their living rooms. Although I could never figure out why anybody wanted Milton in their living room; he was in my living room many times, and he always got flour all over the furniture. Look, television in those days was like Hammerstein's, if you got you name in the newspaper, you could be a guest star.

Durante probably worked with his guests better than anybody else. Television had come along at the right time for Jimmy. He wasn't working that much, and within a very short period of time his wife, his father and Lou Clayton had died. Probably the only reason he even went into TV was because Clayton had told him, a few months before he died, that TV was going to be very big. "It's going to be much better than radio for you," he said, " 'cause they're gonna have the schnozzola to look at." And Jimmy always listened to Clayton.

He went on the air in 1950. Right from the start he had a gimmick that was very different from Milton's—character material. See, Milton never created a character for himself. Unless you consider loud a character. So every dress Milton wore had to be funny. But, just like Jack, Durante had spent a lifetime creating his character—Durante, the street guy wit' the big smile and de bigger nose, at war with the forces of culture. The unstuffer of stuffed shirts. At that time the most successful highbrow show on the air was "Omnibus." Jimmy's shows could have been called "Omnibust." Most of his guests were stars in worlds Jimmy didn't understand at all: people like opera stars Helen Traubel, Lily Pons and Patrice Munsel; dramatic actresses like Ethel Barrymore and Bette Davis; classical musicians like Liberace, and Presidents' relatives like Margaret Truman. And he was great with all of them. All you had to do was think about Durante working with an opera star and you already got the joke.

Opera star Helen Traubel was the perfect stooge for Jimmy because she had a great sense of humor. But before she went on his show for the first time they had some problems. The producers wanted her to sing one of Jimmy's standard songs and she wouldn't do it, telling them that it just wasn't her kind of music. "Whattya mean, it ain't her kinda number?" Durante said when he heard what she said. "If she can't sing, what am I gonna do with her in the act?"

Somebody told Jimmy that she was one of the

greatest singers in the world, she just didn't want to do a honky-tonk number.

Jimmy thought about that for a minute. "All right then," he asked. "Can she strut?"

On the show they ended up doing a parody of an opera. Helen Traubel played a diva wearing a suit of armor, and Jimmy played her lover, who kept trying to figure out how to pin a corsage on her armor. I think the verdict was that Jimmy won this "crash of cultures": Helen Traubel ended up doing a nightclub act while Jimmy never sang in the opera.

No matter what Jimmy's guests did in show business, when they were on his show it always came down to some version of "Can they strut?" For example, when Liberace and his violin-playing brother, George, were on the show, Jimmy had them doing a soft-shoe number. Ethel Barrymore sang and played ragtime piano. Even Bette Davis did a slapstick routine.

Of course, Jimmy never stopped doing the type of material that had made him so popular in the speakeasies. On his very first show, for instance, he went out into the audience and caught somebody watching a competing program on a television set. Jimmy picked up the set and threw it away, screaming, "Nobody watches 'The Goldbergs' when Durante's on!" Then he sang all his old songs and did all the old dances and worked with an old lion.

The lion had a good act. He came running down a long chute, then when he reached the bottom of the chute he just fell over and lay absolutely still. The lion did nothing, which is exactly what you want a lion to do. When Jimmy heard about this lion he went out to the trainer's place with his writers to audition him. How do you audition a lion?

This is a do-it-yourself punch line: "   ."

When they got there the trainer told Jimmy to get into the cage with the lion. Jimmy just looked at him. Then he laughed at him. The trainer insisted it was perfectly safe, so Jimmy did the smart thing—he insisted his writers go in the cage first. Once everybody was cowering in the cage, the trainer gave Jimmy a chair. "That's all right," Jimmy said, "I'll stand."

The trainer told him that he was supposed to use the chair to fight the lion. Jimmy laughed at him again. Then he said, "I got an idea. You stand here with the chair. I'll stand over there."

That wouldn't work, the trainer told him. "No one can stand between you and the lion," he said, "because you're the star."

Jimmy would do almost anything for a laugh; being picked up by an elephant in its trunk, singing with Helen Traubel, dancing with Liberace, getting in a cage with a lion. Even in vaudeville I wouldn't have worked with a lion, I wouldn't have wanted to make the seal jealous. Besides, working on the same bill with Jolson was dangerous enough. But as Jimmy stood in the cage the lion came down the chute and fell over. "Gees," Jimmy said, "dat's funny." The lion was booked.

In this case Jimmy didn't care if the lion could strut, he just wanted to make sure he couldn't chew.

When they did the show the lion came running down the chute, and Jimmy stood at the bottom of the chute holding a chair, waiting for him. The lion reached the bottom of the chute and stood there. Then he started walking around. The one thing he didn't do was fall over. The trainer ran into the cage and started throwing things at the lion to get him to go back up the chute. Jimmy didn't care what the trainer threw at the lion, as long as it wasn't his chair. I'm sure there was only one thought in Durante's mind as he watched this lion strutting around the cage.

I'll tell you something; remembering this show, it makes me sad that W. C. Fields hadn't lived to be on television. I knew Bill a long, long time, and believe me, he would have fallen down.

Jack Benny and Gracie and I didn't go into television right away. I read a lot about television and I knew how dangerous it could be—every day I read stories about people falling off their roof trying to put up an antenna. Besides, I didn't have to worry about Milton stealing my act, she was sleeping right next to me.

It was obvious to me right from the beginning that television was going to be the biggest thing yet, and when Wynn was doing his show in Hollywood, we'd all get dressed up and go to the studio to watch how he did it. And we watched and we learned. When Jim and Marian Jordan,

"Fibber McGee and Molly," were signed by a milk company to represent them on TV, Carnation Evaporated Milk—the milk that came from contented cows—decided to find a couple to represent their product. Charlie Lowe, who later married Carol Channing, thought that Gracie and I would make the perfect "contented couple." So that's how we got on the air. But there was one question I always wanted to ask our sponsor, and never did: If they got powdered milk from contented cows, what did you get from discontented cows? Sour cream?

I've been waiting almost four decades to tell that joke. Maybe I should have waited a little longer.

We did our show live for the first two seasons. Actually, it was Gracie who figured out how we should work on television. "The most important thing," she told me, "is that we have to talk slowly. Because when we're on the air at seven o'clock people are eating, and if we talk fast, the people who are watching us will eat fast, and then they'll get indigestion and they won't like us." So we talked slowly and nobody got sick to their stomach from watching us and we were a big success. And I think the fact that we had great writers and a terrific cast helped too. And the fact that I never asked our sponsor that question.

Television really was the toughest thing we'd ever done. Even when we weren't working in the studio, we were somewhere working on the show. In vaudeville, we did the same material twice a day for different audiences. In radio, we read from a script. But in television we had to do different material every week for the same audience, and we couldn't read from a script. In vaudeville and in radio our costumes had consisted of "What are you going to wear to the theater?" In television we had to change costumes several times each show, and each costume had to be fitted. In vaudeville we wore a little pancake makeup. In radio Gracie wore lipstick. In television we had to have real makeup and I had to have my toupee combed. In vaudeville we could do our seventeen minutes in about twenty minutes. In radio, we did a half hour in twenty-four minutes, not counting commercials. But in television, once we started filming the show, it sometimes took us ten hours to do a half hour.

I think that once we started filming the show it got easier for everyone except Gracie. When we were doing the show live we had to do the scenes in the right order, which made it a little easier for Gracie to remember her lines because they made more sense. They never made a lot of sense, but they made more sense. But when we started filming the show to save time we had every set prearranged and prelighted, and we just moved from one set to the next set and did whatever scene took place there. We didn't necessarily work in order, and that made it much tougher for Gracie to remember her lines. Try counting to ten from the inside out; that's how tough it was for Gracie to do her lines.

When filmed situation comedies became popular another member of the Round Table, Danny Thomas, became one of the biggest stars on TV. His show, "Make Room for Daddy," was number one for two seasons. Danny tells this wonderful story about one of his writers on that show, a very short man named Artie Stander. One day Danny walked into the men's room and there was Stander, standing up on the toilet, doing what you do standing up. When Danny asked him what he was doing, Artie explained, "I always wanted to know how Gary Cooper felt."

Jack got into television about the same time we did. Jack and I talked about TV a lot, trying to figure out the best way to do it. Finally we decided that there was not secret to it: you had to make people laugh. It didn't really matter what we did, as long as we made people laugh.

Jack didn't have to worry. Television was the perfect theater for him. So much of Jack's humor depended on his facial expressions, and that had been lost on radio. In fact, forget everything I wrote in chapter four. After you saw Jack working on television, you knew how lucky he'd been to make it on radio.

Jack made his TV debut on a special program presented by KTTV in Los Angeles when the station went on the air for the first time in 1949. Probably thanks to Jack's appearance, that special immediately became the top-rated show in the whole history of the station. On the show Jack did a wonderful violin duet with Isaac Stern—Stern played all the music and Jack plinked his strings three times. All right, maybe I underestimated Jack's talent, they were nice plinks. Okay, great plinks. Then Jack played the fiddle in a hillbilly spoof called "Spike Benny of the Old West." I remember that skit, it probably should have been called "Old Spike Benny of the West Coast."

Jack told everybody that he wasn't at all nervous about being on television; in fact, he was so not nervous that for days before the show all he could talk about was how not nervous he was. Jack was nervous. Jack was always a little nervous before a performance. He was always afraid that the audience wasn't going to love him. Of course, he was the only comedian I've ever known who felt that way.

If you believe that, I have some swampland in downtown Beverly Hills to sell you. Well, I told you I didn't know anything about real estate.

Let me tell you how insecure Jack was, even when he was one of the biggest stars in show business. At one time somebody took a poll and found out that 97 percent of the people they asked liked and respected Jack Benny. When Jack found out about that, instead of being thrilled, all he could do was worry, "What did I do to the other three percent?"

See, Jack was the kind of person who would start worrying when everything was going too well for him. I think the only time he really didn't worry was when he had a lot to worry about. He was just a nervous person; he was a very light sleeper. I mean, his writers used to say that by the time they woke up in the morning Jack had already been awake and worrying for two hours.

On his first show, in fact, Jack told his viewers, "You see, unless you're nervous before a show you're not a true artist. I'm a wreck."

Jack's television debut went so well that even Mary didn't complain. His own show went on the air on CBS a year later. Jack's opening line on national TV was, "I'd give a million dollars to know what I look like." Then he explained, "Ladies and gentlemen, I must tell you why I decided to go into television at this time. You see, it got to be a little embarrassing . . . so many of my fans kept asking me why I didn't get into this particular medium. They wanted to know if I was afraid of it. Well, of course that's ridiculous—I wasn't afraid. It was my sponsor who didn't have the nerve!"

Can't you just hear him saying that?

Jack did his half-hour show for fifteen years, then did hour specials for another nine years. He won eight Emmy Awards, plus the first Trustees Award ever given by the Academy of Television Arts and Sciences. But when he started out, nobody was really sure the character that had worked so well on radio would work on TV. The problem with television is that it takes no imagination—so instead of imagining Jack's vault and his Maxwell and his living room with the pay phone in it, the viewer could see it. Here's another show business tip for you—the concept of an alligator is funnier than a real alligator.

It took some time, and Jack had to make some adjustments, but eventually his writers came up with enough visual material to make Jack's character work on television. I'll give you an example: On one show Jack's trousers were hanging on a rack, and when a boy delivered a package Rochester took a quarter out of one of the trouser pockets and tipped him. A few seconds later Jack walked into the room, picked up his pants and paused. "Rochester," he asked, "who took a quarter out of my pants?"

Jack's cheap character worked so well on TV that he could fit into any format. Here's another question for you: What did Jackie Gleason's "Honeymooners" have in common with Hal March's "$64,000 Question"?

I know, I know, you're still trying to figure out the three-letter beverage. But the answer to this question is that Jack appeared on both shows as a guest star. Listen, Jack was on every popular show on television as a guest star, what made these two special was that they never had guest stars. How do you guest star on a quiz show?

On "The Honeymooners" Jack played Ralph and Alice Kramden's landlord. That's all you have to know to get the joke. And on "The $64,000 Question he played a contestant named Jack Benny. That was Jesse Block's idea; when he heard the kind of money quiz shows were giving away he knew it was a perfect format for Jack. Jack agreed to do it right away, too—as long as he could keep the money he won. Jack's subject was "The Violin and Violin Music." He actually looked a little nervous when the host, Hal March—who had played Harry Morton on my show for one season—asked him the first question. I don't remember the question, I think it was something like: Who wrote Beethoven's Fifth Symphony? When Jack answered it correctly, Hal March said, "That's right for sixty-four dollars, want to go for a hundred and twenty-eight?" "No," Jack said. He wanted to take his $64 and leave. He became the first person to win $64 and not go on.

Years later it came out that some of the quiz shows had been fixed. But I don't think Jack participated in anything illegal. I think Jack and his writers simply knew the answer to that question.

Part of Jack's great appeal on television was that he made it look so easy, and it took a lot of hard work to do that. If I stared at the camera, I looked like I was staring at the camera; but when Jack stared at the camera, his audience laughed. I figured there was only one possible reason for that —Jack had funnier cameras. That, plus the fact that his character was so well developed that the audience always knew exactly what he was thinking. That was the incredible thing about Jack, the audience knew what was going on in his mind. How many other characters in the entire history of television can you say that about? Besides Lassie, who you just knew was always thinking about her next meal. I mean, you certainly never knew what was going on in Gracie's mind. Even when

375

she told you. But the audience always knew what Jack was thinking.

One of the last TV shows Jack did was "Jack Benny's First Farewell Special." The gimmick was that all of the guest stars had come to wish Jack well in his retirement, while he kept telling them that he wasn't *really* retiring, that this was only his first farewell special. Next year, he insisted, he was going to host his second farewell special, and the year after that . . . But at the end of the show Ronnie Reagan came onstage to give Jack a retirement present: the curtain lifted to reveal a brand-new, fully equipped Rolls-Royce. Jack just stared at the camera, believe me, everybody knew what he was thinking.

Late in Jack's career he started doing commercials. A lot of people made a big deal about that, wondering why someone who had as much money as Jack did would sell himself like that. In fact, a reporter asked Jack why he'd done the commercial, saying, "It couldn't possibly be for the money."

Jack just looked at him. I told you, even when you're just reading about him you know what he was thinking.

Actually we all did commercials. Durante got as much as $100,000 for a one-minute spot. We were vaudevillians; we weren't worried so much about artistic integrity as we were that the check might bounce. Jack signed a multimillion-dollar deal with Texaco that included doing commercials, sponsorship of his specials and personal appearances. It was a complete package. "Show business has changed," he said one day, explaining why he'd agreed to do the commercials, "and I'm changing with it. There's no class in show business today, you just do anything, and everything . . ."

Now that really wasn't true. As long as Jack Benny was in show business there was a lot of class in it. William Saroyan, the great writer who was Carol Matthau's first husband, probably described Jack as well as anybody ever has when he wrote, "Jack Benny had style from the beginning. He stood straight and walked sideways as if being shoved by the touch of genius—and knew it, and you'd know it too, in a moment. Style. If you've got it, you don't need much else. If you haven't got it, well . . . it doesn't matter what you've got."

Believe me, my friend Jack Benny had it.

11

One afternoon a couple of years before *The Jolson Story* put Jolie back on top again, he was playing cards in his suite at the Sherry Netherland with his friend Harry Akst. This was during the time I was still getting sturgeon from him. They heard some music coming from the street and Harry went over to the window. "Hey, Al, look," he said, "it's a parade." Jolie just sat there. "Com'on, Al," Harry urged, "come take a look. You love a parade."

Jolson didn't even look up. "Not when it passes you by."

The only thing permanent in show business is insecurity. No matter how successful you are, that's the one thing you never lose. Cantor was so nervous about his career that he didn't even like riding in a down elevator. I was with Walter Matthau the night *The Sunshine Boys* opened. Walter was already one of the biggest stars in the movie business and *The Sunshine Boys* had gotten great reviews. Instead of enjoying that, I remember him saying, "You know George, if I ever get another picture. . . "

He wasn't kidding. Comedians kid about life and love and sex, marriage, politics, death, you know, all the funny stuff—but you never hear a comedian making jokes about his career. That's serious. There's nothing funny about that. Somebody like Fred Allen should have said that the worst thing about success is that it really makes you appreciate how terrible failure is. Fred should have said that, because I can't. That's much too smart for me. Look, the only thing for certain in show business is that eventually you're going to fail. Failing is easy. You don't have to be good to fail. I did it even before I knew what I was doing. I guess it just came naturally. Success is tough. It helps to be good, but you also have to be lucky. That's why I was so lucky—I was a success at failing. And most of the time success is temporary. Even the seal ended up working in some two-bit aquarium for fish heads.

A lot of the biggest stars in vaudeville, people like Lou Holtz and Sophie Tucker, never made it in radio. And big radio stars like Jack Pearl and Fibber and Molly failed in the movies and on television. In fact, whether you're talking about show business, sex or Japanese acrobats, one thing is true—nobody stays on top the whole time.

Who knows why really talented people like Fred Allen, Cantor, Fanny Brice and Jessel didn't make it on TV. Fred Allen once said, "I didn't make it in television because of ill health. I made people sick." He wasn't that bad, he just didn't make them laugh. Fred never felt comfortable on television. I mean, he didn't even like watching TV. Bob Hope told me about the time he was in New

York City, and staying at the Algonquin Hotel on 44th Street. When he checked in, the manager sent up a big basket of fruit and flowers, and the bellboy just happened to put it on top of the TV set. Fred came over to join him for dinner, and when he walked in the room and saw the basket, he smiled and said, "You know, that's the best thing I've seen on television yet."

Fred tried a few different formats, but none of them were really right for him. He had a weekly variety show, he hosted a version of "Allen's Alley," he was even the moderator of the quiz shows "Two for the Money" and "Judge for Yourself." He finally became a regular panelist on "What's My Line?" Maybe Fred's problem was that he forced the audience to think, and in those days people were so thrilled to have television in their homes that they didn't want to think. No one wondered why Milton blacked out his teeth and wore a dress. They just knew it was funny.

I don't think Fred's failure on television made him depressed; he was depressed long before television was invented. But it did make him a little bitter. "I've finally figured out why they call television a medium," he said. "It's because nothing in it is well done."

That wasn't really fair. Besides, I thought Milton looked sort of cute in a dress.

Fanny Brice also hated television. She knew she couldn't play Snooks on the air and she thought she was too old to go back to her old stage material. That sad thing was that other people believed that too. I remember after Ed Wynn's first TV telecast we all crowded into his dressing room to congratulate him. While we were there the phone rang and he had a brief conversation. "That was my dear friend Fanny Brice, the funniest woman in the American theater," he said when he hung up, or something like that. "She just called to tell me that she thought the show was great." Well, Ed was just thrilled by that call. I guess the next week, after his second show, Fanny called again, and again Ed got excited that his dear old friend had taken the time to call him. This went on for a few weeks. Now, by the sixth week, Ed had used up most of the material he'd done in vaudeville and in the theater and was starting to depend on guest stars. He needed to have some big names on his show to compete with the New York shows. So he met with his writers to figure out who to get for the show. They threw out a lot of names, and finally Sy Jacobs asked, "How about your dear old friend?"

"What dear old friend?" Ed asked.

"Fanny Brice."

"What?" Ed snapped at him. "Are you kidding? What the @#%#%& can she do?"

Well, as it turned out, she might have helped him stay on the air, that's what she might've done.

Maybe Fanny's problem was that she didn't let herself get older. I don't mean she should have played Snooks as a nine-year-old, I mean she should have allowed herself to mature. Sophie Tucker was great on TV because she didn't try to be something she wasn't. "The older a woman is, the better she is," Sophie used to say, "and I ought to know, baby, 'cause I'm older than hell." Sophie didn't try to do the same things when she was seventy-five years old that she'd done when she was starring in vaudeville. When she was young, for example, she sang a song called "Papa Goes Where Mama Goes, Or Papa Doesn't Go Out at Night," and she sang it like she was a red-hot mama. Her meaning was clear—Papa followed Mama because she was sexy. But as she got older she knew it was silly to try to convince an audience that Papa was following Mama for sex. So she still sang the song when she was in her seventies—but when she sang it, she kept a gun pointed at Papa.

Blossom Seeley was another woman who wouldn't let herself get old. She tried to sing "Toddling the Todalo" when she was eighty years old the same way she'd sung it when she was twenty-five. That was ridiculous, nobody can toddle the todalo at eighty like they could when they were twenty-five. Whatever it means, you just can't do it as well. She even wore white gloves when she performed so that people couldn't see her veins. What's wrong with veins? At least she didn't try to wear her tiger's head.

Georgie Jessel wouldn't change his act as he got older. And older. I mean, the first time he went on TV he did the same kind of telephone routine he'd been doing since 1915, he had a conversation with his mother. Nobody believed that. His mother would have been maybe a hundred years old. You know what a real conversation with Georgie's mother would have been like: "HELLO, MAMA? IT'S ME, GEORGIE. GEORGIE. I SAID GEORGIE. THAT'S RIGHT, MAMA, GEORGIE, YOUR SON. NOT GUN, MAMA, SON. GEORGIE. G-E-O-R . . . ."

I think Georgie felt that since he had been in show business long before television had been invented, television was going to have to adjust to him. Well, it just didn't work that way. Nobody wanted to turn on the Georgie, they wanted to watch television. He just didn't understand TV. "To be television," he told us at the club one day, "a show has to be live. A show like 'I Love Lucy' is nothing but a two-reeler, although it's a damned good one. This business didn't start out to be telling the audience, here's something we filmed last year. . . ."

Georgie tried several different types of TV shows. He was the host of a variety show called "The All-Star Revue." He hosted another show called "Comeback," which told the stories of one-time stars whose careers had gone downhill and who were trying to make a comeback. Well, this show had no chance. The public is pretty smart, and this was a show featuring people the public had already decided they didn't want to see. That's why their careers had gone downhill in the first place. So why would they watch performers on this show when they didn't want to see them anywhere else? They didn't.

The show that should have worked for George

was a half-hour version of the famous Friars Club roasts. Georgie sat at a long table and told some of his old stories, then introduced his guests. It was almost exactly the same show Dean Martin did successfully a few years later. The problem with the show was that Georgie insisted on doing the whole show himself; he starred in it, wrote it, picked the talent, he told the director what to do. I mean, who did he think he was, Frank Fay?

I told him it was a great idea, but I begged him to hire some writers and a producer and let them do their jobs, but he wouldn't do it. Maybe it was his ego, maybe he wanted to keep more of the budget, but he really believed he could do everything himself. "When I started in television," he said, "they told me I couldn't do a show by appearing as an after-dinner speaker, just standing at the table and talking. They said I had to move around. I said, 'Doesn't Heifetz stand still and play the fiddle?' I can talk as good as he plays."

The show lasted only a few weeks. Actually, he didn't just stand still on the stage. He let his guest stars do some sketches. I think I can sum up how good this show was by describing a typical bit to you: Georgie had Eddie Fisher and Margaret O'Brien doing a scene from *Romeo and Juliet*.

As I said, I just don't think Georgie understood TV.

I just don't think Cantor understood TV either. And apparently it was mutual. Georgie and Eddie had been successful for so long doing their own material their own way, they just wouldn't change.

384

Just a few years after Cantor's radio show had been canceled because he spoke out against fascism, he became the first person to be censored on TV. In 1944 Eddie's show was the first program to be telecast from one city to another by relay, meaning that the television waves were transmitted from one relay tower to the next, where the signal was amplified, then transmitted. The reason I know how that works is that I'm a member of the Academy of Television Arts and Sciences, and that was part of the sciences. On Eddie's show, which was broadcast from New York to Philadelphia, Eddie sang a duet called "We're Having a Baby, My Baby and Me," and the NBC censor decided that some of the lyrics were objectionable. I think he said that people who watch TV didn't have babies. So when Eddie started singing the objectionable parts of the song, they cut off the sound. So I guess it could be said that Eddie's career stretched from silent movies to silent television.

And they didn't just censor the lyrics. Let me tell you how much TV progressed in just a few years: In 1956, when Elvis Presley sang on the Sullivan show and the Berle show, the camera shot him from the waist up because of the suggestive way he moved his hips. But in 1944, when Cantor was singing his song, they also shot him from the waist up—because from the waist down he was doing the hula. Excuse me, he was doing a suggestive hula. I'll tell you what it suggested—it suggested that Cantor couldn't do the hula. So they censored Cantor's hula. It was ridiculous. What

385

you saw when Matthau dropped his pants was more suggestive than Eddie Cantor's hula.

Eddie got really upset, and said that since he was older than television he knew what was best. "No man can be in this business for thirty-five years and do vulgarity and last," he said. "I've been at it longer than NBC or television."

Cantor was never a big television star because, just like Jessel, he wouldn't change his act. His first comedy special in 1950 was a big hit because people wanted to see him. And on that show he did his stage act, he sang all his old songs, "Ain't She Sweet," "Ma—He's Making Eyes at Me," "Bye Bye Blackbird," "Makin' Whoopee!" "Waitin' for the Robert E. Lee," and, of course, "Ida," as the camera showed a close-up of Ida sitting in the audience. And he danced around the stage and waved his arms and jumped into the air, he even did some of his material in blackface. It was a great show, but it had taken him forty years to prepare for it. After that he had two weeks to get ready for his next show. Maybe "Bye Bye Blackbird" is a nice song for the first six weeks, but after that you wish the blackbirds would leave already.

Eddie just didn't trust new material. Once his writers went to his house for a meeting and found him lying naked on a massage table in his back-yard. They'd written a cute sketch parodying professional wrestling, which was big on TV at the time. When they described it to him, he got off the table and got down on the ground on his hands and knees and twisted his body. "You mean I do this?" he asked. Then he twisted some more, "And then I do this? And this?" He went through the whole routine, doing all the moves. Then he climbed back onto the table and shook his head. "Nah," he said, "that's too tough for me. I can't do all that stuff." For Eddie, taking a risk meant singing "Ain't She Sweet" in whiteface.

I didn't have too much trouble making the transition to television; I didn't have an act, so I didn't have to change. I had talked to Gracie in vaudeville, I had talked to Gracie in radio, I had talked to Gracie in the movies. The big change I made for TV was that I talked to Gracie—and then I talked to you. But it was much tougher for people like Cantor and Jessel and Jolson. They had an act, they'd become big stars by doing that act for forty years. It was just too tough for them to change. Cantor wasn't Berle, he looked terrible in a dress. All right, maybe not terrible, but he was too short to look very good.

Jolson died of a heart attack before he got into TV. I don't think he would have liked it though, I think he would have decided it was too restricting for him. He was on television once in his whole life. A few months before he died he performed at a big charity benefit sponsored by the *Chicago Tribune* at Soldiers Field. Colonel McCormick, who owned the *Tribune*, was too sick to attend the show, but he loved Jolson so much that they set up a special closed-circuit system from the stadium to his house and telecast the show. And that was the only time Jolson was ever on TV.

He talked about going into television though; he used to say he had a plan. I'll tell you about Jolson's plan. One night he had dinner with Wynn, and Wynn asked him to come on his show. Jolson agreed to do it. So Wynn sent his head writer, Hal Kanter, out to Jolson's place to make plans for his appearance. "What do you want to do on the show?" Hal asked him.

"What show's dat?" Jolie asked.

"Ed Wynn's show. You told Ed you'd come on the show."

Jolie laughed a little. "Oh, you ain't gonna believe that, are you? I ain't gonna do no Ed Wynn show."

"Then why'd you tell him you were?"

"Ah," Jolie said, "how could I say no to an old man like that? I'd break his heart. I mean, you look at that sweet face, how you gonna say no?

"But see, I know how I'm gonna go into TV. When Jolson goes on the air, there's gonna be but one sponsor, maybe I gonna get me somebody like General Motors. What's gonna happen is that there's gonna be no commercials. It's gonna start out with somebody like General Eisenhower, he's gonna come out and say, 'Ladies and gentlemen, General Motors takes great pleasure in presenting Al Jolson.' Then I gonna come out, I gonna sing a few songs, and then I'm gonna sit down at the footlights the way I used to do it at the Winner Garden and I'm gonna tell a few stories, then I'm gonna sing a few more songs, then I'm gonna bring a guest star out, maybe I'm gonna get Bingie on the show, and we gonna do a few jokes and then we gonna sing a song or two, then he'll leave and I'll finish up with a medley. And at the end of the night, General Eisenhower, he gonna come back out and say, 'Ladies and gentlemen, that was Jolson, brought to you by General Motors, and good night.'

"That's how I gonna go inna TV. So I ain't doing no Ed Wynn show."

And you know what, it would have been beautiful. It was the second week that would have been the problem.

In vaudeville we never ran out of new audiences. Television was so different. Ed Wynn called television the monster that was never satisfied—it just ate up material. Television used up so much material I can't even think of anything else to say about it. After a while nobody could keep the monster fed. Including Wynn and Berle. Wynn's show was a hit for one season, then struggled along for three more years. Berle lasted a little longer than that.

After five years, Milton's audience had seen everything in his closet. He tried to change, but then he wasn't Milton. I mean, after you've seen a man wearing a dress and a wig, with two blacked-out front teeth, standing in a tank of water, getting hit in the face with a powder puff while a wind machine blows whipped cream all over the stage —four times—everything else is a little anticlimactic. Milton really got desperate—he hung up his dress and hired Goodman Ace to take over the show. Goody tried to tone down Milton, then he turned the variety format into more of a musical comedy. That worked for a season. But when his ratings started going down again, Milton moved the show to Hollywood and started doing a show with a single plot each week. One week, for example, Gore Vidal wrote a script for him that ended up with him being the Dictator of Russia. I don't think the audience was ready to accept Milton as the Russian dictator—everybody knows that a Russian dictator would never wear a dress.

The show that finally knocked Milton off the air was Phil Silvers as Sergeant Ernest Bilko. Bilko was a great television character, he was the total con man—they described Bilko as "The only American soldier during the entire conflict of World War II to capture a Japanese prisoner and hold him for ransom." Phil Silvers was a big Broadway musical comedy star, and when he was offered the role he asked Jack what to do. Jack was pretty firm in his advice. "Don't get into that TV trap," he told Silvers. "You're a smash on Broadway, stick to the stage. It has dignity, and you're one of the best in it."

Okay, maybe Jack wasn't always right. Silvers took the part and became one of the biggest stars on television. In fact, after Bilko had passed Berle in the ratings and beaten Jack's show for an Emmy, Jack wired him, YOU SON OF A BITCH. YOU WOULDNT LISTEN TO ME!

I was being very serious when I wrote that no-body stays at the top forever. Even General Motors had to get more specific. I've always tried to look at failure as a positive thing; 'course, I've always tried to look at it from a long distance too. But you know what it's like to fail and I've tried to learn from it. Maybe that's how I learned so much about show business.

Every performer experiences failure. It's part of the business. It's just that some failures last longer than others. Jack Pearl's failure, for example, lasted longer than his career. Look, even Jolson went through some bad times. I'll never forget them either, best sturgeon I ever had.

I think that failing was so tough for Jolson because he had the furthest to fall. When Jolson wasn't working he'd hang around his house all morning, go to the club for lunch, maybe go to the track in the afternoon, but he was very lonely. When the poolman came to clean his swimming pool, for example, Jolson would come out of his house in a robe and follow him around while he cleaned the pool. I remember at Jolie's funeral, Cary Grant was sitting in the front row and he didn't know the man sitting next to him. "I'm Cary Grant," he said, offering his hand, "and you're—"

"I'm the poolman," he said.

Jolson's comeback was the greatest in show business history. In fact, his comeback after *The Jolson Story* was released was so big that they made a picture about that, called *Jolson Sings Again*. All of a sudden Jolie was more popular than he'd been in a decade. "The Al Jolson Album," a collection of his old songs, became the best-selling album of all time. His single, "The Anniversary Song," sold over a million copies in a few weeks. For Jolie, it was just like the old days. I mean, just like the old days. For example, he was making a personal appearance at the Oriental Theatre in Chicago to promote the second picture. In those days they sometimes had a stage show with the movie. Coincidentally, Jessel was the headliner of the show at the Oriental. So before the show began, Jessel told Al Rylander, who was working with Jolson, "I gotta introduce Al. I'm the star of the show and it won't look good if I don't."

Jolson and Jessel hadn't really gotten along since *The Jazz Singer*, but Rylander talked Jolson into letting Jessel do the introduction. "Okay," Jolie said, "but here it is. He says, 'Ladies and gentlemen, Al Jolson.' Not one word more, not one word less."

Jessel agreed. After the movie was over the band started playing Jolie's theme song, "California, Here I Come," and Jessel came out to introduce him. But before Georgie could open his mouth, Jolson walked out onstage and said, "I don't need no introduction. They know who I am."

Like I said, just like the old days.

Ed Wynn's comeback was almost as great as Jolson's. After Ed's television show was canceled he had a tough time getting work. I remember Jack had him on as a guest star once. It was a cute bit. Louella Parsons had written that Jack was so good he could get laughs reading names out of the phone book. So he tried it. He stood in front of the audience reading the *G*'s. Louella was wrong. Then Ed Wynn came out and told Jack that he wasn't reading it right. "Try again," he said. This time, as Jack read names out of the phone book, Ed took out a pair of scissors and cut off his tie. Then he cut off his jacket. Then he started on his pants, one leg at a time. It turned out that Louella was absolutely right, Jack could get laughs reading names out of the phone book.

But except for appearing with Jack and Gobel and Red Skelton as a guest star, Ed couldn't get a job. He never lost his sense of humor, though. One day he was walking along Madison Avenue and a fan stopped him. "Ed Wynn," she said, "I thought you were dead."

"I am," he told her politely. "Welcome."

Ed had been through tough times before. Three marriages had failed, he'd lost a fortune in the stock market, he'd lost another fortune when his radio network failed, he'd had to pay the government more than half a million dollars in back taxes, and for years his son, the great actor Keenan Wynn, didn't speak to him. But this was serious. So Ed's 800 funny hats, 300 funny coats and one pair of oversized clown shoes just sat in his closet.

I don't know how you feel right now, but I got sad just writing that. By 1956 most people who watched television thought of Ed Wynn as Keenan Wynn's father. That year José Ferrer was directing a TV drama and asked Ed to play a small role. Ed had done something like seven different vaudeville acts, twenty-one Broadway shows and his own TV variety show—and he'd never done one serious line. He turned down the offer. "Oh, I couldn't do that to my public," he told Keenan, "they expect me to be 'The Perfect Fool.'"

"What public?" Keenan asked. "Then why aren't you working?"

Ed finally accepted the part, a six-minute monologue in a filmed drama called "The Great Man." He did a good job. Not too long after that "Playhouse 90" producer Martin Manulis was casting Rod Serling's new teleplay, "Requiem for a Heavyweight." He wanted to offer a part to Keenan Wynn, but somehow another part got offered to Ed. Now that Ed was an experienced actor, he accepted.

If this book gets made into a movie, make sure they put a drum roll right here. The rehearsals were terrible. This was a heavy drama, Ed was playing the manager of a boxer getting his big shot, but Ed insisted on playing it for laughs. In one scene Jack Palance, playing the fighter, punched him, and Ed did a pratfall, the kind of slapstick fall he'd done in vaudeville. Keenan worked with him every day, and the producer secretly had another actor rehearsing the role, ready to take over.

This is some dramatic story. I can't wait to see how it comes out, so I'd better keep writing.

In another scene Ed had to cry. He couldn't do it. Manulis told him to go home and sit in front of a mirror and practice. The next day Ed told him, "I worked in front of a mirror like you said, but every time I looked at myself I got hysterical."

Things got so bad that the director wanted to replace him. Rod Serling said that if Wynn wasn't fired he wanted his name taken off the credits. Even Keenan, who was costarring, thought Ed should be removed from the cast. But Manulis insisted that Wynn could do it.

Keenan went through every line, every movement, with his father, and Ed learned to imitate him. And when the show was broadcast live—big drum roll here—Ed was great. He cried on cue, he fell down like he had been punched, he remembered every line. After the show Keenan stood in a corner and said, happily, "Here I am, Ed Wynn's son all over again." Ed was so good that he won the Emmy as Best Supporting Actor that year.

Ed was seventy years old, and suddenly the kid had a whole new career as a dramatic actor. He got all kinds of offers. He starred in several other TV dramas, one of them a play called "The Man in the Funny Suit," which told the whole behind-the-scenes story of what went on during the rehearsals for "Requiem." Ed played himself in the play, that's typecasting, and he was as good as himself as anybody else could have been. He was offered the lead in five different Broadway shows, he co-starred in big movies like *Marjorie Morningstar, Mary Poppins,* and and he was nominated for a Best Supporting Actor Oscar for his work in

The Diary of Anne Frank. He even did a series for my production company, McCadden Productions.

Ed was a famous actor. Personally, I was afraid he was going to take up with some ingenue like that Helen Hayes or Ruth Gordon. But he didn't let his new stardom change him at all. "You know," he said, "I've been around longer than RCA or General Motors. I'm a brand name, like Heinz 57. In the old days you could see me for fifty cents. And look how I've progressed—now you can see me for nothing."

Almost all of the critics loved his work. No matter what he did, they gave him rave reviews —all except one guy. A television critic at *Variety.* He hated everything Ed did, everything. And Ed couldn't figure it out. "Why doesn't this man like me?" he'd ask. "I don't even know this man. Why is he criticizing me all the time? Doesn't he have anything better to do?"

One day Ed was having lunch at the Brown Derby when this critic came in. As he went past Ed's table, somebody told Ed, "That's so-and-so." This was the first time Ed had ever seen the man. He was not a good-looking man. Even for a critic he was not a good-looking man. He was tall, and much too thin, and he had a hooknose and a squashed face and big ears and bad skin. Ed looked at him, and smiled, and said quietly, "I'm glad."

But you know what? I think that even with all the success he had as a dramatic actor, Ed missed making laughter. There just isn't any other sound in the world like the sound of an audience laughing. Applause is nice. A cash register ringing is great. But laughter . . . there's nothing that compares to it. I remember once I was in a meeting with Ed, we were talking about the show he was going to do for me, and suddenly he said, "You know, George, there's something radically wrong when they hire me to make people cry and Perry Como to make people laugh."

The only thing wrong with making a comeback is that first you have to be a failure. If you could make a comeback without having to fail, comebacks would be much more popular. Almost all of my friends tried to make comebacks during their careers—except Jack; he never had anywhere to come back from. In fact, for a while it seemed like everybody was trying to make a comeback. A good New York comedian named Jack Osterman was walking along Broadway on an icy day when he saw a police horse trip and fall. The horse had a rough time getting up. A big crowd gathered around to watch. Finally, the horse struggled to its feet, and when it did, Osterman applauded and yelled, "Nice comeback!"

Wynn wasn't the only comedian to make a comeback as a dramatic actor. I used to think that an actor was a comedian with bad material, but it turned out to be a lot tougher than that. But Berle, Jackie Gleason, even Cantor and Harpo all tried to make it doing dramatic parts. Red Buttons won an Oscar for 'Sayonara.' Of course, for Milton, wearing a suit was serious acting.

When Milton's comedy shows all failed he tried other types of shows. In 1958 he hosted a half-hour variety show that had what he called a "no-format format." It also had a "no-audience audience" and got "no-laughter laughter." Two years after that show was canceled he hosted "Jackpot Bowling," on which he did a few minutes of ad-libs between bowling matches. I don't know, if Milton had sung songs like "Strike Up the Band," "Brother, Can You Spare a Dime," or "Roll Out the Barrel," the show might have worked, but whatever he did, the show was no funnier than this entire sentence. A few years after that he tried another variety show, and that failed too. Listen, it's easy for a comedian to know when his material isn't working: if you get hit in the face with a powder puff and nobody laughs, your material isn't working. It's much tougher to know in drama: in drama, if you get hit in the face with a powder puff and nobody laughs, it's working.

So Milton had been doing drama for a few years before he started doing serious roles. But when he did, he turned out to be a terrific actor. Maybe that shouldn't be a surprise, because he'd become a kid star in vaudeville doing dramatic sketches —of course, in those days he'd step on his costar's feet to get her to cry in their big scenes.

Let me tell how good an actor Milton is. He told me, "As a comedian, the fact that someone could forget I was Berle was an insult. But to me, the greatest compliment came from people who watched me doing dramatic roles, and said that after the first thirty seconds they forgot they were watching Berle." And when he said it I believed him. That's how good an actor he is.

Cantor tried acting too. Eddie really wanted to work, but tastes had changed. The television audience was looking for something a little more sophisticated than bugeyes. They wanted large . . . personalities. And they wanted them in tight sweaters. Finally, Eddie was hired to do an hour-long drama on NBC called "George Has a Birthday." He played George, and his big scene was having a birthday. Then he got killed. That's why I don't like birthdays, they're much too dangerous. He did the show with Mae Clarke and Lillian Gish, two terrific actresses. Both of them knew how nervous Eddie was, so at 5:30 A.M., the morning of the telecast, Mae called a convent to ask the sisters to pray for the success of the show. She woke everybody up. And when she told Eddie about the phone call, he told her, "Of course you woke them up. At that hour God isn't even awake."

That was a shame, because I think God could've helped. Eddie wasn't an actor. Times had really changed—as an actor Eddie got the laughs he didn't get as a comedian. He just couldn't stop bugging out his eyes and mugging for the camera. At least Eddie's career ended with the sound of laughter.

Harpo wasn't right for television either. What was he going to do on TV? I mean, Harpo was known for three things: never saying a word, wearing a curly blond wig and playing the harp. Television depended on speaking, the picture was in black and white, and they didn't even play the harp on "Omnibus." Harpo on TV had all the excitement of a photograph of Jolson. One night Ed Murrow visited Harpo and Susan on his "Person to Person" show. Murrow opened the program by warning Harpo, "I hope it's not your intention to monopolize the conversation this evening." Murrow was funny, but he was no Ed Sullivan. Anyway, Harpo spent the half hour grinning, whistling, blowing bubbles and playing his harp. And at the end of the show Susan said that Harpo was really "A quiet man. Very philosophical. He uses his head." While in the background he proved that was true—by standing on it.

After that, Harpo appeared on TV every once in awhile. He played his first serious role in 1960, being cast as a mechanical man working in a department store window who witnessed a murder. After that show he admitted, "You don't know what a relief it is not to have to get laughs." His last starring role on television was in a Christmas special titled "The Wonderful World of Toys."

On that show, Harpo's voice was played by Carol Burnett.

The truth is that Harpo really did speak onstage a few times. Once, when the Marx Brothers were touring to promote their movie *Go West*, he did a harp solo. When he pulled the wrong strings, or whatever it's called when you make a mistake on the harp, he said, "I'll get the darned thing right yet." In vaudeville once, a fire broke out in the theater, and Harpo kept people calm by reciting his bar mitzvah speech. And in 1941 he played the role of Banjo in a summer theater production of *The Man Who Came to Dinner*. How bad could he have been in the role? George S. Kaufman had based the character on him. So Harpo played Banjo, who was really Harpo. Marx Brothers casting. The first line he said onstage in almost twenty years was "I can feel the hot blood coursing in your varicose veins." You want my opinion? He should have kept his mouth shut. After all that time, you'd think he'd come up with something funnier. Maybe something like "Don't ever use that sea bass line again, Groucho."

Maybe the show didn't go so well, because he didn't speak onstage again for another twenty-two years. Then he surprised everybody at a charity concert in Pasadena by telling them, "I'm going on seventy-five and I want to play golf, relax and travel," then announcing he was retiring from show business. But can you imagine that, forty-two years to come up with that ad-lib? You know, after all this time, I think I finally figured out why he never spoke—he didn't have anything to say.

When he announced his retirement he sent a picture of himself taken from behind to gossip columnist Hedda Hopper, with a note reading, "You weren't in on the beginning of my show business career, but you're in on the end of it."

A year later he died. That's what he got for opening his mouth.

Not every comeback went well. For instance, none of Benny Fields' and Blossom Seeley's comebacks worked out, and they made more comebacks than a boomerang. Benny made his first comeback in the mid-1930s as a nightclub singer, but then World War II started and put most of the clubs out of business. After the movie about Blossom's life without the tiger's head between her legs, *Somebody Loves Me,* was released, they tried another comeback in the nightclubs, but they weren't really successful.

Finally, Blossom and Benny made another comeback playing the smaller rooms in Las Vegas. A few weeks before Benny died in 1959, he taped an appearance on Ed Sullivan's variety show, singing his biggest hit, "Lullaby of Broadway." That show was telecast a few days after he died. And it didn't matter how good he was on the show, that was one comeback even Benny wasn't going to be able to make.

Frank Fay was so talented he was able to turn one of the great comebacks in show business history into an even bigger failure. That sort of renewed my faith that nice things happen to nice people. And other things happened to Fay. Faysie's career ended about the same time as his marriage to Barbara Stanwyck. After that nobody would hire him. "What Fred Allen is to dancing," he told people, "I am to unemployment." He spent most of his time sitting next to his swimming pool, which he couldn't even afford to fill up with water. Then a Broadway producer started looking for an actor to play a drunk named Elwood P. Dowd, who was the only person able to see a friendly 6'1" white rabbit named Harvey. Fay was a natural for the part. The night *Harvey* opened, Fay became a star again. One critic even wrote, "Fay now overacts his underplaying."

Somehow it was a little comforting to see that Fay's years of failure hadn't changed him at all. When the rave notices were printed, he said, "I must phone my mother to congratulate her on having me." The only thing he couldn't figure out was why the critics were surprised he could act. In his usually modest tone, he said, "Why, I was playing Shakespeare and Ibsen when they were playing patty-cake." And I'm sure he was a better patty-cake player than Shakespeare.

Fay was probably more popular than he'd ever been. He played the role of Elwood Dowd on Broadway and on the road for five years and made another fortune. But then Fay made another mistake; he started taking himself seriously, and that's the worst thing a comedian can do. He got involved in politics.

Now, in all the years I've been performing I've never done political humor. Like Fred Allen must have said sometime, I leave political humor to the politicians. Left wing, right wing, all I knew about wings was that I wasn't supposed to step on the seal's. Maybe I'm wrong, but I've always felt that comedians are supposed to make people feel better after the politicians have done their job. Jack used to say that the closest he ever got to politics was once being invited to dinner at 1590 Pennsylvania Avenue. And I agreed with him completely. It's like I told my old friend, President Ronnie Reagan, "You don't sing country-western songs, I won't invade Grenada." The last time I had anything to do with politics was in 1940, when Gracie ran for President as the candidate of the Surprise Party. Maybe you heard, she lost.

But a lot of other comedians have gotten involved in politics. Cantor, for example. I remember telling Eddie I thought he was making a big mistake. "Just keep trying to save the world, Eddie," I told him. "Don't waste your time on politics."

Fay made that mistake. At a huge rally at Madison Square Garden, called "The Friends of Frank Fay," he told 15,000 people that several entertainers, including Cantor and Frank Sinatra, were Communists. Cantor told people that that was probably the funniest thing Fay had said in years. Sinatra said, "He's been living with an imaginary rabbit so long that now he's seeing imaginary Communists."

The night after the rally Fay went into Toots Shor's place. Toots sat him at a table right up in front, where everybody could see him. And he sat there alone the whole night. Nobody said one word to him. Fred Allen watched him sitting there, who knows, maybe Harvey was with him, and said sadly, "Last night he had fifteen thousand friends. Tonight he hasn't got one."

Fay's career ended when *Harvey* finally disappeared. Sometimes he'd show up at political rallies and he worked in some clubs, but he never got another starring role. Because of his politics? Who knows. But when he died in 1961 he had a few bucks and a lot of enemies. And he got both of them the same way—he earned them.

Georgie Jessel made the same mistake Fay did. He got so involved in politics that he forgot he was supposed to be a comedian. Everywhere he went he'd wear his USO uniform with all his medals pinned to the jacket. Some people were still laughing at him, but this time he was trying to be serious. It was a very sad time for all of us who loved him, and knew how much good he had done for so many people, to see him end up like this. But Georgie wouldn't listen to anybody. He had always been someone who believed so much in peace that he was willing to fight anyone to get it. George believed in democracy, and he felt that everybody had a right to an opinion. His. And sometimes that made things rough for him.

During the Vietnam War, for example, he was being interviewed on the "Today" program and the host, Edwin Newman, cut off the interview because he kept referring to the *New York Times* as *Pravda*, the Russian government newspaper. That was Georgie's subtle way of hinting that he thought the *Times* was too liberal; of course, he was about as subtle as Berle with a police whistle.

Nobody wanted to give him a job. Finally, I was doing a television special and I wanted him on my show. The network told me I couldn't have him on the show; I told the network that this was my show and I wanted him. "When you do your own special," I said, "don't have Jessel. I want him." So I put him on. And you know what, even then, even when his career wasn't going so well for him, he hadn't changed at all. As soon as Irving Fein told him he was going to be on the show, he asked, "Can I get paid in advance?"

Toward the end of his life Georgie was performing in vaudeville revivals, working in some of the same small towns he'd played fifty years before. In fact, a big part of his act was telling the audience that he'd played their town half a century earlier, then making up stories about the town. The kid was stealing my act. But who remembered what had happened fifty years earlier? Would anybody really know that Lincoln didn't say Alexandria, Minnesota, was his favorite town in America?

Some of these tours were well managed, but others were just thrown together. Georgie somehow managed to get involved with the bad ones. I knew Georgie for almost sixty years, I don't know why that should surprise me. But one night he ended up in Greensburg, Pennsylvania, sharing a six-dollar-a-night motel room with Jack Carter. Believe me, even for six dollars a night, Georgie wanted more than Jack Carter.

No, that's not true, Jack was a good friend to

him. Jack had started out in show business doing impersonations of Jolson and Jessel and all the rest of them, so he had a real appreciation of show business history. Georgie's life was show business history. I mean, he was there when Irving Berlin played "Alexander's Ragtime Band" for Jolson for the first time on the piano at Polly Adler's place. So Georgie talked and Jack listened and they got to be pretty good friends. That night in Greensburg the tour got to be too much for Georgie, and he asked Jack to take him home. Home to Los Angeles.

This particular tour was being run by a shady promoter who was later murdered. Georgie had the perfect alibi. He was dead at the time. But to keep the tour together this promoter had hired local policemen to "protect" his stars. Also to keep his stars from walking out on him. So at four o'clock in the morning, Carter snuck into the motel manager's office and gave him fifty dollars to drive him and Jessel to the airport in Pittsburgh. For Georgie it was just like old times—sneaking out of town in the middle of the night.

When they got to the airport Carter got a wheelchair for Jessel. Georgie really didn't need a wheelchair, but it made him a little more comfortable. They bought their plane tickets and waited in the lounge. And while they were waiting in the lounge they had a few drinks. Georgie really didn't need them, but they made him a little more comfortable. Now, all this time Georgie was wearing his USO uniform, which was blue with gold trim.

407

And coincidentally, that was exactly the same color uniform that the pilots working for this airline wore. When the announcement was made to board the plane, Carter wheeled Georgie right up to the front of the ramp. All the other passengers waiting for the plane stood there watching as Georgie, who was dressed just like the pilots, and maybe having had a little too much to drink, was wheeled onto the plane . . .

. . . and then they all rushed the ticket desk to cancel their tickets. I mean, would you get on an airplane if you thought Georgie was the pilot? I didn't even like getting on an airplane if Georgie was a passenger.

Georgie Jessel came home, and that was the last time he ever worked onstage. He didn't retire, the audience retired him. Very few people in show business ever really retire; Gracie did. Harpo did. Mary Benny did. But pretty much everybody else I knew just went on a long vacation. I never even thought about retiring. For what? There's no money in sunbathing. Besides, if I spend too much time in the sun my skin's going to look terrible when I get old. Jack used to tell me that he was going to retire a few weeks after he died. Durante said, "If ya retire, ya decay. What am I gonna do if I retire, swim? When Durante swims, nobody watches." I remember when Benny Rubin decided to retire and move into the Old Actors Home. He thought he was going to be there with all the old vaudevillians and they'd sit around all day telling lies about the seal they'd worked with in Altoona.

But as soon as he found out all the people living there were old actors, he moved right back out.

Look, it takes a lot of experience to grow old. I don't care how smart some of these younger kids are, it's going to take them a long time to learn how to do it. Because it takes a long time to get old. And you have to be very lucky. Look, I'll be very honest, being old is not the best thing that ever happened to me. But it's a great alternative.

Some people get old better than others. Sex symbols, like Marilyn and Blossom, have a tough time getting old. But not me, and not Jack. Of course, we weren't really sex symbols. We were just followers. On Jack's eightieth birthday Frank Sinatra threw a big party for him. They asked me to give the toast. "We've been friends for fifty-five years," I told Jack. "That means we met when you were twenty-five and I was twenty-three . . . and there's not a damn thing we did then that we can't do better now." Then I admitted to everyone at the party, "That gives you an idea how pathetic we were when we were young."

Listen, you can't help getting older, but you don't have to get old. I always liked the attitude of Adolph Zukor, who used to run Paramount. On his 103rd birthday we threw a big party for him at Hillcrest. We all sang "Happy Birthday." Then they wheeled out a cake with 104 candles on it, and fourteen or fifteen of us got together and tried to blow them out. During the party I went over to him and asked, "Mr. Zukor, how does it feel to be a hundred and three?"

"George," he told me, "right now I feel just as good as I did when I was a hundred and two." I liked that answer a lot, and the good news is that I'll be able to steal it years before Berle gets old enough.

The truth is that the only thing it's easier to do when you get old is get sick. Everything else becomes a little harder. Well, not everything. Being sick can be a real pain—or it can be an imaginary pain. For Cantor and Durante, it was very real. Both of them had serious heart attacks. The first day the doctors let Eddie sit up in bed after his heart attack Jack went to visit him. Jack told me how sad it was, here was the most energetic performer who had ever worked onstage, and he was thrilled because the doctors told him he could dangle his legs over the side of his bed. Cantor told Jack that that was a big improvement—the first time he'd tried to read a newspaper in bed the nurses wouldn't let him turn the page because it took too much energy.

But within three months Cantor was out of the hospital and back at work on his television show, his radio show, and recording songs for the soundtrack of the movie *The Eddie Cantor Story*. The story I heard was that Eddie was actually scheduled to die when he had his heart attack, but he just didn't have the time.

Durante spent the last few years of his life in a wheelchair after his stroke, but he was still The Schnozzola. "I'm feeling better," he told Berle one day. "It's slow. But don't forget, it takes a lot of strength to support a nose like mine."

There were always a lot of people at Durante's house. Berle was there a lot, and Sammy Fain, the great songwriter; jockey Willie Shoemaker, Ernie Borgnine, Jack Carter, Joey Bishop, Groucho when he was feeling okay, and usually a priest or two. Jimmy used to tell people about the priests, "Perry Como sends 'em over."

It was sort of surprising that it was Jimmy's heart that went bad, because that was the biggest part of him. Yeah, even bigger than the schnozz. But his mind was always sharp. One day, for example, Jack Carter and Joey Bishop had been there to see him and they were getting ready to leave. Jimmy was sitting in his wheelchair, his fedora on top of his head at a rakish angle, his unlit cigar clenched in his teeth—still "Jimmy, the Well Dressed Man." Margie brought him into the hallway to say goodbye. But as Carter and Bishop got to the front door, they started doing their best Durante impersonation. They opened with "Ya Gotta Start Off Each Day Wit' a Song," and then went right into "Inka Dinka Doo." Jimmy watched them working for a while, then looked up at Margie and asked, "Which one a them bums is de real Durante?"

A few months before Jimmy died, Margie threw a party for him at the house. It got to be a little too much for him, so he went into his bedroom and lay down. He was just lying there quietly when

Carter went in to see him. "You all right?" Jack asked.

Jimmy smiled. "Oh yeah," he said, "I'm all right. But I got this room covered, why don't you go work the other room?"

Now, some of the pains my friend Jack Benny had were imagined. Jack was just a little bit of a hypochondriac. I mean, I'm being honest here, how many people do you know who like to hang out at their doctor's office? Just in case. That was Jack.

I remember once Jack did have a little problem and he had to get a series of shots in the-part-that-Matthau-showed-me-that-wasn't-funny. Jack had to get two shots a week, one in each side, and the nurse kept forgetting which side she'd stabbed last. So one day Jack went into the office and dropped his pants—and printed on one side was the word TUES, and on the other side, THURS.

Jack was an expert on doctors and hospitals. He got just as enthusiastic over a nurse who gave a great needle as he did over a fluffy towel. While he was entertaining soldiers in the South Pacific during World War II, he'd spent a few days with Dr. Charles Mayo, one of the founders of the great Mayo Clinic. Maybe twelve years after that, Danny Kaye wanted to check into the Mayo Clinic, and Jack called up Dr. Mayo to arrange it. And ten more years later, Jack decided that he wanted to check into the Mayo Clinic himself. So he called up, and when he got Dr. Mayo on the phone, he said, "Hello, Charlie. This is Jack Benny."

And Dr. Mayo said instantly, "What? Again?" I'm telling you something, the one thing no comedian needs is a doctor who has better writers than he does.

Because Jack was a bit of a hypochondriac, I don't think we really believed him when he started complaining about stomach pains. The doctor took every possible test, but he couldn't find anything wrong. "He told me I'm imagining it," Jack complained.

"So tell him to imagine you paid his bill," I said.

Meanwhile, I got sick. I had to have a heart bypass operation. This was a lot different from the agent's bypass, where they just bypass your heart and go right to your wallet. This was the doctor's bypass, in which they fix your heart, *then* they go right to your wallet. So after my operation I was lying in bed at home and Jack called me from Dallas where he was doing a concert. "I have a bad stomachache," he told me. Jack was the only person I knew who could call me after I'd had a serious heart operation to tell me how he was feeling.

"That's too bad," I said. "I'm lying here dying and you're complaining about a stomachache."

"Well," he said, "I just think I sho—" So I hung up the phone on him. That was me, always willing to do anything for Jack to help him feel better.

413

When Jack died, I cried. I cried more for me than for him, because I knew how much I was going to miss him. I knew that I was going to have to spend the rest of my life completing every phone call I ever made. And where was I going to find another audience like that? I wasn't really crying for Jack, that wouldn't have done any good. Besides, how bad could death really be? I mean, you never hear anybody complaining about it.

I just can't waste time worrying about it, I have too many other things to worry about. And I think it's silly to worry about it. I remember when Harry Ritz was sick. I called him up and asked him how he was feeling. "I'm finished, George," he said. "I'm gonna die."

"Really?" I said, "then, Harry, maybe you could do me a favor. I've never had anybody die on the telephone. Could you die for me on the phone?" He had some nerve, instead of dying, he started laughing. "See, Harry," I told him, "you're not so smart. You can't tell anybody when you're going to die. Somebody else handles that. They knock on the door, you can die. But you can't die on the phone."

There are some people who think everything is a joke. With some of those people, I wouldn't even put dying past them. Fortunately, Milton hasn't tried to steal that act. I remember when Fanny Brice got sick. Fanny was one of those people who believed that the cure for everything was aspirin. Headaches, fever, lost loves, opening night nervousness—take two aspirin. After she'd had her heart attack in 1951, she was in the Cedars of Lebanon Hospital and her good friend Spencer Tracy went to see her. He sat down next to her bed and took her small hand in his. "What is it, Fanny?" he asked.

She opened her eyes and took a deep breath, then she said weakly, "Too many first nights." Spencer nodded his head, and maybe he even wiped away a tear. And then Fanny added, in a clear, loud voice, "And taking all that sonofa-bitchin' aspirin didn't help either!"

Ed Wynn knew he was going to die for the last six weeks of his life. I think that was probably a booking he could have lived without, but when you're booked . . . He was a happy man until the day that he died. In fact, a few days before he died, he woke up feeling very good, so he im-mediately called his doctor and told him, "I think you'd better get right over here. I feel good, some-thing must be wrong. I think you must have given me the wrong pills or something."

Ed's son Keenan had had the same maid for years, and Ed wanted to leave her something in his will. Now this maid was a big woman; I don't mean "big" in the show business way, I mean "big" in the fat way. Ed didn't remember her last name, so when he was making out his will he called Keenan to ask what it was. "Peters," Keenan said. The next day Keenan called back to correct him-self. "Her name isn't Peters anymore," he said, "it's Martin. I forgot that she got divorced."

"Oh," Ed said, a little surprised, "all of her?"

Supposedly, just before Ed died, he wrote a letter to Keenan telling him how he wanted his funeral to be handled. After giving him the letter, which wasn't to be opened until it was necessary, he called Keenan to tell him there was one more thing he'd forgotten to put in the letter. "Promise me one thing," he said. "No Jessel."

The only good thing that came out of all of these people dying was that it gave Jessel something to do. Maybe it wasn't the best work he ever had, but at least it was steady. For years Georgie gave the eulogy at every big Hollywood funeral. A lot of places have official greeters; Georgie was Hollywood's official dispatcher. He gave the eulogy at more than 300 funerals, including George M. Cohan, George Gershwin, even Will Rogers. People used to say that you weren't officially dead until Georgie gave the word. I remember once he was introducing former President Truman at a luncheon. Just before he went up to the microphone, Truman said to him, "Georgie, do me a favor. Don't get too sentimental about me. Every time you do, I think I'm dead."

Let me tell you how good Georgie was at funerals. James and Pamela Mason had beautiful cats that they loved very much. When one of their favorite cats died, they decided to bury him in their backyard. Jessel offered to say a few words. A few days after that I ran into James Mason and asked him about the little ceremony. "Oh, George," he said, "it was really quite moving. You know, I'd had that cat for seventeen years, but

416

until the other day I'd never realized how much he'd done for the State of Israel."

Nobody gave better eulogies than Jessel. Of course, nobody had as much practice. But Georgie appreciated the beauty of the English language, and used it so well. I'll give you an example: At Jolson's funeral, Jessel said, "And not only has the entertainment world lost its king, but we cannot cry, 'The King is dead; long live the King!' for there is no one to hold his scepter. Those of us who tarry behind are but pale imitations, mere princelings. . . .

"I am proud to have basked in the sunlight of his greatness, to have been part of his time, and to have only a few days ago—hugged him and said, 'Good night, Asa, take care of yourself. . . .'"

I mean, Georgie was so good at this that he could make you cry when a cigar died. "The poet Goethe once wrote a sonnet to which Tchaikowsky composed music," he said at Fanny Brice's funeral. "This was known to us as 'None But the Lonely Heart.' But the meaning of its original tongue is more poignant which, translated from the German means, 'Only he who has known nostalgia knows my heartache.' The older I get the more I realize, as we all should, that all is vanity, all things go back from whence they came—and only words are left behind. . . .

"But the great Playwright of this ever-beginning, never-ending plot, the Master Director who so skillfully stages this tightly woven, disconnected spectacle of tragic nonsense, has planned it otherwise. . . ."

Now, Georgie didn't just bury the stars, he was usually willing to give a nice send-off whenever he was asked, even if he sometimes didn't know the person. Once, for example, when a hood died, a friend of Georgie's in the mob asked him to wish the deceased well from the boys. "He left the scene just a few days ago and went to his Maker," Georgie said, "quite unexpectedly. But I must say in all honesty, that his hasty departure from the play of life doesn't excuse his bad performance. . . ."

Evvrreeee . . . body's a critic. Maybe Georgie's greatest regret was that he didn't get to work his own funeral. He used to tell people that he was going to tape his own eulogy, but he never did. That would have been something to hear, "A funny thing happened to me on the way to my grave. I met a man who said he hadn't had a bite in two thousand years. . . ." Instead Berle gave the eulogy at Georgie's funeral. Milton said that, if Georgie were there, he'd probably complain, "Milton is doing the eulogy? Well, why not? He's taken everything else from me."

Well, there were some funerals that Georgie missed. At Durante's funeral, for example, Jimmy's battered old fedora sat on top of his casket at a rakish angle while Bob Hope and Danny Thomas both gave eulogies. Desi Arnaz, who had been in charge of organizing things, said, "I was s'posed to read the eulogy myself, but Jimmy helped me with my English, so maybe it wouldn't come out so good."

In show business, as soon as somebody does something successfully for the first time, everybody else wants to do it. Jolson's funeral was such a big success that, as Durante might've said, evvvreeee-body wanted to get inna de act. For a while I was going to so many funerals that I was afraid to send my dark suit to the cleaners. I mean, I thought that all day dying was silly. Even if the funeral was a big hit, what could you do for an encore? Want to know what I think: Don't die, it's been done. Try something original. Live.

Jolson started it, in 1950. That figured, Jolson always had to be first. He was in San Francisco to do a radio show with Bing Crosby when he had a heart attack. As John Huston said, "He was too good a man to get sick. When the time came, he just died." Jolson was playing cards with Harry Akst and another friend when he felt the pains in his chest. "Boys," he told them, "this is it." But Jolson never got off a stage that quickly in his life. Or in his death. He survived for hours while doctors tried to save him. But finally he announced, "Oh, I'm going," and he died.

His funeral drew a bigger crowd than most people's openings. For some people, crowds show up just to make sure, but not in this case. This was Jolson. More than 20,000 people stood outside the synagogue during the service. He was buried in the Hillside Cemetery, which immediately became known as "The Jolson Cemetery." Figures, dead or alive, no matter where he was, Jolson always had to have top billing.

Ed Wynn's last request was "Bury me where you will. God will find me." Groucho was a little more demanding, saying, "Bury me next to a straight man." He died in 1977. He was pretty weak his last few years, but he didn't change at all either. Among the people he got friendly with at that time was Robert Shields, of the mime act "Shields and Yarnell." I think Groucho liked Shields because he reminded him of Harpo a little.

At one point Shields and Yarnell were the opening act in Vegas for a popular country-West Hollywood singer, and Groucho and Erin went to see them opening night. But the headliner insisted that he had to introduce Groucho to the audience, even though he knew that Groucho had come to see Shields and Yarnell. That was fair, he was the star, but he took it too far. "I'm greatly honored tonight," this singer told the audience, "'cause a man we all love and admire is here to share this night with me. . . ." And he went on like that, telling the audience that Groucho had come to see him perform.

Now, maybe Groucho was weak, but he was Groucho, and he knew exactly what this singer was doing. And he didn't like it. So finally, after this singer had finished giving Groucho this big self-serving introduction, he walked over to Groucho and stuck the microphone near his mouth and asked him if he wanted to say something to the audience. It wasn't that easy for

Groucho to speak, but he gathered his energy, leaned forward and said, "There was a young Roman named Caesar; who told a fat girl he wanted to squeaser; But the girl with a blush, pulled her . . ."

Still too much Groucho.

His family didn't even have a real funeral when he died in 1977. Maybe it was better that way. Knowing Groucho, they probably would have served those . . . same . . . goddamn . . . green . . . beans . . . and sea bass.

Maybe you know by now that I'm really not a very sentimental man. Of course, I've always loved a good old joke, but I've always felt that people are better off looking ahead of them than looking back. I know where I've been, I've already been there. Jack felt exactly the same way. "The hell with the past," he used to say, "I'm only concerned with how good my last show was, and how good the next two will be." But when I do look back, there were only three times that I can remember crying. When Gracie died, I cried. That was the first time. The second time was when I played the Catskills for the first time. It had nothing to do with playing the Catskills, I played the Concord and it was a very nice hotel. There were a lot of nice single girls there, and I think that some of them would have thrown the keys to their room to me, but unfortunately they couldn't lift them.

When I came onstage I looked out into the audience and sitting in the front row was my old partner, Billy Lorraine, of "Burns and Lorraine, Two Broadway Thieves." I hadn't seen him in . . . in a very long time. I brought him onstage and introduced him to the audience. I explained that when I'd met Billy, he stuttered when he spoke, but not when he sang. Once our hotel room had been robbed and he tried to tell me about it. "Ge . . . Ge . . . Ge . . ." he said.

"Sing it, Billy," I told him.

"We've been robbedddddd!" he sang beautifully.

The audience laughed, and Billy said, "Ge . . . Ge . . . Ge . . ." so I asked him to sing something for us. One song. If Jolson only got one song, Billy Lorraine only got one song. Now, Billy had been on vacation for decades, but he didn't even hesitate. He spoke to my piano player, Morty Jacobs, then took the mike, looked at me and started singing, "It's Just Like Old Times."

I couldn't take it. Seeing Billy again after all those years, hearing him singing that song, I started crying. There had been times in my life when I'd made the audience cry, but I'd never cried for the audience. That was the only time in my life that I've had to leave the stage in the middle of my act.

The third time I cried was when Jack died. Jack got sick for the last time in 1974 when he was doing that concert in Dallas. He had a very mild stroke. He flew home on a hospital plane, and by the time he got to Los Angeles he was fine. In fact, when the plane landed they wanted him to lie down on a stretcher, but he wouldn't do it. Instead, he treated the pilots, his nurse and the two attendants from the ambulance that had met the plane to lunch at the airport coffee shop. I think he said that that was the greatest airport coffee shop he'd ever eaten at. He particularly admired the brown paper towels in their men's room. And after lunch one of the attendants climbed in the back of the ambulance while Jack sat up front reading a newspaper, and they drove him to the hospital.

Was it our fault we really didn't think it was that serious?

But Jack kept getting weaker and weaker, and the pain in his stomach kept getting worse. Dr. Kennemar took every test, but everything seemed normal. I'll admit it, a lot of people thought Jack might be imagining it, but he knew the old joke, "If the pain's in my head, why does my stomach hurt?" The pain finally got so bad that he stayed in bed, except to go to the doctor's office or to go to his violin lesson. I was glad his violin playing had finally made someone feel better.

Just before Christmas we found out that Jack really was sick. His stomach pains were being caused by pancreatic cancer that didn't show up on any tests. By the time they found it, it was too late. There's nothing I like less than a phony hypochondriac.

Jack never knew how sick he really was. He just lay down one day and didn't get up. I didn't think that was fair; after all those years, I thought

Jack should have had the satisfaction of knowing he'd been right the whole time—there really was something wrong with him.

I was just devastated. If I hadn't just had a heart operation, I know I would have needed one. I'll tell you how terrible I felt; I felt so terrible that I would have gladly listened to him practicing his fiddle. So if you'd ever heard Jack play the fiddle, you now know that I really can be sentimental.

Jack stayed upstairs at home, in bed, partially sedated to ease some of the pain. Jack never knew he was dying. Or if he did know, he didn't act like he did. We never talked about it. We talked about the same things we'd always talked about —the shows, the ratings, the gossip. We were in show business, we weren't in the dying business. Everybody knows there's no future in the dying business.

I was at the house when Jack Benny died. There were a lot of people there, because Mary had called everybody to tell them that Jack was dying. The day before, Christmas Day, Irving Fein, the manager who was about to lose half his clients, and Don Rosenfeld, Jack's lawyer, went to the cemetery to pick out a coffin and a sarcophagus, the place where the coffin would be put. There were two spots available, one on the first floor of the building, the other one on the second floor. They picked the one on the first floor. "Jack would want to be in the orchestra," Don said. "I just can't picture him in the balcony."

It was just before noon, on December 26, when

Mary came downstairs and said, "Jack's dead." Just like that, "Jack's dead."

"I'm going up," I told her.

"You can't," she said, "the doctor said—"

"I knew him longer than the doctor did. I'm going up." Jack was lying there with his hands clasped together on his chest, just barely touching his chin. From the man who had turned silence into a punch line, the silence was just awful.

We had had some great friendship. Knowing how enthusiastic Jack was about things, he probably would have said it was the greatest friendship that two men have ever had, then told everybody they had to go and have one. I'll tell you this though, I knew him fifty-five years, and I never once walked out on him when he was playing the fiddle, and he never laughed when I sang. I think that's pretty good.

There were thousands of people at his funeral. Groucho made it, and Georgie and Matthau and Danny Thomas, Jack Carter, Ronnie Reagan, Berle, Sinatra, Hilly Marks, and Benny Rubin and his former wife, Mary. Benny and Mary had gotten married in 1927, just after Jack and Mary— but they'd gotten divorced seven years later. They hadn't seen each other in four decades, but the night before the funeral Mary phoned Benny and said, "We were there at the beginning; let's be there together at the end."

Hope and I gave the eulogies. Well, Hope and I were supposed to give the eulogies; I tried, I just couldn't do it. I started, but after saying a few words I had to stop. I guess you could say that that was the last time I hung up on him.

Hope more than made up for me. "If a memorial service is for those who are left behind, for those who mourn the loss of a loved one," he said, "then this service is for the world. . . . [Jack] didn't just stand on a stage, he owned it. For a man who was the undisputed master of comedy timing, you would have to say that this was the only time Jack Benny's timing was all wrong. He left us too soon. He only gave us eighty years. It wasn't enough. . . . This was a man. God keep him, enjoy him. We did for eighty years."

Jolson, Jessel, Cantor, Wynn, Groucho and Harpo, Danny Kaye, Fanny, Jack Pearl, Haley, Fields, Blossom and Benny, Jesse Block . . . Jack. All the others. I miss them all. And most of all, Gracie. Hell, I even miss the seal, and that seal was the worst roommate I ever had. He always wanted to flip me for the lower bunk.

Bob Hope once had a good comedy writer named Barney Dean working for him. When Barney was dying, Bob went to see him. Barney signaled Hope to come closer, and when Bob leaned over, Barney whispered, "Anything you want me to tell Jolson?"

Listen, my first hundred years have been great. So far. I just hope the next thirty or forty years are as good. I don't kid myself, I know I'm not as young as I used to be. Hey, most people aren't old enough to be as young as I used to be. But I have no intention of going anywhere for a long time. I can't afford to die. I'd lose a fortune. Besides, I'm booked; and I haven't missed a booking since vaudeville. I'm scheduled to play the London Palladium for two weeks in 1996 to celebrate my 100th birthday.

That's if the Palladium is still there.

I know that sometime there's going to be a knock on my door, and when I open it somebody'll give me back my pictures. And I'll go. But I'm telling you something right now; when I go, I'm taking my music.

You never know.

Thank you, you've been a wonderful reader. Good night.

(APPLAUSE)

(APPLAUSE)

Thank you, thank you again, thank you. Please, sit down. Oh, you are sitting down, aren't you. I hope you enjoyed being here with me. Now, I'd just like to take a few sentences to thank some people for their help.

First, I'd like to thank my accompanist, David Fisher on the typewriter.

And I'd also like to thank my conductor, the person who made this whole performance possible, Phyllis Grann. Take a bow, Phyllis. That's nice . . .

Don't tell anybody, but she bought that outfit just for this appearance. Now, finally I'd like to thank the chorus, those people who helped me remember. There are too many people to mention them all by name, but you know who you are, and you know how much I appreciate your help.

And most of all, I'd like to thank all of you for spending this time with me.

You know, normally, for an encore, a performer usually sings their big hit song or does a great dance number. I'll tell you the truth, I'd considered typing a few bars of my biggest hit, "I Wish

I Was 18 Again," but instead I thought I'd tell you a little story. I hope you enjoy it.

The truth is that I loved being in radio, and I loved being on television and I loved making movies. I even loved making videos. But you know what, if you started in vaudeville like I did, no matter what you did afterwards, you were always a vaudevillian.

Everything I know about show business I learned in vaudeville. We all did. Well, once, a long time ago, Jesse Block and Eva Sully were on a bill at the Chicago Theatre with Fanny Brice. They were in the number-four spot, Fanny was the headliner, and she took a liking to them. After the show she invited them to go with her to a party at Al Capone's house that he was throwing in her honor. The party was great, and afterwards they all went to a club called the College Inn to see Ben Bernie. It was some great time.

Now, that was the last time Jesse saw Fanny for years and years. But not too long before she died, Jack Benny took Jesse with him when he went to see her at her house. Fanny's memory wasn't too good by this time, and she didn't remember working with Jesse and Eva. "We played the Chicago Theatre together," he reminded her.

"No." She shook her head. "I never played the Chicago Theatre."

"Sure you did," Jesse insisted, "and after the show you took us with you to a party at Al Capone's house."

"Al Capone, huh? No, I never went to Al Capone's house."

"And after the party we all went to the College Inn to see Ben Bernie."

Fannie laughed. "You're wrong. That never happened. Sorry."

"Yes," Jesse said, "believe me, it did. You were the headliner. They paid you seventy-five hundred for the week."

"Eighty-five hundred," Fanny said.

Ladies and gentlemen, believe me, it was an erra.

Thank you from the bottom of my heart. I love you. Good night.

(APPLAUSE)